Answering Terror:
Responses to War and Peace after 9/11/01

edited by Sharon Hoover

Friends Publishing Corporation
Philadelphia, Pennsylvania

Cover Design: Cathleen Benberg

Cover photo: ©iStockphoto.com/Gloria-Leigh Logan

Answering Terror: Responses to War and Peace after 9/11/01

ISBN: 0-9779511-0-3

This book is dedicated to Friend Tom Fox, whose body was found in
Baghdad on March 10, 2006.
He made the ultimate sacrifice for his faith,
and in so doing he followed
his Guide with utter integrity.

Contents

Introduction

When three U.S. commercial airliners were used by members of the militant, fundamentalist, Islamic group al-Qaida on a sky-blue September morning in 2001 to attack strategic landmarks in the United States, the resulting death, destruction, and fear shocked people all over the world.

Friends found that they needed the support of each other for work that immediately presented itself—mitigating the results of trauma, grief, homelessness, and feelings of helplessness, anger, and confusion. They also found, however, that they needed first to center down into that silence which is God. Only then would they have the calm, the energy, and the wisdom to comfort, heal, feed, and inform. In addition, it was only after centering themselves in the Spirit that individuals could know what work was theirs to do and what to leave for others.

FRIENDS JOURNAL began to use its pages to print communications among Friends, and it continued to do so for the following months and years. The staff relied on its readers and contributors, its friends and supporters, to determine what to present. At the same time, however, they trusted that they would be led by the Spirit to select those things that might speak to the condition of the magazine's constituents.

A rich outpouring of engaged conversations filled the pages of the magazine for months. Numerous people who examined these fertile "experimental" ideas concluded that the collection of articles, viewpoints, letters, and poems presented an outstanding opportunity for Quakers to consider their positions on aggression and pacifism anew. Such consideration is necessary in each generation and each era. It is part of our destiny to leave for our descendants the ongoing stories of Friends worshipping, studying, and witnessing in today's traumatic times. Friends must continually tell new stories to testify to the transforming Power in whose light we seek to live.

In this spirit, the editors of FRIENDS JOURNAL decided to compile an anthology of work from the three years following the attacks. The first step was to make a preliminary collection of the applicable items to determine if there was enough material of sufficient quality and diversity to warrant such a book. These steps were begun by two summer interns.

Alex Koppelman collected and organized a preliminary group of selections and Sara Sharpless evaluated it. Robert Dockhorn, senior editor, then continued the selection and handed the materials to me, Sharon Hoover, to organize into a coherent collection. Another summer intern, Melissa Minnich, then laid out the pages.

Long before I knew there was a plan to create an anthology of the works, the breadth and depth of the contributors and the contributions I was finding month after month in FRIENDS JOURNAL had impressed me. At the time, however, like many others, I was busy volunteering. First, I volunteered for a short time with the American Friends Service Committee in New York City, then involved myself with local, regional, and yearly meeting reponses to the needs of our many constituencies.

As I have read and reread the contributions people offered in those issues of FRIENDS JOURNAL between late 2001 and 2004, I recalled the processing I witnessed people undergoing after the attacks. I quickly realized that the first thing many Friends needed was a safe environment to vent their anger and express their grief. Many of the Friends I know live in and around New York City, and many of them were too young to have had to invest themselves in responses to previous wars. I found that even more distant and older Friends, however, were often surprised by their own levels of anger and grief.

The first step in healing was to acknowledge the anger and grief both individually and in corporate bodies. FRIENDS JOURNAL received hundreds of letters in which individuals asked their questions and gave their tentative answers. Many people felt an urgent need to speak out and to hear others speak out. We were thirsty to hear the responses of those with spiritual wisdom and broad encounters in international concerns.

Although the statements of organizations and of the first individuals to respond in the pages of FRIENDS JOURNAL reminded us to remain calm and faithful, it was only after people could acknowledge their overwhelming feelings that they could begin to heal. After recognizing their own grief, they could begin to enter imaginatively into the experiences of others. They began to reflect, pray, and worship together, often sitting in long silences—waiting, as Quakers have done for centuries, to feel that covering of the Spirit that signals that we may be finding something akin to Truth. The Religious Society of Friends, says Howard Brinton in *Friends for 300 Years*, "is peculiar in being a group mysticism. This mysticism resides not in theory but rises from community worship.

After such worship, we can 'walk in the Wisdom of God answering that of God in every one'" (his paraphrase of George Fox). It was only then that we were ready to undertake considered action to assist in the long-term recovery.

These steps are not entirely linear, of course. They represent overlapping stages that I observed Friends traveling as we searched for our way through the maze of responses to the tragedy. I found the same kind of pattern in the writings in FRIENDS JOURNAL in the months that followed the disaster. People spoke to the issues of confusion and grief, of imaginatively entering another's experience, of meditating, of listening to others, of learning, and of finding ways to respond personally and with their communities.

I have organized the selections under these same general headings, beginning with the earliest statements by organizations and individuals and the outpourings of confusion, especially stimulated by Scott Simon's public break with pacifism. Then we begin to see Friends embark on healing. There are reflections and meditations, then articles filled with information and thoughtful analyses to help us comprehend the issues. After silence, worship, prayer, and seasoned thought, we found ourselves truly ready to ask the question, "what shall I do—what actions do I take to create greater peace?"

One of the lessons over the months, for me personally, was that the stages could not be skipped or rushed, and that my task was to hear what God was calling me to do at this time: not what someone else should perhaps be doing, or what I have done before or may do in the future— but right now. Through worship, Friends learn what God would have us do now. Through worship, I learn what God would have me do now.

As I read the selections you will find in this book, questions—queries if you will—often rose to my mind. I found the materials a rich mine of queries for Friends as we move through this so-called War on Terror that apparently has no envisioned end. Each of us has our own learning to do and our own tasks, but we must also remember that searching and working corporately is important. We test our leadings within the community. Since queries have such an established use among Quakers, and since we can ponder queries together, and we can answer them as a group, I have chosen to add queries to the different sections of the anthology. These are meant to be neither exhaustive nor definitive, but to suggest possible avenues of discussion. I encourage you to rewrite them, delete them, or add to them as you find yourself moved. Their purpose, as I see it, is to aid us in preparing ourselves to become more centered Friends and citizens, thereby strengthening ourselves for whatever lies ahead and for whatever God calls us, and our children, to do.

—Sharon Hoover

Immediate Responses from Quaker Organizations and Individuals

The first public reactions of Friends came from Quaker organizations and leaders—pastors, experienced clerks, long-time activists, and writers. Friends in Quaker organizations immediately convened ad hoc meetings and struggled with absorbing the new shock waves into their knowledge of the world and their commitment to the ideals of the Sermon on the Mount. They then put into words their dedication to that of God in all creation and in each person in that creation, and subsequently released their statements immediately to Friends and to news media. Semi-official statements immediately following a crisis of such magnitude serve an important purpose. They remind Friends and others that we are present and that we will speak and act as best we can in our differing positions relative to the disaster. The statements are based on our testimonies of truth telling and peacemaking. They are based on past experience and will guide us in the present circumstances.

Individuals also saw the need to speak of the personal turmoil they were experiencing and to remind others of the healing power of worship. They recognized that Friends needed to hear calm words of reason. Many readers eagerly looked forward each month to the light that Friends shed on our assumptions, conclusions, and questions following the attacks.

At the end of this section is the statement that Rep. Barbara Lee delivered on the floor of the U.S. House of Representatives. It reminds us that there are public voices, too, that speak calmly in tumultuous times, and that we should affirm those voices when we hear them.

Statements of Quaker Organizations

September 11, 2001

As organizations of the Religious Society of Friends (Quakers) and as members of the human family and children of God, we are profoundly grieved at the loss of life, the suffering, and the sorrow that result from today's tragic events. The God of love and mercy whom we worship and serve surely grieves too in the face of these acts of anger and hatred and the suffering they cause. We pray earnestly for comfort and strength for those who are injured and grieving. So too we hope with all our hearts that, in responding to today's tragic events, all persons will find ways to end the violence that is consuming our world.

We offer our gratitude and prayer to those who are responding to this tragedy, rescuing and caring for those who are injured, comforting those who are grieving, and working for peace and reconciliation.

The Religious Society of Friends since its inception in the 1650s has been led to eschew war and violence for any end whatsoever. Time and again we have ministered to the victims of war and violence. We believe that the challenge before us all is to break the cycle of violence and retribution.

—Bruce Birchard, Friends General Conference,
Cilde Grover, Friends World Committee for Consultation,
Thomas Jeavons, Philadelphia Yearly Meeting,
Mary Ellen McNish, American Friends Service Committee

September 12, 2001

Our hearts go out today to the victims of Tuesday's terrible attacks on the World Trade Center, the Pentagon, and the people in the four civilian aircraft. We call on Friends and others across the U.S. to offer prayers, solace, friendship, and aid to the survivors, families, and friends of the victims. We commend the heroic efforts of public safety personnel and the many others who, at great personal risk, are working to rescue and treat the victims of these tragedies.

We join with people across the country and around the world in expressing the hope that those who planned and orchestrated these terrible acts will soon be brought to justice under the rule of law.

We are concerned, however, about how the U.S. government responds now. First, we are concerned that the U.S. not avenge these attacks with attacks upon other innocent people who may happen to be of the same nationality, faith, or ethnic group as the alleged perpetrators. This concern extends to protecting the safety and rights of people here at home. Many in this country of the Islamic faith or of Middle Eastern descent are worried that they may now become the unwarranted focus of suspicion in their communities or, worse, the subjects of unjust persecution.

Second, many in the administration and Congress have declared that a state of war now exists. We are concerned that these public statements may be stirring the popular will and expectation for war. We wonder: War against whom? Cooler heads must prevail in the U.S. government during this time of crisis. War will only compound the tremendous assault on humanity that has already occurred. War is not the answer. The people who committed these acts struck with hatred. They saw the people in the World Trade Center, the Pentagon, and the aircraft as faceless enemies. They denied the humanity of their victims. The U.S. must not commit the same sin by compounding the hatred, violence, and injustice of these attacks with its own acts of terror and war against another people, most of whom are innocent of these crimes.

Finally, the people who planned these suicide attacks were able to draw volunteers from a growing number of people around the world who harbor deep resentment and anger toward the U.S. It is important that we in the U.S. try to hear and understand the sources of this anger. If we in the U.S. do not seek to understand and address the roots of this anger—poverty, injustice, and hopelessness—then the violence may well continue, no matter what the U.S. does to try to prevent it.

As members of the Religious Society of Friends (Quakers), we witness to that spirit of love which takes away the occasion of war. Out of darkness and tragedy, may God show us the path of true and lasting peace.

—Friends Committee on National Legislation

September 12, 2001

As pastors and leaders of Northwest Yearly Meeting of Friends gathered for a study retreat, together we faced the recent terrorist act against our nation. We grieved together, processed together, and felt called to express some of our leadings.

Our hearts, as yours, have been shaken. We meet this tragedy with deep sorrow and compassion, for those lives which have been lost or shattered, for those whose hatred drove them to this act, for those who are lost spiritually and may be further hardened against God.

This incident casts seeds of hate upon the wind. Our natural response is to ingest these seeds and let them grow. Yet this draws us away from Christ and ultimately makes us less of who we are intended to be. Christ's challenge is to turn our attention and appetite to the often difficult words and example of Jesus: "Love your enemies, and pray for those who persecute you, that you may be children of your Father in Heaven." (Matt. 5:44-46)

We urge each of us to resist the temptation to use nationalism, retaliation, or demonization of others to rebuild a false sense of security. Rather, let us discipline ourselves to find our true security in Christ, and be merciful to all as we have received mercy. Let us work to respond to the causes of violence and "learn war no more." (George Fox)

We urge each of us to be aware of the tensions between our natural reactions and the responses to which Christ calls us. These tensions are the fertile ground where God is working and inviting us to deeper Christ-likeness.

To assist us with the tension between the world's values and God's values, we offer these queries for personal and corporate reflection:

• How well are you making room in your life and the life of your faith community for the honest expression of grief, fear, and anger, as well as hope and healing?

• Are you faithful to pray for those who are among the victims and injured, and their families, those who struggle to rescue and heal, and for the spiritual conditions of all involved?

• Are you able to commit to God that area where you are feeling the most tension between your natural response and the way Christ calls you to respond, asking for insight, strength, and healing?

• How consistent is your response with the values reflected in the Beatitudes (Matt. 5:1-12) and the Truth taught in James 3:17-18. . . . "But the wisdom from above is first pure, then peaceable, gentle, willing to yield, full of mercy and good fruits, without a trace of partiality or hypocrisy. A harvest of righteousness is sown in peace for those who make peace."

• In the violence and instability in which we suddenly find ourselves, are you able to keep your ministry and relationships centered in Jesus' call: "The Spirit of the Lord is upon me, because he has anointed me to bring the good news to the poor. He has sent me to proclaim release to the captives and recovery of sight to the blind, to let the oppressed go free, to proclaim the year of the Lord's favor." (Luke 4:18-19)

May you experience comfort and peace in the loving presence of God and in the compassion and prayers of your pastors and leaders.

—The pastors and leaders of Northwest Yearly Meeting

September 17, 2001

We grieve over the September 11, 2001, disaster that has taken so many lives. We share in mourning with all those who have lost loved ones and give thanks for the heroic efforts of rescuers. The loss will live with us for years to come.

For over 300 years, Quakers (the Religious Society of Friends) have endeavored to build a just and nonviolent society. The Quaker United Nations Office in New York has collaborated with the UN since 1947 to encourage a focus on people as well as politics, and on peaceful ways of including all groups and hearing their needs. In the wake of this tragedy, we will continue to strive for increased international under-standing and cooperation.

As Friends at the UN, we cannot overemphasize the importance of a humane and rational response. Although many feel an urgent need to react strongly, some even violently, vengeful retaliation will not make the world safer from such threats. Indeed, it will only feed the cycle of violence behind these horrific acts. Rather, the security of nations and peoples must be based on human well-being, strengthened international cooperation and norms, and respect for the rule of law.

We call on all individuals and decision-makers to reject the clamor of war and work with the global community to prevent further violence.

In the short term, focus needs to be on securing the arrest and trial of those responsible and assuring fair judicial process in collaboration with the international community. Governments, communities, and indi-viduals should take responsibility not to scapegoat any nation, faith, or ethnic group. In the long term, the difficult process of addressing the anger, resentment, and hatred that fueled the attack must begin. It is disingenuous to regard non-state terrorism as simply aberrant attacks of fanatics when such incidents have become commonplace in much of the world and often enjoy popular support from aggrieved peoples. A clearer understanding of the roots of such violence is needed, including recognition of the extent to which national and international policies have contributed to creating and sustaining the despair and frustration behind these extreme acts.

Finally, we agree with Martin Luther King Jr., that violence is "a descending spiral, begetting the very thing it seeks to destroy . . . adding deeper darkness to a night already devoid of stars. Darkness cannot drive out darkness; only light can do that. Hate cannot drive out hate; only love can do that." We pray that the citizens and leaders of the world will rise to this challenge and move with generosity toward healing and reconciliation.

—Quaker United Nations Office, New York

September 21, 2001

Now that the initial shock of the terrorist attacks of last week has passed, deep grief and profound anger have set in for many of us. Now the critical questions that confront us all are several: How can we best comfort those who mourn? How can we begin to heal some of the wounds to all of our souls as well as our bodies? How can we see that justice is really done? How can we build bridges of understanding and reconciliation among all people so that there is no more harm done and no more hatred sown? How can we begin anew the work of creating a world where there can really be peace, addressing the injustice and despair which are so often the seeds of violence, so there will be no more victims?

These are the tasks to which a God of love calls all members of the human family. How will we respond?

As organizations of the Religious Society of Friends (Quakers) and people of faith we find ourselves challenged to continue to respond to the tragic and horrific events of September 11. Indeed, we feel called—and believe all people of good will are called now—to respond to these events and the hurts they have caused in ways that are deeper and more sustained than our initial shock and grief may have allowed. In particular, we believe the work of building a different and better world, one in which all persons are seen as sacred because we are all children of God, one where this kind of act would not happen again, is the calling of all of us who worship a God of truth, grace, and mercy.

To our dismay, we have heard people in the highest levels of our government calling for retribution rather than justice. To our astonishment we hear the talk of war and plans for war in which our nation in turn would cause the death of innocents—the sin which so appalled us—asserting this will somehow put things right. To our sorrow, we have seen people from many walks of life in our own communities striking out in their anger against other people in our communities just because of the faith they profess, the color of their skin, or the country of their origin.

We say with certainty that these statements, plans, and actions will not lead us to healing, justice or peace; and we pray they will cease.

In contrast, we commit ourselves to reach out to all who have been injured in any way by the events of the past week; and to offering comfort, solace, and practical support in any way we can. We commit ourselves to reach out to those whose backgrounds, cultures, and faith may be different than our own; and to listen and learn, in hopes of building the foundations of understanding and respect on which peace can be built. We support the prosecution of those who perpetrated this horrendous crime; and commit ourselves to the achievement of justice under law and due process, including international law.

Finally we commit ourselves to praying and working for righteousness and reconciliation, as the God of Abraham, Jesus, and Mohammed has taught us, so that there may be no more victims of hate and terror anywhere.

—*Bruce Birchard,* General Secretary, Friends General Conference,
Susan Corson-Finnerty, Publisher and Executive Editor, Friends Publishing Corporation,
Cilde Grover, Executive Secretary, Friends World Committee for Consultation, Section of the Americas,
Thomas H. Jeavons, General Secretary, Philadelphia Yearly Meeting,
Mary Ellen McNish, General Secretary, American Friends Service Committee

Statements of Quaker Meetings

September 13, 2001

On this day of horror, Friends in this Regional Meeting, which covers most of the State of New South Wales in Australia, reach out . . . with love and caring, tenderly holding you all whilst you come to terms with the magnitude of the violation against yourselves and your fellow countrymen. We grieve for you, we weep with you, and our imagination replays a little of the dismay you must be experiencing.

How concerned you must feel that the years you have spent encouraging nonviolent viewpoints and reconciliation are going to be so severely tested in the weeks to come. Our care for you will continue in the difficult times ahead, holding you steadfast in the Light, believing firmly that the transforming ability of love and truth will help you through. If there is any way we can ease your load we will gladly do so.

—*Cathy Davies*, Regional Meeting Clerk, Sydney Regional Meeting, Australia

September 16, 2001

Friends Meeting of Austin shares in the sorrow and grief over the tragedy of September 11, 2001. We mourn, pray for, and hold in the Light those who died and those who suffered and continue to suffer from the tragedy of that day. We are horrified at the attacks in New York City, Washington, D.C., and Pennsylvania.

As Quakers we condemn all acts of violence. We are called to seek and honor the Light, that which is God, in all people. We feel compelled to provide a visible witness to peace and reject the idea that retaliatory and retributive violence will somehow make this horrific situation right. We pray that we ourselves and our leaders will be blessed with wisdom and inspiration during this difficult time.

We call on all people to discern how we can open the way to peace. We deeply believe that all of the world can "live in that Light that takes away the occasion of war." We also call on Friends and others to meet the hatred and animosity towards all people, and especially those of the Islamic faith and towards those of Middle Eastern or South Asian descent, with love, compassion, and action.

We believe that out of this violence, the opportunity to affirm and spread a message of peace, justice, love, and tolerance can occur. We commit ourselves as individuals and as Friends Meeting of Austin to work towards that goal.

—*Austin (Texas) Meeting*

September 17, 2001

We share in the sorrow of people around the world at the loss of life in Pennsylvania, at the World Trade Center, and at the Pentagon. We abhor violence that has occurred to so many innocent people. The evidence of compassion, courage, and love evoked by the disaster heartens us deeply.

We join the many who caution against reacting to this tragedy with hatred or vengeance. The Religious Society of Friends, since its inception in the 1650s, has been led to eschew war and all forms of violence for any end whatsoever. We believe that the challenge before us all is to break the cycle of violence and retribution. As we seek justice in the aftermath of this tragedy, let us do so under the system of international law. Let us do it in a way that strengthens international institutions like the United Nations, whose purpose is to achieve security and stability for all peoples.

In response to this tragedy let us commit ourselves to eliminate terrorism by correcting the causes of hatred upon which it feeds. Over half of this year's U.S. discretionary budget already is going to support the U.S. military, and close to one percent for nonmilitary aid for developing countries. A disproportionately rich and heavily armed society can never be secure in a world of the suffering poor. We will have far more security in a world we approach as helpful friends than in one we arm ourselves against as potential enemies.

Let us also remember that there is a force more powerful than bombs or knives or weapons of war. That force is love—as Gandhi told us: "Love is the strongest force the world possesses, yet it is the humblest imaginable." Let us dare to move forward in love.

—*Tina McMahon*, Clerk, Multnomah Meeting in Portland, Oreg.

September 23, 2001

Dear President George W. Bush and leaders of the government of the United States,

This is a letter of concern to you and to all members of the United States government regarding the response to the September 11th attacks on the World Trade Center in New York and on the Pentagon in Washington, D.C., including the demolition of the four hijacked planes, one of which went down in Pennsylvania.

In this time of national tragedy, we would unite with the great outpouring of compassion for all of the victims, the dead, the wounded, and the families of those who have been taken from us.

We have endeavored to understand the motivations for this attack, that we might more clearly comprehend an effective response to it.

At this point in time, it appears that the attacks were carried out by members of an Islamic fundamentalist underground group, perhaps not unrelated to the same group which endeavored to bomb the World Trade Center several years ago. These people seem to have primary allegiance to no particular country, but they have a common passion to uphold a world view which has come to consider American and Western civilization as Satanic and a moral threat to Islamic values. Those who share this religious passion consider martyrdom for their cause to be a holy calling. While most Islamic peoples are opposed to this radical philosophy, the fundamentalists seem to have much popular support in Palestine, Iraq, Afghanistan, and other Islamic countries suffering deep poverty and conflict with Western powers.

We have witnessed how you, President Bush, and other leaders of the United States government have vowed swift reprisals against those responsible for these terrorists attacks, promising, if need be, military incursions into Afghanistan or wherever the leaders of these campaigns of terror may be hiding. However, it will be very difficult or impossible to separate the terrorists from those in the Islamic world who are innocent of terrorist intentions. If Afghanistan is made the target, that country has already been desolated by 20 years of bombing and warfare. Armed attacks upon specific countries will only serve to galvanize antagonism against America and the West. Regardless of one's militaristic or pacifist orientation, it must be recognized that armed might cannot triumph in this situation.

The American government must realize that, if these terrorist elements are to be apprehended, cooperation must be obtained from all nations of the Middle East and of the larger world community. At this time of crisis, regardless of past wars and ideological disputes, we must re-establish diplomatic relations with all nation states. This includes Libya, Iraq, and Cuba. We must remove those sanctions which are causing so much hardship and suffering in these countries. We must even seek to keep communications open with the oppressive Taliban government of Afghanistan. Our government must become more actively engaged in bringing an end to the Israeli-Palestine conflict. We should refrain from carrying on and expanding the missile defense program, which causes much anxiety on the part of governments such as Pakistan, China, and North Korea. The United Nations should be utilized as a forum for international discussion and action.

At this time, we must come to understand that the threat of terrorism can only be overcome as we unite with all peoples and religions, including especially the adherents of the Muslim faith, in upholding a morality of universal justice. This morality will not tolerate terrorist activity, but it will seek to root out the causes of the fear and animosity from which terrorism arises. This will make possible true security and peace in our world.

—Jacquelyn Leckband, Clerk
on behalf of the Bear Creek Monthly Meeting
of Friends (Conservative)

Statements of Individuals

September 12, 2001

The following was delivered in Saskatoon, Saskatchewan, at an evening prayer vigil attended by about 300 people:

Friends, these are terrible events that we have just witnessed. Nothing that we could now say or do will alter them. Their history—though yet to be written—is already beyond our power to change. Let us focus ourselves, then, on that history that can be changed, the history of the response to these terrible events—a history not yet enacted that will unfold over the next days and weeks.

Much of the talk yesterday—as people were still reeling under the first shock of the enormity of these deeds—was talk of retribution, talk of hunting down and punishing, talk of vengeance decked out in the language of justice. Such talk, I fear, will prevail at last—as if the evil of violence could be eliminated by violence.

As we mourn the dead and fear the future, the deeds that we have just witnessed should also give us pause for reflection. It is altogether too facile to say that the responsibility lies completely with a single party that we can identify, isolate, vilify, and crucify. I think that tonight and in the days to come we should ask what it is in ourselves and in people like us—in what we say and do—that can drive others to hate us so much, that can drive them to such a pitch of fury.

We should, I think, amidst all the talk of the defense of freedom, consider what type of freedom the World Trade Center and Pentagon might symbolize, not only to the small group of people that attacked them, but to people everywhere made desperate by the apparent hopelessness of their conditions. What do the World Trade Center and the Pentagon symbolize other than our freedom—the freedom of people of wealth and privilege—to dominate the world by whatever means we can grasp: cultural, commercial, and military?

It makes no difference to victims of violence whether those raining death down upon them are self-appointed, covert operatives or publicly elected officials following meticulously detailed norms of procedure. Nor should it make a difference to us. Terror is always terror, whoever the terrorists might be.

The poor people in New York and Washington who have suffered and died from these reprehensible acts now join their names to those of the poor people who have suffered and died from other acts of terror—other acts in what Winston Churchill called the "lamentable catalogue of human crime." They join their names to those of the poor people of Hiroshima, Nagasaki, Hanoi, Baghdad—to all who have suffered terror, injury, and death from the skies.

What, we might ask, can we—the people of Saskatoon—do in the face of these terrible events? What contribution might we make? There is nothing we can do for the dead. There is probably little we can do to avert the terrible acts of retribution now being planned. But there is much that we can do to change the familiar world of our everyday lives—to change the way that we relate to one another—the way that we interact between and among ourselves. We can study to bear with one another better than we do. We can study the arts of compassion and forgiveness. We can teach ourselves that there is no way to peace: peace is the way. We can learn that there is no way to nonviolence: nonviolence is the way.

—*Jay Cowsill,* Prairie Monthly Meeting

September 13, 2001

Last night, I slept and dreamt of tornadoes coming toward me. But "we" sheltered in a motel-like structure and survived. It's an improvement over the night before when I found that I could not go through my usual routine of getting ready for bed. So at 2 a.m. I lay down on top of my bed in all my clothes and slept for six hours dreaming of a rattlesnake that kept escaping and that, when found, was impossible to kill.

I woke yesterday surprisingly clear and energized to another perfect September day—cool and crystalline, not a cloud in the sky. I went out about 10 a.m. to see if my Middle Eastern newsdealer was open. I wanted, after five years, to tell him that my name was Carol and to ask if he and his family were okay. His store was open, but the papers were gone and there was another much younger man in his place. We stood there a minute looking at each other. And finally I said something like, "He is not here?" And the man shook his head, no. So I stumbled out my message anyway to this stranger, asking that he relay it—not even knowing how much English he spoke or understood. Evidently he understood enough. His face lit up and he nodded, Yes! I choked up with tears and fled.

Mayor Giuliani has advised all Middle Easterners who wear identifiable garb—turbans, caps, veils—to stay off the streets of New York for their own safety. He did so with grace and regret.

There are no coffee carts on the sidewalk, very few cab drivers, very few newsdealers open.

I came home and got very busy on phone and e-mail trying to connect with 15th Street Quakers myself and figure out ways we could stay connected with each other when travel is so impaired and communication channels screwed up. My Quaker meeting is the center of my life. I wasn't trying to do good work. I was fighting for my sanity—fighting the isolation and the powerlessness. The post traumatic stress syndrome that I am so familiar with from the events in my own life of 1981 when I was a crime survivor. (Hey! I'm tough! I'm a veteran! I'm a pro! I know about this stuff! Welcome to my world!)

By 2 p.m. a tension headache was immobilizing me. So I knew I had to move. Thank God for Motrin. I thought of the people in Iraq as I took two.

Outside the air had turned smoky for the first time since this began. The wind had, in fact, changed somewhat, but later that night I learned that it was the collapse of One Liberty Plaza. There also happened to be two firetrucks standing in front of a small apartment building at 2nd Avenue and 89th Street. Evidently someone had phoned in an alarm. All seemed to be well, but, of course, it made me wonder what is going on in the rest of the five boroughs in terms of our "ordinary" New York City emergencies? It was good to be out in the neighborhood. The sidewalk cafes were busy. I'd heard that restaurants were serving limited menus because they're out of things like bread and eggs. But there did seem to be enough for people to assemble some kind of meal.

Most of the stores on 86th Street (our shopping strip) were closed. Barnes & Noble, closed. Ben & Jerry's (that was a blow, let me speak plain). The movie houses were open. Federal Express, of course, dark. As was the Post Office.

The churches were wide open. Park Avenue Methodist had put a lectern on the sidewalk so people passing by could write names of those to pray for. I wrote down my two names and spoke a word to the pastor who was standing in his robes out front, just hanging out, just being there, a presence to chat with as you went by. It was wonderful.

I walked around to the other neighborhood churches. It was healing to see all those open doors. Announcements of prayer services taking place at different times in different churches are taped up all around the city streets.

I was headed for Central Park. It was filled with people. Quiet people, but people sitting in the sun, walking their dogs, wheeling their kids in strollers, people sitting in the shade reading. I passed one Park Avenue matron sitting there silently reading her Bible.

I went into The Ramble. Made a quick pass by Azalea Pond— birdwatching central. There were folks sitting there, but none of them were birders. I'm sure that new community of mine was out there somewhere, because it is coming on to the height of the fall warbler migration, but I had to leave the park to find a bus down to midweek meeting for worship.

When I got to the edge of the park at Fifth Avenue and 72nd, I saw a line of flatbed trucks with bulldozers and backhoes on them parked in a line that stretched south as far as the eye could see down the avenue— parked there, waiting to go in.

At Lexington Avenue and 72nd, I heard a siren wailing toward me, saw a car with lights flashing, barreling down Lex. Traffic scattered. It was a New York State Trooper's car, a puzzling sight. And then I realized what was happening. It was escorting a Shoprite trailer truck full of groceries into the city!

We all cheered as the trooper and the truckdriver flew by.

I caught the 2nd Avenue bus to the meetinghouse. Along about 60th Street, I saw a man and a woman get on dressed in hospital scrubs. They came and stood near me at the back of the bus. I remembered what Diane (the chaplain at St. Vincent's) had told me to do. I went over to them and asked, "How're you doing?"

The young man nodded and looked away. The woman and I looked into each other's eyes for as long as it took.

I got off the bus and continued to do that, as I was led, whenever I saw someone in scrubs or when I saw police officers.

Diane is right. It is the thing to do.

We worshiped for two hours at 15th Street.

After the worship, on my way home as I checked my messages from my cell phone, I learned that one of the two names I had put on the prayer list at Park Avenue Methodist was alive—and well. Unbeknownst to me, he had left for vacation in Italy on Friday morning. That leaves my young neighbor two floors below.

I walked north up Third Avenue for a while taking in the news that Kieran was alive. The streets were busy with people seeking each other out, being together. I thought of Sarajevo. At 34th Street, traffic was stopped while a police towing vehicle went through pulling a police van behind it. Its windows were shattered and it was covered in the white ash I'd been seeing on TV.

When I got home, I saw on TV that the Empire State Building was being evacuated, along with Penn Station. That was two blocks away from where I'd just come.

Later that night I got a call from the McAllisters in Los Angeles. It was wonderful to hear from them. They grew up in Northern Ireland at the height of The Troubles. Seamus lost a high school mate to a bomb explosion when they were 15. He talked to me a lot about life in Belfast. You get through, he said, by doing what New Yorkers are doing. By staying connected. By telling your stories and listening to other people's. By catching the eye of someone on the street and nodding or saying, "How's it going with you?"

We're learning here. We're learning.

Seamus, who loves New York like I do, said it's so gratifying to have people amazed at the way New Yorkers are living into this. They had no idea, out there, in the rest of the world, who we are.

That makes me smile.

And Seamus and I spoke of Mayor Giuliani. We both had occasion to meet him in the course of our lives, and found him to be deeply weird. The strangest vibe coming off another person I've ever felt. He couldn't make eye contact with me when we were introduced, among other things. But he's been terrific in this. He's been our mayor. I never in my entire life dreamed I'd be saying such things about him. But a transforming work had begun in this man months before this happened. We could all see the changes in him. And now here he is. And, say what you will about his political views, the man knows this city.

And thus my day ended with words of praise for the man I'd gotten arrested in protest against at One Police Plaza in the wake of the Diallo shooting. And I'd walked down Second Avenue asking the cops that I saw how they were doing and thanking them.

After a long silence here, thinking about what to write next, this is all I can come up with. There is a great work going on here.

Stay connected. Don't isolate. Talk and listen. How's it going with you?

—*Carol Holmes*, 15th Street (N.Y.) Meeting

September 14, 2001

Dear President Bush: We don't want any wars in America or any other countries. We want to catch and punish the people responsible for the horrible things that have been done, but we don't want a war. We are determined to prevent a war from happening. Please help.

—*Mira Sigal-Feldman*, age 10, in a petition circulated among and signed by many individuals at an interfaith gathering in Chestnut Hill, Pa.

September 14, 2001

How can we find security? How do we build security for our people and all people in the world? It seems to me that the trillions of dollars this country has spent on the military and weapons of mass destruction, the CIA, and having the most powerful military force in the world was unable to prevent the terrible destruction and loss of life in the horrendous attacks in New York and Washington last Tuesday.

Will bombing some other country which is sure to include killing thousands of innocent civilians make us more secure? I believe not. It is likely to only further the flames of hatred and counter-hatred. As Mahatma Gandhi said, if we pursue the eye for an eye philosophy, we will end up with the whole world blind. Is there a better approach?

I believe that the only way we can build *real security* for the American people is for the United States to become a real friend of all the world's people. Instead of hundreds of billions of dollars for weapons of destruction, we should allocate hundreds of billions for feeding the world's hungry, housing the homeless, healing the sick, and helping heal the wounds of war and hatred around the world. This would do more to win friends and real security than Star Wars and all the weapons in the world combined. It is time to understand the unity and interconnectedness of all people around the world and build our security system based upon that understanding.

May we use this horrible nightmare as a springboard for a new beginning.

—*David Hartsough*
San Francisco, Calif.

September 15, 2001

When I approached New York Yearly Meeting for support in my refusal to subscribe to the Feinberg Certificate at SUNY in 1964 (a refusal which eventually led to a landmark Supreme Court decision), Larry Apsey asked me an unforgettable question: Is this something you cannot not do? I answered that it was. I still appreciate the brilliance of the question, and I still mull over what sort of necessity that was and how it comports life, with identity, and with Quaker ways. It is a question which goes to the root of commitment and serves to distinguish true conscience from prudence and politics. I realized then, and I appreciate even more today, that my affirmative answer contributed significantly to my determining who I am, to my identity as a Friend. True conscience, in my experience, goes hand in hand with building a rich fellowship of the Spirit.

I think of Larry's question and the power of conscience again in connection with the events of this second week of September, 2001.

Conscience can lead to a fellowship of evil. I have no doubt that the hijackers asked themselves Larry's question and answered it affirmatively. They must have known that they were defining themselves, determining their personal and social identity. A monstrous hateful identity, to my mind, but no doubt one born of profound conscience, alas. It has been said that conscience is the voice of God, but I wonder if that is not too wishful.

What is sacred, perhaps even what is godly, is not only awesome but sometimes also violent. (Réné Girard wrote a book about this.) That is obvious not only in pagan sacrifices but also in the "Christian" burnings of witches and heretics, and in holy wars, whether a "crusade" or a "jihad." It was a memorable experience to visit Montsegur, last bastion of the pacifist Cathars in southwestern France, which was betrayed to the Crusaders in 1244 and whose 200 peaceful residents were then burned alive in a huge pyre on the plain below. That was perhaps a sacred duty, a Christian act blessed by the Pope, one of the last moments of the Albigensian Crusade.

Revenge or retaliation is often a sacred duty, another form of holy violence. President Bush spoke of retaliation in the National Cathedral, and his firm resolve seems to make retaliation a kind of sacred duty.

We should neither lose sight of the holy, conscientious side of acts of violence which invoke the sacred, nor praise or condone them just because they are sacred or conscientious. I have no doubt that the hijackers were extraordinary human beings moved by a sense of divine mission, but their acts were heinous. Revenge and retaliation are also (I do not say "equally") heinous and violent, and also anathema to us Quakers.

The nation, along with our friends around the world, has united in grief and quiet resolve. We Quakers unite in the grief and in that resolve, and also in prayers for the victims and for people all over the world, that their lives and ours may be lived in the Spirit that takes away the occasions for violence. We cannot, however, unite in a resolve for revenge, nor join the forces for retaliation. We must instead articulate and focus attention on alternatives to revenge, as we focus on alternatives to violence on other occasions.

The hijackers displayed profound courage and devotion as well as considerable technical skill, resources, and organization. They are now dead, so what we confront is other people who have equal skill, resources, and devotion. Some of these people and their resources, as well as people supporting and nurturing them, will be destroyed in the course of the retaliation. An alternative to destroying such people and resources would be to turn them to constructive ends, and we need to consider how that might be possible. To do that we will need to understand and turn around their hatred for America.

How have we earned such hatred? Is that a question we as a nation can seriously address? To do so we will have to take a close look not only at the right sharing of world resources (Ps. 24:1) but also at our stereotypes of Arabs, of Islam, of Israel, of energy use, and of free trade. That is a big order. Not one of those issues is simple, especially when we need to understand radically different perspectives. And smug self-righteousness may make it impossible to get started.

Was the "Battle Hymn of the Republic" at the National Cathedral meant to convey such self-righteousness? It certainly contrasted with the hymn at the close of another stirring talk I heard over 50 years ago. Bayard Rustin, to my mind the greatest Quaker of the 20th century, spoke at Swarthmore College about the "Journey of Reconciliation," in which an interracial group traveled on interstate tickets through the South to test state and local compliance with the Supreme Court ruling that segregation is unconstitutional in interstate travel. His story in-cluded not only harassments, beatings, arrests, and weeks on a chain gang, but also turning a "red neck" guard into a friend. Heroic stuff. But at the end he was anything but triumphant or self-righteous, ending with the spiritual "It's not my brother, it's not my sister, but it's me, Oh Lord, standing in the need of prayer." What can that teach us?

It may be helpful to recall what George Fox wrote in the midst of difficult times in 1663 (Letter 227): "Sing and rejoice, ye children of the day and of the light, for the Lord is at work in this thick night of darkness that may be felt. As truth doth flourish as the rose, and the lilies do grow among the thorns, and the plants atop of the hills, and upon them the lambs do skip and play."Alternatives to retaliation need not wait until the business of revenge is finished. They can work cheerfully alongside or burrow playfully underneath. The time to nurture them is now. There is, as Fox once wrote to his parents, no time but this present.

—*Newton Garver*
East Concord, N.Y.

September 18, 2001

Even now, when rage is so justified, we pray that greater wisdom will prevail in the hearts of our leaders and our citizenry. Many who, in the heart of this hopeless moment, agree that forgiveness is impossible, are the same people who condemn warring factions in the Middle East for their futile cycle of provocation and revenge. Many who agree are the same people who are mystified by the centuries of intractable violence in Ireland and the Balkans. Many who agree are the same people who profess to follow Jesus, or Buddha or Mohammed or the Talmud— and yet still behave as if this world will never require excruciating acts of forgiveness.

I do not suggest that justice be ignored. I do not suggest that the isolation, apprehension, and control of terrorists is anything but complex and absolutely necessary. I do suggest a path different from the path drawn by our heartfelt need for retribution. I do suggest that before we act we must understand our rage for revenge.

We are capable of anything, including, with prayer, the wisdom to measure our own actions and to distinguish this unconscionable atrocity from the reasons that motivated it. With such wisdom, we can forge our response to terrorism on higher ground than provocation and revenge.

We offer a prayer of support and a prayer of divinely inspired forbearance for our President, his advisers, and the rest of us as we discern our next steps in the tortuous path everyone on our planet will be walking together.

—*Steven Baumgartner,* Executive Director,
Pendle Hill Quaker Religious Community, Wallingford, Pa.
[Letter to the editor, Philadelphia Inquirer, *September 18, 2001, p. A22]*

September 18, 2001

Together with millions of people throughout the U.S. and the world, the American Friends Service Committee's national Lesbian, Gay, Bisexual and Transgender (LGBT) program was stunned by the indefensible and horrifying attacks that occurred in New York City and Washington, D.C., on September 11, 2001. We grieve deeply for those lost and injured in the attacks, and for their families and friends. In the name of justice, the individuals and groups responsible for planning and carrying them out must be held accountable. But what vision of justice is large enough to confront this violence with responses that lead to healing rather than the spilling of more blood?

LGBT people know only too well what happens when we are cast in the role of the despised other and our rights and humanity are denied. If we look deeply into our own hearts, surely we will find the courage to declare that we must never do the same thing to other people, or stand by in silence while our government undertakes actions that are a mirror image of hate violence. We have a special obligation to act with care, compassion, and integrity in this perilous time.

A dangerous mood is being fueled across the land. Who will call us home to our better, more just, and compassionate selves? Our political leaders are preparing us for war that will, in its turn, bring violence and devastation to civilian populations elsewhere. The impulse to destroy those who have hurt us is leading to terrible forms of "vigilante violence" within our own country. Where is the justice in this?

At the root of all hate violence, war, and injustice is the violence of "us" and "them"—those considered "good" (worthy), and those who are "evil" and therefore expendable. To fully claim our common humanity, it is necessary for all individuals, all political and identity groups, all nations to stop locating violence outside ourselves and recognize a painful but necessary truth: that we who are victims of violence and injustice in some situations may also be, in other situations, perpetrators of violence and injustice.

Increasingly, we see people stricken by grief and rage in this country threatening and targeting for harassment and assault friends of Middle Eastern and South Asian descent. Already, one good man, Balbir Singh Sodhi, a gasoline station owner, has been murdered. An Arab American worker has been attacked by a machete-wielding assailant. A Hindu temple has been firebombed. Mosques have been vandalized. Muslim schoolchildren are being threatened.

We urge all people to stand publicly in solidarity with Middle Eastern and South Asian communities, and to speak out boldly in defense of the constitutional, civil, and human rights of all, without exception.

The danger is very great that people in the U.S. will permit the erosion of the Bill of Rights in order to secure an illusory "safety." But authentic and lasting safety will not be created by the surrender of fundamental rights. The already widespread use of racial and ethnic profiling is escalating. The government is likely once again openly to permit political assassination. The use of secret evidence against persons suspected of being or associating with terrorists—virtually any person of Middle Eastern or South Asian descent—has been contested with some success in various courts in recent years, but is now likely to enjoy new support. Due process rights have long been in jeopardy. Already powers are being given to the federal government to detain and deport "suspects" on the basis of no evidence at all. Such broad powers invite wide use and abuse.

However unjustifiable the attacks of September 11, they possess a long history and arise within a broader social, political, and economic context. Can our hearts open sufficiently to realize that that the U.S., too, is implicated directly and indirectly in the violence, injustice, poverty, disenfranchisement, and despair felt by many in the Middle East and elsewhere around the world? People within the U.S. are capable of great generosity and compassion, and have shown it time and time again. Yet too many of our own nation's policies and actions—including the use napalm and anti-personnel fragmentation bombs against civilian populations; covert actions; carpet bombing; support of and sales of arms to undemocratic, repressive regimes and groups that rely on torture, terror, and death squads — have often caused great hardship and unimaginable suffering to families in other parts of the world. Fear, hatred, resentment, and the desire to obliterate those perceived as "enemy" thrive in such violent and unjust conditions. We reap what we sow.

Massive military retaliation and repressive policies abroad and at home will further inflame hatreds and cause the violence to escalate on all sides. If the suffering is to cease, only imaginative, bold, and ceaseless public activism and international diplomacy, rooted in universal affirmation of human rights and commitment to social and economic justice for all, offer us hope for a different, more just, less violent, more secure future. Within the larger LGBT/queer community, we have before us the opportunity to allow our own experience of violence and injustice to illuminate our understanding of the destructive power of hatred and strengthen our determination that no peoples shall be demonized, dehumanized, and considered expendable.

Let us redeem the lives of all those lost to this senseless violence by finding practical ways to transform the ashes of destruction into the love of healing justice, in which the integrity of means and ends is ultimately life giving for all.

—*Kay Whitlock*
Missoula, Mont.

September 20, 2001

During a meeting for worship last evening at Bethesda (Md.) Meeting, I found myself wondering what would Gandhi do, or what would Rev. Martin Luther King Jr. be preaching today. Others will have greater insights than mine, but it came to me to believe that they would be planning a peace effort in Afghanistan. I also concluded that if Clarence Pickett were alive he would be seeking meetings with the Muslim clerics in Afghanistan. This may be crazy but this morning I e-mailed Bob Edgar, the general secretary of the National Council of Churches and a former Congressman from Pennsylvania, urging him to lead a delegation of international religious leaders to Kabul seeking cooperation from the Taliban for an end to terrorism and religious war. For those interested, his email is <redgar@ncccusa.org>.

—*David Runkel*
Silver Spring, Md.

September 20, 2001

I got a clear message during meeting that Martin Luther King Jr. and Gandhi both would have chosen actions that lead to life over death, both here in this country as well as around the globe. I was with an African American preacher the other day, a wise man with years of experience in the Civil Rights movement. He called us to see that movement as a model of what a war on terrorism could be.

—*Liz Yeats*
Austin, Texas

September 21, 2001

Friends in Atlanta called a meeting for worship last Tuesday night, September 11, and met with Bet Havarim, a Jewish congregation who rents space from us for services. As I prayed, the words of Gandhi came to mind, "An eye for an eye will leave the whole world blind." I cried for all those around the world who now seem bent on creating blindness and wonder where are the leaders with the moral authority of Gandhi who can confront evil in nonviolent ways. Later I realized that this kind of thinking is part of the problem—looking for the savior, denying our own part in creating the tragedy, and being unwilling to do what we can to respond. We have supplied and dropped weapons of mass destruction on others expecting never to pay the price for our actions. As I prayed for guidance, this story sent by a friend seemed God's way of telling me we all need to do what we can.

The Hawk and the Dove:

"Tell me the weight of a snowflake," a hawk asked a wild dove.

"Nothing more than nothing," was the answer.

"In that case I must tell you a marvelous story," said the hawk. "I sat on the branch of a fir, close to its trunk when it began to snow. Not heavily, not a raging blizzard, no, just like in a dream, without any violence. Since I had nothing better to do, I counted the snowflakes settling on the twigs and needles of my branch. Their number was exactly 3,741,952 when the next snowflake dropped onto the branch— nothing more than nothing, as you say—the branch broke off." Having said that, the hawk flew away. The dove, since Noah's time an authority on peace, thought about the story a while and finally said with resolve, "Perhaps only one person's voice is lacking for peace to come about in the world."

—*Mary Ann Downey*
Atlanta, Ga.

September 21, 2001

Like most people in North America, I have been horrified, shocked, and saddened by the past week's events in the U.S. A scenario imaginable only in the movies took place pretty close to home. Undoubtedly, the loss of a great number of innocent lives makes this an immense tragedy. However, with all the subsequent saber-rattling and threats of retaliation on a massive scale, one cannot but help feel there are other things that are fueling the outrage of many Americans, among them injured national pride and a sense of invulnerability removed. Not to mention a military-industrial complex with its own vested interests and an insatiable appetite for an ever-greater share of the national budget, and opportunistic political leaders who will do what is expedient to score points, no matter what the long-term results.

As a Canadian, I am concerned that we may be taken headlong into a doomsday scenario, unless we stop and think carefully about what we are being fed by much of the media, and about where a U.S.-dominated NATO wants to go. We must maintain an independent voice at the UN, and within NATO. While support of friends is worthy, there is also a time for critical questioning of friends when their actions threaten the well-being of others or themselves. Being a cheerleader is not always very helpful.

President Bush has stated that "The terrorists, and those who harbor them, will be hunted down and rooted out." One has to wonder if those who train terrorists will also be called to account. I wonder how many North Americans are aware of the fact that it was the American CIA-run School of the Americas in Georgia that trained many of those now being blamed for last week's attack, when they were useful for fighting the former Soviet-backed leadership of Afghanistan from bases in Pakistan. The enemies of my enemies do not always remain my friends!

I believe that violence begets violence, and that there would not be terrorism unless there was first repression. This is not in any way to excuse or rationalize what happened last week, but we need to carefully think about what reaction our responses will inevitably provoke.

Fundamentalism, both religious and political, sees the world in simplistic, black and white terms, demonizing whatever is different or whatever it does not understand. Add to this the modern desire for "quick (technological) fixes," and we have a potent recipe for further disaster on a world scale. The reality is that whatever military action is taken in the next days and weeks will either decrease or increase the size of fundamentalist terrorist hotbeds. And thoughts of American invulnerabilty from further attacks are totally illusory. It is quite likely that any terrorists remaining have long since left Afghanistan for distant places, if Afghanistan was in fact ever their base. "Star Wars" type defense shields would be of little value when any terrorist could easily carry in a pill bottle enough deadly poison or disease-causing organisms like anthrax to contaminate an entire city's water supply, killing millions before it was even detected.

I do not believe there are any quick fixes. I believe that the U.N. should be a forum for countries to continue to reach agreement on dealing with terrorists if and when they are actually identified, not just suspected. Cooperation between police forces at all levels and in all places should be the priority, rather than those between military forces. The difference in my mind is that police actions are, or should be, limited in scope and force, focused, subject to well-understood rules, and account-able for every bullet that is fired. Military actions, on the other hand, especially in the past half century, seem so often to have no limits on the amount of force used or who it is aimed at, and little or no accountability to those they are supposed to serve.

It is, and should be, much the same as the way the Mafia, a group with roots in Sicily, is dealt with. Despite the connection of the Mafia with illegal drugs, coercion by gang-style murders, and prostitution, there are no threats or efforts to bomb Sicily, even if some Sicilians benefit from the illegal activities of its more notorious citizens. Likewise, one does not eradicate a cancer with indiscriminate and massive blasts of radiation or chemotherapy or by using an axe; rather the area to be treated is carefully and cautiously targeted, so that healthy surrounding tissues are not harmed or destroyed. In the long run, as with cancer, the causes of the problem must be dealt with, not just the symptoms. Extreme poverty, continuing injustice, lack of democratic options, hopelessness and utter desperation feed directly into terrorism. If you have absolutely nothing to lose, what difference does it make if you lose your life to kill others?

So much of the U.S. is now a gated community, where the rich elite that has, seeks to have more, and keep what it has from the hordes outside the gates. Sometimes a few from those hordes write graffiti on the gates, or even steal or harm those who strive for total security within. But so far in Canada and the U.S., constrained by the laws of the land, we have wisely and fortunately not seen fit to allow bombing of or mass retaliation against whole communities of the deprived from which a criminal element has arisen.

The human desire for vengeance creates a vicious cycle of revenge, re-revenge, re-re-revenge and so on. One has only to look at the history of Northern Ireland and so many other places to see the truth of this. Is this really what we want here? I for one, do not. For our children's sakes, let's choose life. Justice is called for, but taking revenge is by no means an adequate substitute for justice.

—*Brent Bowyer,* Lucknow and area worship group of Kitchener Monthly Meeting. Wingham, Ont.

September 23, 2001

You may find this hard to believe, but this morning during meeting in Des Moines, after about 15 minutes of worship, a member, Bob Henderson, exclaimed out of the silence, "Look, there's a dove sitting right there on the wall between us and the flag across the street." All eyes immediately turned and saw the amazing sight and recognized its haunting significance. Indeed, that dove, never observed before, sat calmly on the wall for what seemed like several minutes, then disappeared. The symbolism of the dove between the flag and our terrorism-troubled meeting led to a gathered meeting few will forget.

—*Wilmer Tjossem*
Newton, Iowa

Viewpoint: Enemies

... wrestle with spiritual weapons and not with flesh and blood, but wrestle with the power of darkness that leads from God ... in the love that thinks no evil, but loves enemies.

—*The* Journal *of George Fox*

Many Friends are having difficulty with their feelings about the September 11 attack on the U.S. This isn't like Vietnam or Grenada or even the Gulf War. During those conflicts, we could easily distance ourselves from the policies of our government. This time, we have been attacked—and it is impossible to avoid being included in that "we."

We have been declared an enemy and we don't like it.

For Friends, opposition to war is rooted on the belief that there is that of God in every person. We quote George Fox saying, "Walk cheerfully over the Earth, answering that of God in every one." Somewhere deep within us, we resonate with the old Irish maxim: No one is a stranger, just a friend you haven't met—we'll even capitalize Friend. We like to think that we do better than just loving enemies—that indeed, there are no enemies.

And yet, we have been declared an enemy and attacked.

One way to deal with this situation is to decide that it is a mistake. Those who are being called terrorists have legitimate grievances, but not with us. We are not part of the problem; we are not part of the power structure; we are not among the oppressors; we are not the enemy. Those people have not met us—they don't yet know us as friends.

But we who are citizens of the United States, Canada, Germany, the United Kingdom, and other Western nations do enjoy the benefits and privileges of that citizenship. Our comfort is unparalleled in history. To much of the rest of the world, even our poor look wealthy. When our governments act, they do so in the name of the people (and we are included) and they act for the benefit of those people (and we are included). When their actions raise grievances among others, all the people who benefited are responsible (and we are included).

We cannot cast off the label of enemy by a declaration of solidarity. Even if we were to renounce our citizenship, give up our material goods, and move penniless to a Third World country, we would bring with us accumulated wealth that we cannot simply let go: skills, education, health, immunizations, friends, families, and more. Birthright is hard to relinquish. We could live among others, but we could never be others.

And is this what God is calling us to do?

Our Peace Testimony is not a call to run away, but a call to faithfulness. It is a testimony and we need to testify—not to the poor and downtrodden, but to our own neighbors and friends. We need to say uncomfortable things to people we know and live with and love. Uncomfortable for them to hear maybe, but certainly uncomfortable for us to say.

Pacifism is easy if there are no enemies. It's like turning the other cheek when no one is threatening to hit you. The Quaker message is to love your enemies, not to pretend they do not exist. George Fox called on Friends to "wrestle with the power of darkness." This means we have to accept the reality of evil and with love to resist it.

We have had it easy; now we are called to faithfulness when it will be hard.

—Paul Buckley

Paul Buckley is a member of 57th Street Meeting in Chicago. He and his wife, Peggy Spohr, were co-clerks for the 2002 Friends General Conference Gathering in Normal, Ill.

Peace Is Not

Peace is not a testimony
when uttered
behind the fortress
of suburban landscapes;
or whispered
in the bedrooms
of indignant sufferers of fools
who wish the world
could only be like us;
the way we used to be
(like no one).

Peace is not a testimony
when it shields us from the pain
of those who bear the burden
of our indifference,
as we in condescending tones
of well-protected comfort
instruct the victims
of our greed to wait
in patience for their
coming turn.

Peace is not a testimony
before the rage has even
seethed within our blood
against the godlike arrogance of men
who try to slaughter
their own fears
they see reflected
in the eyes of little children.

Peace is not a testimony
until we are so
bored with explanations
of our political correctness
that no one needs
to suffer or affirm
the hollow righteousness
that echoes in our cause.

Peace is not a testimony
until we freely give
what cannot be requested;
and we ignore
the ever-present fact of death
and still move on
because the life we feel
is more compelling
than the fearful future
we would otherwise protect.
Peace is not a testimony
until we realize that
the good that turns the world
is not our formula or instrument
but we are carried by it
like a river into other lives
if we don't shut our hearts
against the terrifying
torrent of its force.
Peace without price
is apathy dressed up
to look like principle
and self-protection
of the status quo
interpreted to sound
like saintly sacrifice.

Peace is only peace
when love is more than life
and truth the only duty
to our souls
and all salvation sinks
beneath simple silence
of our inevitable Being.

To find this Peace
we must leave our homes
and stand naked
in the rain of darkened night
until the drops fall through us
into thirsty soil
from which the morning
flowers spring.

All else is war.

—*Phil Lord*

Phil Lord is a member of Chestnut Hill (Pa.) Meeting.

September 14, 2001

A Lone Dissent to the Use of Force Resoluton

I rise today with a heavy heart, one that is filled with sorrow for the families and loved ones who were killed and injured in New York, Virginia, and Pennsylvania. Only the most foolish or the most callous would not understand the grief that has gripped the American people and millions across the world.

This unspeakable attack on the United States has forced me to rely on my moral compass, my conscience, and my God for direction.

September 11 changed the world. Our deepest fears now haunt us. Yet I am convinced that military action will not prevent further acts of international terrorism against the United States.

I know that this use-of-force resolution will pass although we all know that the President can wage a war even without this resolution. However difficult this vote may be, some of us must urge the use of restraint. There must be some of us who say, let's step back for a moment and think through the implications of our actions today—let us more fully understand its consequences.

We are not dealing with a conventional war. We cannot respond in a conventional manner. I do not want to see this spiral out of control. This crisis involves issues of national security, foreign policy, public safety, intelligence gathering, economics, and murder. Our response must be equally multi-faceted.

We must not rush to judgment. Far too many innocent people have already died. Our country is in mourning. If we rush to launch a counter-attack, we run too great a risk that women, children, and other non-combatants will be caught in the crossfire.

Nor can we let our justified anger over these outrageous acts by vicious murderers inflame prejudice against all Arab Americans, Muslims, Southeast Asians, or any other people because of their race, religion, or ethnicity.

Finally, we must be careful not to embark on an open-ended war with neither an exit strategy nor a focused target. We cannot repeat past mistakes.

In 1964, Congress gave President Lyndon Johnson the power to "take all necessary measures" to repel attacks and prevent further aggression. In so doing, this House abandoned its own constitutional responsibilities and launched our country into years of undeclared war in Vietnam.

At that time, Senator Wayne Morse, one of two lonely votes against the Tonkin Gulf Resolution, declared, "I believe that history will record that we have made a grave mistake in subverting and circumventing the Constitution of the United States. . . . I believe that within the next century, future generations will look with dismay and great disappointment upon a Congress which is now about to make such a historic mistake."

Senator Morse was correct, and I fear we make the same mistake today. And I fear the consequences.

I have agonized over this vote. But I came to grips with it in the very painful yet beautiful memorial service today at the National Cathedral. As a member of the clergy so eloquently said, "As we act, let us not become the evil that we deplore."

—Barbara Lee, on the floor of the U.S. House of Representatives

Queries

What was my immediate response to the attacks on September 11?

What was my response during the next few days?

If I had had to write a statement of response, what could I or did I say?

If my meeting wrote a response, what did it say? If not, what might we have said?

Why did we or did we not respond in the days following the attacks?

What were or might have been the benefits of having to write a personal response? Of writing a corporate response? What did we or might we have done with a corporate response?

Extended Responses
of Seasoned Friends

S ome people perceived immediately the depths of shock that many of us felt in the aftermath of September 11. Their experience in the world and their wise faith helped to calm many Friends who were facing conflicted feelings toward violence in the heightened atmosphere of national and personal vulnerability for the first time.

As one who believes deeply in nonviolence, John Paul Lederach captures well the first moments we faced after the attacks. In the first fearful moments of any catastrophe, Friends call on the best lessons they have learned from their practice. John Paul Lederach relied on lessons he had learned in 20 years of daily dedication to his work as a mediator.

Stephen Cary's article challenges us with basic questions that search deeply into our Peace Testimony. Many of us love the United States, its hills, plains, ranches, cities, rivers, seashores, plants, animals, peoples, and stories, even though some of the stories make us feel sad. Nevertheless, there is sometimes talk about moving away to Central America, Canada, or New Zealand. Stephen Cary leads us to ponder a question that may face us wherever we go: "Do I have the depth of conviction I need to live out my beliefs under a government and in a culture that does not value and may actively oppose those who believe in the values of the Sermon on the Mount?"

Mary Lord is able, in the following article, to remind us to be humble in the face of our complicities with militarization. She reminds us, too, of the ingrained cultural myths of good and evil in our society that we celebrate in vivid color and surround sound, such as Star Wars. Most of all, however, she reminds us of the basis of our testimony: "It is not our Quakerism, or our pacifism, or our knowledge, or skill, or emotion that overcomes hate and violence. . . . The power is not ours, it is God's."

She early sounded a clarion call to worship that many people heard.

Finally, we have a short piece by George Rubin. Since experiencing the devastation of war many years ago, he has worked unceasingly for peace while he lived his daily life in business. He reminds us that the road we travel is not a lonely one, no matter our occupation. We have God with us, and the stories and histories we know, and we have one another. The Religious Society of Friends is just that—based in Spirit, we are friends, and we journey together.

The Challenge of Terror: A Traveling Essay

by John Paul Lederach

So here I am, a week late arriving home, stuck between Colombia, Guatemala, and Harrisonburg, Virginia, when our world changed. The images flash even in my sleep. The heart of America ripped. Though natural, the cry for revenge and the call for the unleashing of the first war of this century, prolonged or not, seems more connected to social and psychological processes of finding a way to release deep emotional anguish, a sense of powerlessness, and our collective loss than it does as a plan of action seeking to redress the injustice, promote change, and prevent it from ever happening again.

I am stuck from airport to airport as I write this, the reality of a global system that has suspended even the most basic trust. My Duracell batteries and fingernail clippers were taken from me today and it gave me pause for thought. I had a lot of pauses in the last few days. Life has not been the same. I share these thoughts as an initial reaction recognizing that it is always easy to take potshots at our leaders from the sidelines, and to have the insights they are missing when we are not in the middle of very difficult decisions. On the other hand, having worked for nearly 20 years as a mediator and proponent of nonviolent change in situations around the globe where cycles of deep violence seem hellbent on perpetuating themselves, and having interacted with people and movements who at the core of their identity find ways of justifying their part in the cycle, I feel responsible to try to bring ideas to the search for solutions. With this in mind I should like to pen several observations about what I have learned from my experiences and what they might suggest about the current situation. I believe this starts by naming several key challenges and then asking what is the nature of a creative response that takes these seriously in the pursuit of genuine, durable, and peaceful change.

Some Lessons about the Nature of Our Challenge

1. Always seek to understand the root of the anger. The first and most important question to pose to ourselves is relatively simple though not easy to answer: how do people reach this level of anger, hatred, and frustration? By my experience, explanations that they are brainwashed by a perverted leader who holds some kind of magical power over them is an escapist simplification and will inevitably lead us to very wrong-headed responses. Anger of this sort, what we could call generational, identity-based anger, is constructed over time through a combination of histori-cal events, a deep sense of threat to identity, and direct experiences of sustained exclusion. This is very important to understand, because, as I will say again and again, our response to the immediate events has everything to do with whether we reinforce and provide the soil, seeds, and nutrients for future cycles of revenge and violence, or whether the cycle changes. We should be careful to pursue one and only one thing as the strategic guidepost of our response: avoid doing what they expect. What they expect from us is the lashing out of the giant against the weak, the many against the few. This will reinforce their capacity to perpetrate the myth they carefully seek to sustain: that they are under threat, fighting an irrational and mad system that has never taken them seriously and wishes to destroy them and their people. What we need to destroy is their myth, not their people.

2. Always seek to understand the nature of the organization. Over the years of working to promote durable peace in situations of deep, sustained violence, I have discovered one consistent purpose about the nature of movements and organizations that use violence: Sustain thy-self. This is done through a number of approaches, but generally it is through decentralization of power and structure, secrecy, autonomy of action through units, and refusal to pursue the conflict on the terms of the strength and capacities of the enemy.

One of the most intriguing metaphors I have heard used in the last few days is that this enemy of the United States will be found in their holes, smoked out, and when they run and are visible, destroyed. This may well work for groundhogs, trench, and maybe even guerilla warfare, but it is not a useful metaphor for this situation. And neither is the image that we will need to destroy the village to save it, whereby the population that gives refuge to our enemies is guilty by association and therefore a legitimate target. In both instances the metaphor that guides our action misleads us because it is not connected to the reality. In more specific terms, this is not a struggle to be conceived of in geographic terms, in terms of physical spaces and places that if located can be destroyed, thereby ridding us of the problem. Quite frankly, our biggest and most visible weapon systems are mostly useless.

We need a new metaphor, and though I generally do not like medical metaphors to describe conflict, the image of a virus comes to mind because of its ability to enter unperceived, flow with a system, and harm it from within. This is the genius of people like Osama bin Laden. He understood the power of a free and open system and has used it to his benefit. The enemy is not located in a territory; it has entered our system. And you do not fight this kind of enemy by shooting at it. You respond by strengthening the capacity of the system to prevent the virus and strengthening its immunity. It is an ironic fact that our greatest threat is not in Afghanistan, but in our own backyard. We surely are not going to bomb Travelocity, Hertz Rent-A-Car, or an airline training school in Florida. We must change metaphors and move beyond the reaction that we can duke it out with the bad guy, or we run the very serious risk of creating the environment that sustains and reproduces the virus we wish to prevent.

3. Always remember that realities are constructed. Conflict is, among other things, the process of building and sustaining very different perceptions and interpretations of reality. This means that we have at the same time multiple realities defined as such by those in conflict. In the aftermath of such horrific and unmerited violence that we have just experienced this may sound esoteric. But we must remember that this fundamental process is how we end up referring to people as fanatics, madmen, and irrational. In the process of name-calling we lose the critical capacity to understand that from within the ways they construct their views, it is not mad lunacy or fanaticism. All things fall together and make sense. When this is connected to a long string of actual experiences wherein their views of the facts are reinforced (for example, years of superpower struggle that used or excluded them, encroaching Western values that are considered immoral by their religious interpretation, or the construction of an enemy-image that is overwhelmingly powerful and uses that power in bombing campaigns and always appears to win) then it is not a difficult process to construct a rational worldview of heroic struggle against evil. Just as we do it, so do they. Listen to the words we use to justify our actions and responses. And then listen to words they use. The way to break such a process is not through a frame of reference of who will win or who is stronger. In fact the inverse is true. Whoever loses, whether tactical battles or the "war" itself, finds intrinsic in the loss the seeds that give birth to the justification for renewed battle. The way to break such a cycle of justified violence is to step outside of it. This starts with understanding that TV sound bites about madmen and evil are not good sources of policy. The most significant impact that we could make on their ability to sustain their view of us as evil is to change their perception of who we are by choosing to respond strategically in unexpected ways. This will take enormous courage and courageous leadership capable of envisioning a horizon of change.

4. Always understand the capacity for recruitment. The greatest power that terror has is the ability to regenerate itself. What we most need to understand about the nature of this conflict and the change process toward a more peaceful world is how recruitment into these activities happens. In all my experiences in deep-rooted conflict, what stands out most are the ways in which political leaders wishing to end the violence believed they could achieve it by overpowering and getting rid of the perpetrator of the violence. That may have been the lesson of multiple centuries that preceded us. But it is not the lesson learned from the past 30 years. The lesson is simple. When people feel a deep sense of threat, exclusion, and generational experiences of direct violence, their greatest effort is placed on survival. Time and again in these movements, there has been an extraordinary capacity for the regeneration of chosen myths and renewed struggle.

One aspect of current U.S. leadership that coherently matches with the lessons of the past 30 years of protracted conflict settings is the statement that this will be a long struggle. What is missed is that the emphasis should be placed on removing the channels, justifications, and sources that attract and sustain recruitment into the activities. What I find extraordinary about the recent events is that none of the hijackers was much older than 40 and many were half that age.

This is the reality we face: recruitment happens on a sustained basis. It will not stop with the use of military force; in fact, open warfare will create the soils in which it is fed and grows. Military action to destroy terror, particularly as it affects significant and already vulnerable civilian populations, will be like hitting a fully mature dandelion with a golf club. We will participate in making sure the myth of why we are evil is sustained and we will assure yet another generation of recruits.

5. Recognize complexity, but always understand the power of simplicity. Finally, we must understand the principle of simplicity. I talk a lot with my students about the need to look carefully at complexity, which is equally true (and which in the earlier points I start to explore). However, the key in our current situation that we have failed to fully comprehend is simplicity. From the standpoint of the perpetrators, the effectiveness of their actions was in finding simple ways to use the system to undo it. I believe our greatest task is to find equally creative and simple tools on the other side.

Suggestions

In keeping with the last point, let me try to be simple. I believe three things are possible to do and will have a much greater impact on these challenges than seeking accountability through revenge.

1. Energetically pursue a sustainable peace process to the Israeli/ Palestinian conflict. Do it now. The United States has much it can do to support and make this process work. It can bring the weight of persuasion, the weight of nudging people on all sides to move toward mutual recognition and stopping the recent and devastating pattern of violent escalation, and the weight of including and balancing the process to address historic fears and basic needs of those involved. If we brought the same energy to building an international coalition for peace in this conflict that we have pursued in building international coalitions for war, particularly in the Middle East; if we lent the same significant financial, moral, and balanced support to all sides that we gave to the Irish conflict in earlier years; then I believe the moment is right and the stage is set to take a new and qualitative step forward.

Sound like an odd diversion from our current situation of terror? I believe the opposite is true. This type of action is precisely the kind of thing needed to create whole new views of who we are and what we stand for as a nation. Rather than fighting terror with force, we enter their system and take away one of their most coveted elements: the soils of generational conflict perceived as injustice used to perpetrate hatred and recruitment. I believe that monumental times like these create conditions for monumental change. This approach would solidify our relationships with a broad array of Middle Easterners and Central Asians, allies and enemies alike, and would be a blow to the rank and file of terror. The biggest blow we can serve terror is to make it irrelevant. The worst thing we could do is to feed it unintentionally by making it and its leaders the center stage of what we do. Let's choose democracy and reconciliation over revenge and destruction. Let's do exactly what they do not expect, and show them it can work.

2. Invest financially in development, education, and a broad social agenda in the countries surrounding Afghanistan rather than attempting to destroy the Taliban in a search for bin Laden. The single greatest pressure that could ever be put on bin Laden is to remove the source of his justifications and alliances. Countries like Pakistan, Tajikistan, and yes, Iran and Syria should be put on the radar of the West and the United States with a question of strategic importance: how can we help you meet the fundamental needs of your people? The strategic approach to changing how terror reproduces itself lies in the quality of relationships we develop with whole regions, peoples, and worldviews. If we strengthen the web of those relationships, we weaken and eventually eliminate the soil where terror is born. A vigorous investment, taking advantage of the current opening given by the horror of September 11, shared by even those whom we traditionally have claimed as state enemies, is immediately available, possible, and pregnant with historic possibilities. Let's do the unexpected. Let's create a new set of strategic alliances never before thought possible.

3. Pursue a quiet diplomatic but dynamic and vital support of the Arab League to begin an internal exploration of how to address the root causes of discontent in numerous regions. This should be coupled with energetic interfaith engagement, not just of key symbolic leaders, but of a practical and direct exploration of how to create a web of ethics for a new millennium that builds from the heart and soul of all traditions but that creates a capacity for each to engage the roots of violence that are found within their own traditions.

Our challenge, as I see it, is not that of convincing others that our way of life, our religion, or our structure of governance is better or closer to truth and human dignity. It is to be honest about the sources of violence in our own house and invite others to do the same. Our global challenge is to generate and sustain genuine engagement that encourages people, from within their traditions, to seek that which assures the respect for life that every religion sees as an inherent right and gift from the Divine, and how to build organized political and social life that is responsive to fundamental human needs. Such a web cannot be created except through genuine and sustained dialogue and the building of authentic relationships, at religious and political spheres of interaction, and at all levels of society. Why not do the unexpected and show that life-giving ethics are rooted in the core of all peoples by engaging a strategy of genuine dialogue and relationship? Such a web of ethics, political and religious, will have an impact on the roots of terror far greater in the generation of our children's children than any amount of military action can possibly muster. The current situation poses an unprecedented opportunity for this to happen, more so than we have seen at any time before in our global community.

A Call for the Unexpected

Let me conclude with simple ideas. To face the reality of well-organized, decentralized, self-perpetuating sources of terror, we need to think differently about the challenges. If indeed this is a new war, it will not be won with a traditional military plan. The key does not lie in finding and destroying territories, camps, and certainly not the civilian populations that supposedly house them. That will only feed the phenomenon and assure that it lives into a new generation. The key is to think about how a small virus in a system affects the whole and how to improve the immunity of the system. We should take extreme care not to provide the movements we deplore with gratuitous fuel for self-regeneration. Let us not fulfill their prophecy by providing them with martyrs and justifications. The power of their action is the simplicity with which they pursue the fight with global power. They have understood the power of the powerless. They have understood that melding and meshing with the enemy create a base from within. They have not faced down the enemy with a bigger stick. They did the more powerful thing: they changed the game. They entered our lives, our homes, and turned our own tools into our demise.

We will not win this struggle for justice, peace, and human dignity with the traditional weapons of war. We need to change the game again.

Let us give birth to the unexpected.

Let us take up the practical challenges of this reality perhaps best described in the Cure of Troy, an epic poem by Seamus Heaney, no foreigner to the grip of the cycles of terror, who wrote:

So hope for a great sea-change
On the far side of revenge.
Believe that a farther shore
Is reachable from here.
Believe in miracles
And cures and healing wells.

John Paul Lederach is Professor of International Peacebuilding at the Joan B. Kroc Institute for International Peace Studies at Notre Dame University and a Distinguished Scholar at Eastern Mennonite University's Conflict Transformation Program. E-mail: <JPBus@aol.com>.

A Response to September Eleventh

by Stephen G. Cary

As a Quaker, a pacifist, and one of the 9 percent of U.S. citizens who dissent from our country's current response to the September 11 attack, many friends belonging to the 91 percent majority have asked me to explain my position. Piecemeal answers are time-consuming and unsatisfactory, so I have drafted this fuller statement that I can share with all interested.

It goes without saying that I share the view of all in the U.S. that what happened in New York and Washington was an unspeakable crime. I, too, want the perpetrators identified and brought to trial—preferably under international auspices. Those are givens.

There are two roots to our national anguish, either painful in itself, but together responsible for causing a level of shock as deep or deeper than Pearl Harbor. The first is our sadness over the terrible loss of lives and the pain we feel for those whose days will never be the same. The second is the harsh recognition of a new national vulnerability. For 300 years we have been secure behind our oceans. For 300 years we have been in control of out fate. The coming of the atomic and missile age actually ended that happy state of affairs a half-century ago but did not seize the nation until September 11, when it came like a bombshell. Citizens of the U.S. knew then that our world would never be the same. It was a stunning shock.

The question we face now is how to respond to this new reality, and this is where the 91 percent and the 9 percent part company. How do we differ? As I understand it, the 91 percent, under the President's leadership, hopes to regain control and restore at least a measure of invulnerability by building alliances, tracking down evildoers, and taking military action. In his words, "It is America's mission to rid the world of evil. We must root out the terrorists and stamp out terrorism, and we will do so." It is a new kind of war, against civilian populations, and not fought by opposing armies. Our military response will be measured, designed to flush the guilty from their hiding places and punishing enough to persuade those who harbor them to turn them over. The war's end is indefinite, but it will be long and will continue until the threat of terrorism is eliminated. The U.S. will stay the course. Justice will prevail.

The people of the U.S., traumatized by events, find comfort in a new national unity, based on a fervent patriotism that finds expressions in showing the flag, singing "God Bless America," arranging for 40 million children to simultaneously recite the pledge of allegiance, and congratulating ourselves on our role as the champions of justice and the torchbearers of freedom. This outpouring is reinforced by the full weight of the government, the media, and the entertainment, sports, and corporate communities, and leads to unquestioned backing of the bombing of Afghanistan as the opening phase of the new war.

There is a need for comfort in trying times. The decline in partisan bickering and the coming together of our diverse society are welcome. But acquiescence has a downside in the present crisis because it silences dissent and the serious discussion of alternative policy directions. From my perspective, this is a dangerous state of affairs because the path down which we are going is likely to lead to more terrorism rather than less, and to decreasing security rather than rebuilding it.

Why? First, because retaliation, whether identified as "punishment" or "justice," does not teach the enemy a lesson or lead it to change its ways. Retaliation stiffens, angers, and invites counterretaliation. If we have not learned that over the last half-century in the Middle East and Northern Ireland conflicts—to name just two of many settings where the tit-for-tat game has been on daily display—I don't know where we've been. Retaliation as a way to prevail against an enemy has, short of annihilation, been a failure. Has any benefit really accrued from the daily bombing of dirt-poor, starving, and chaotic Afghanistan? Has this really reduced the threat of terrorism?

Second, we will likely see more terrorism because our bombing will increase alienation, and in many countries, especially throughout the Arab world, add to hatred. It is already doing so. Polls taken in Turkey and Pakistan have shown that a shocking 80 percent of Turks and a majority of Pakistanis oppose our bombing, and a dangerous number even supports bin Laden. It is just this hatred that produces the fetid soil from which the terror masters recruit their troops. (Compare: the rise of Hitler in an embittered Germany in the wake of a vindictive Versailles.) If we succeed in capturing bin Laden, there will be plenty of others prepared to take his place. Increasing hatred assures more terrorism. In sum, I believe the President's "crusade against wickedness" will fail.

What is my alternative? How seriously should I take the instructions for dealing with enemies given to me by Jesus, whom I claim to be my guide, my brother, and my master? There is no doubt about where he stood. He made it clear in the greatest of his sermons when he preached to the multitude from a mountaintop: "And why beholdest thou the mote that is in thy brother's eye, but considerest not the beam that is in thine own eye? . . . Thou hypocrite, first cast out the beam out of thine own eye; and then shalt thou see clearly to cast out the mote out of thy brother's eye." (Matt. 7:3-5)

Reflecting on these words is not a popular exercise for Christians these days. Brushing them aside has been made easier, first, by the efforts of theologians who for 2,000 years have found them too uncompromising and have looked for ways to temper them without repudiating their preacher; and, second, by claiming that Osama bin Laden is a new and more terrible devil than the world has ever known, who must be dealt with differently.

Neither of these rationalizations is satisfying. I believe Jesus meant what he said because his words are no less than a faithful reflection of the vibrant witness of his own life. Nor can I accept the convenient bin Laden argument. Jesus' world was at least as brutal as our own, his country under military occupation, and its terrorist differing from ours in name only. His name was Herod and his al-Qaida was his army.

These reflections have made me think about motes and beams. What are the beams in our American eyes that make people hate us? And if we can remove them, won't that lessen hatred and reduce terrorism? Human beings do not fly civilian airplanes into buildings to kill 3,000 innocent people without harboring a depth of anger that makes them easy targets for a bin Laden to persuade them that in doing so they will become God's martyrs. We in the U.S. live with illusion if we do not recognize that there are millions, especially in the Arab and Muslim worlds, who harbor this kind of feeling toward us. Doesn't it make sense in such a circumstance to ask what options are open to us to ease this dangerous situation? A few voices are doing so, but I have yet to hear a single word on the subject from any government source. Indeed, to the contrary, President Bush has been widely quoted as saying that he, "like most Americans, is amazed that people would hate us because I know how good we are." With all due respect, I am appalled at the shallowness of such a comment from the most powerful man in the world.

I think there are things that we can do that would point us in a new and more hopeful direction. I identify them in what follows in the hope that they will provoke thought:

Aid to Others

We need to take a fresh look at our outreach to the world's poor, its hungry, its oppressed and illiterate, its sick, its millions of refugees. We think of ourselves as generous and caring. The reality is otherwise. The U.S. is by far the most miserly of all the world's industrialized nations in the percentage of resources it allocates to nonmilitary assistance to the underdeveloped world. I think we should be troubled when we glance at our current budget: $340 billion for the power to kill; $6 billion for power to lift the quality of life of the poor and dispossessed, on whose succor peace ultimately depends.

World Arms Trade

Shouldn't we reexamine our role as the largest player in the worldwide trade in arms? We justify it on the grounds that it helps democratic allies defend themselves against aggressor nations, but often they are dispersed on the basis of two other criteria, (1) the ability to pay, or (2) the recipient's qualification as the enemy of our enemy and therefore entitled to our weapons. It is this armament that frequently ends up in the hands of tyrants and is used to oppress their people or attack their neighbors. A poignant current example: Afghanistan, where we armed the Taliban because they were fighting the Russians, but who then used our largess to seize power, with tragic results. The arms trade is great for Lockheed, but a curse to the world, and a source of slaughter from which hatred is spawned.

Sanctions Against Iraq

Shouldn't we be concerned about the 5,000–6,000 Iraqi children who die every month because of U.S.-supported sanctions? Aren't these lives just as precious as those so wantonly destroyed on September 11? The sanctions are of course aimed at Saddam Hussein, but after years they have left him stronger than ever, and they are being ignored by many nations, including close allies. What purpose are they serving to justify the added burden of hatred they provoke?

The Role of the CIA

Whatever it may have accomplished that we don't know about, what we do know should raise the grave concern of all in the U.S. Particularly egregious has been its role in arranging coups that overthrow governments we don't like, even popularly elected ones. The list is long— Guatemala, Chile, Iran, Cambodia, to name several. Do we in the U.S. have any awareness of the millions of human beings slaughtered by the regimes we installed in their place or opened the way for? I have personally seen the tragedies we wrought in three of those examples: Chile, Guatemala, and Cambodia—and it is an appalling record. Our readiness to interfere in the internal affairs of other nations poisons our image, especially when others see the firestorm that erupts here when foreigners mess into our affairs, even when through relatively innocuous illegal contributions to our political campaigns.

U.S. Policies in the Middle East

This is the most sensitive and difficult concern for me to raise, but because it is probably the most important source of hatred of the U.S. throughout the Muslim world, where the greatest threat of terrorism is centered, I have to speak to it despite my full support of an independent Israel. The problem is the perceived 50-year imbalance in our stance in the Israeli-Palestinian conflict.

I speak to this issue on the basis of three visits to the West Bank and Gaza over the last 20 years, and six weeks living in Jerusalem, with instructions to focus on meeting with Likud officials to better understand their point of view. There are a number of factors that underlie Arab anger:

(a) The harshness of Palestinian life under a half-century of brutal Israeli military occupation—brutal not because it is Israeli, but because any occupation in a hostile environment is brutal. Neither people in the U.S. nor, indeed, many Israelis, have any idea of what the daily life of a Palestinian is like, and has been for 50 years: arbitrary cutting off of livelihoods; daily encounters with checkpoints often involving long delays; land seizures; unfair allotment of water; summary trials in military courts; sudden shutting down of schools and colleges; blowing up of homes; thousands trapped in squalid refugee camps since 1948. I wish U.S. and Israeli policymakers could spend two weeks living with a Palestinian family; they might better understand the rock throwers.

(b) Massive military aid to Israel. This is justified as necessary to assure its security in a hostile environment, but U.S. weapons, from heavy tanks to helicopter gunships, kill Palestinians at a ten-to-one rate and give Israel overwhelming superiority in the brutal game of mutual retaliation. This adds to Arab anger and robs us of the neutrality required of a broker in peace negotiations.

(c) The Israeli settlement program. Deliberately designed to honeycomb the West Bank to make a potential Palestinian state geographically impossible, and involving the seizure of large blocks of land without warning or compensation and the eviction of all who live on it, the program has always been a massive obstacle to any meaningful peace settlement. Yet for over 30 years the U.S. has made only the most modest protests and has made it financially possible by large grants of nonmilitary aid that have served annually to free Israeli funds for its construction program. Some years ago, I was sitting in the office of Mayor Freij of Bethlehem when he pointed across a valley at a settlement under construction and said, "Mr. Cary, I have friends whose family has lived on that land for 700 years. They were just told to get out. We could do nothing. Do you blame us for being angry? I can promise you one thing: the Israelis will never know peace until this sort of injustice is ended. You Americans could have stopped this program, but you weren't interested in doing so."

(d) Highways crisscross the West Bank to assure easy passage between Jerusalem and the settlements. Cars with Israeli license plates can reach most of their destinations in 20 to 40 minutes, while Palestinian cars take several hours because of holdups at military checkpoints.

(e) I've mentioned water. I do so again to underline that because it is in such short supply throughout the region, its allocation is a major issue. Israel controls all water resources, and in the eyes of Palestinians, its allocation is so unfair that it is a source of bitterness, of which they are reminded daily.

(f) Terror. We rightly condemn and give full press coverage to Palestinian terror—the blowing up of Israeli buses and the tossing of bombs into marketplaces—but where has been the outrage, or even press mention, of the Israeli practice over many years of forcibly removing Palestinian families from their homes and bulldozing or dynamiting them because a relative has been accused of being a terrorist? Isn't this cruel retaliation against innocent people also terrorism?

Or, to cite a more recent, specific example of terrorism: the assassination of Israeli Tourism Minister Rehavan Zeevi. You will remember that a few months before his killing the Israelis assassinated two radical Palestinians (in what they labeled "preemptive strikes") by blowing up their cars from helicopter gun ships (U.S. provided). The Palestinian response: nothing—not, alas, by choice, but because they had nothing to respond with. In contrast, the Israeli response to the Zeevi killing: heavy tanks (U.S. provided) sent into ten Palestinian towns, at the cost of 25 Palestinians' lives—all in territory turned over, at least in theory, to the Palestinian Authority. I don't justify assassination under any circumstances, but there's hardly been a clearer example of the imbalance of power (courtesy of the U.S.) that is such a bitter source of Arab anger.

The Arrogance of Power

Throughout history great powers and empires have always been tempted to go it alone, to pursue their own interests without regard for the interests of others. England was the victim of this mindset throughout the 19th century. In the 21st, are the immense wealth and power of the United States taking us down this road? Some troubling evidence:

(a) Our stance toward the United Nations. We call on it when it suits our purposes, but ignore or denounce it when it doesn't. We don't pay the dues we solemnly committed ourselves to pay because some things about the organization displease us. This petty behavior badly hurts our image around the world.

(b) We walk away from treaties we signed and ratified, but which we no longer want to be bound by. A current example is the Anti-Ballistic Missile Treaty, the cornerstone of arms control for the past 20 years.

(c) Ignoring, vetoing, or reneging on a whole range of negotiated agreements that enjoy overwhelming support of the world community, but which we don't like because they may limit our freedom of action. Examples: the Kyoto agreements on global warming, the Nuclear Test Ban Treaty, the elimination of land mines, the Law of the Seas agreement, the establishment of an international war crimes court, and the regulation of international trade in small arms.

Wouldn't a more generous, cooperative role in the community of nations, instead of readiness to go it alone because we are the superpower that nobody can challenge, help to change our image and lessen anti-Americanism around the world?

Earlier, I spoke of identifying and bringing to trial the perpetrators of September 11 as "a given," but I haven't mentioned the subject since. It is still a given, but it has a different priority with me than with the nation's 91 percent.

Blasting Osama bin Laden and his lieutenants from their caves or killing them on the run will satisfy the widespread desire for vengeance, but its price is too high and its contribution to easing the threat of terrorism too low. Destruction of a starving country and blowing up Red Cross relief depots, hospitals, and residential areas—however unintentionally—only add to the anger that is the root cause of terrorism.

I give priority to pursuing other avenues that promise to improve the international climate to the point where diplomatic and legal initiatives can produce the culprits for trial and punishment. Biding our time will prove less costly than dropping megaton bombs.

I have wanted to give some sort of answer to the many friends who are troubled by bombing and retaliation, but ask, often plaintively, "But what else can we do?" My suggestions are of things that in the long run would seem to me to be more likely to free us from terrorism and restore security than rooting out bin Laden by twisting arms to build temporary military alliances, meeting violence with violence, and bombing poor countries.

In making my case, however, I have two problems. The first is how to speak forcefully on so many issues without coming across as anti-American and/or anti-Israel—perceptions bound to produce more heat than light. It's also frustrating because I am as devoted to our nation as any flag-waver. My aim—and my definition of patriotism—is to help a great country become greater, and more worthy of its dreams.

My second problem is the impression I may convey that the United States is the only one responsible for bringing terror on itself, which is patently not the case. We are one player among many. Other countries, including nations in the Arab world, are guilty of sins of omission and commission that have contributed to the present poisoned atmosphere, and which must be addressed. My position is only that we are complicit, and should undertake our response to September 11 where it is easiest and most important to do so—where our own house is out of order and where we can ourselves do things that will contribute to easing the world's sickness.

We must move beyond the naive but satisfying illusion that "we" are good and "they" are evil—that the devil always lives somewhere else: now in Berlin and Tokyo; now in Moscow, Hanoi, and Beijing; now on to Belgrade and Kabul; but never in Washington. The devil lives in the hearts of all of God's children, and until we take responsibility to try to lift up that which is good in us and cast out that which is bad, the scourge of terrorism will continue to torment us.

Stephen G. Cary, who died in 2002, was a member and former clerk of Germantown (Pa.) Meeting, a retired vice president of Haverford College, and was long associated with American Friends Service Committee, including 12 years as clerk of its national board.

Can Love Overcome Violence and Hate?

by Mary Lord

Dear Friends, when you first invited me to speak on the Peace Testimony last summer, I was working at Friends Committee on National Legislation starting up a new program on the peaceful prevention of armed conflict. I had been giving talks on the spiritual basis of our testimony and on the opportunities presented by the emerging field of conflict prevention. I enjoyed telling the stories of heroic peacemaking being done by many people, including Friends in regions of conflict, and of the possibilities for a new vision of the peaceable kingdom. I planned a speech on those lines, and I will do some of that tonight.

After September 11, I agreed to come to Philadelphia, on loan from FCNL, to work as coordinator of the No More Victims Campaign, American Friends Service Committee's response to September 11 and the emerging war. In the months since then, I found that many Friends in the U.S. have struggled with the Peace Testimony because they were not sure what we should do instead of going to war. So I had decided to respond to that need and to talk also about the need to end the bombing of Afghanistan. That was when I picked my title, and I will do some of that tonight.

Both my little world and the world around us have changed again. Tonight, I have a new task at AFSC, as the incoming interim director of AFSC's Peacebuilding Unit, following Judith McDaniel's decision to return to Tucson and a very special new job. As I was writing up the talk for tonight, I began to struggle—while FWCC Executive Secretary Cilde Grover got more and more nervous because the translators were supposed to have had the text two weeks ago. Finally, on Tuesday night of this week, I needed to acknowledge that I was having so much trouble with the speech that I must be working on the wrong message. So in prayer I asked God what I was supposed to say. The response was pretty swift and clear. It is a hard message to give, and probably a hard one to hear. But we live in hard times.

I need also to apologize to Friends coming from outside the United States, because much of my message is directed to those of us who are U.S. citizens and must face the consequences of what our government is now doing. I hope what I say will also be of value to you, and I hope that you dear Friends from other countries will help us, through your prayers and your insights, to be faithful to our witness.

A New Global War

Friends, as events unfold in the world around us, I very much fear that we are on the eve of a new and terrible global war. Even now it could be stopped, but there is not the will to stop it. There is rather the will to threaten and to fight, either by design or lack of thought, blundering forward in a manner reminiscent of the events that led up to World War I. The consequences of the war now beginning will bring immense suffering to many peoples. We as Friends need to do what we can to stop the wars that are already spreading or intensifying. But we also need to be prepared to be Quakers in wartime—never an easy experience.

What leads me to this dire prediction? First, of course, are the statements by U.S. President George W. Bush and other U.S. government officials that we are in a war that will reach into many countries and last perhaps through our lifetime. It is the decision of this government to respond to the present crisis by promising this generation of young adults decades of warfare as their inheritance. There are Friends in Africa, the Middle East, and Latin America who know firsthand what decades of war can mean.

Second are the actions that have accompanied the statements. As the war in Afghanistan apparently begins to wind down, both sides in this war of terror are taking the battle to many other countries. U.S. forces are already in the Philippines in what some believe is a violation of its constitution. Troops are also present or en route to Yemen and probably Somalia. Military aid is increasing to Colombia—intensifying that war which until recently was a war on drugs, and is now a war on terror. Troops are reported heading to the former Soviet republic of Georgia. An invasion of Iraq is almost certain, possibly with tactical nuclear weapons. This expansion of the war to a longer and longer list of countries has little or no support from our allies in Europe, except perhaps Tony Blair, or in the Middle East or Asia. But it is very likely that the U.S. will nonetheless, as Secretary of State Colin Powell told Congress, "go it alone."

Recently the U.S. announced a change in nuclear weapons policy—changes that will make it more likely that nuclear weapons might, for the first time in almost 60 years, actually be used in war. Against the backdrop of insider debates about whether to use mini-nukes in Iraq, the change of nuclear policy is ominous indeed. Listening to all of this, the board of directors of the Bulletin of the Atomic Scientists moved the "Doomsday Clock" two minutes closer to midnight. Having served on that board myself for several years in the past, I can tell you that the hands of the clock are not moved lightly.

Of course, the U.S. was attacked on our own soil in a despicable act that left more than 3,000 dead in New York, Washington, D.C., and western Pennsylvania. These terrible attacks affected the children of my own home meeting, Adelphi, which is near Washington. It was not widely reported that there were a number of school children on the plane that went into the Pentagon. Some of those children were playmates of the children in our meeting, and the adults at Adelphi had the task of trying to help our children understand what happened to some of their friends. Like me, you may have watched the documentary shown on CBS a few days ago about the firemen in the World Trade Center. It gave us a small sense of the horror of the day close up. The attacks had to be answered—but how? What might we have done instead of going to war?

The Road Not Taken

On September 12, the U.S. immediately began to prepare for war. There was another road that might have been taken—the road of international law, working together with other nations to find and arrest the members of the criminal conspiracy. In fact, many individuals were identified, arrested, and await trial in a number of countries, using just such methods.

There is an International Criminal Court that will soon come into force when 60 nations ratify it. Already more than 50 have done so. The current U.S. administration rejects this treaty and refuses to support or cooperate with it. As a nation, the U.S. has declared itself above the law of other nations. We might, on September 12, have supported a special tribunal like that now operating in The Hague and trying Slobodan Milosevic. We might have developed a special court or arrangement, like the Scottish court that operated in The Hague to try the perpetrators of the bombing of Pan Am 103 (on which one of my closest friends lost his youngest daughter).

We might take action to make future terrorist activity less likely. We could ratify international agreements on stopping the financing of terrorist groups, but we have not yet done so. We might support efforts for better information sharing between nations to identify such criminals, but we have not yet done so. We might have tried to limit the trade in weapons to unstable regions, but instead the U.S. almost single-handedly thwarted a special United Nations conference convened for that purpose. We might have sought to strengthen the verification procedures on biological and chemical weapons, but instead the U.S. scuttled that conference also, enraging our British and Australian allies who had worked six years to bring nations together on this treaty. We might have sought to limit the spread of nuclear weapons technology to rogue nations and others, but instead we are dismantling the international agreements that have limited proliferation, and the U.S. appears to be standing ready to resume testing of nuclear weapons. I could go on for some time.

There has been a conscious choice to use U.S. military force rather than international law against al-Qaida. There is a conscious decision to expand the war to countries with whom we want to settle old scores (North Korea, Iran, Iraq), or where we can gain access to oil (the former Soviet republic of Georgia), or where we hope to regain military bases (the Philippines)—whether or not the nations involved have any connection to September 11.

This is a decision to use the tools of warfare rather than the tools of policing and international law. It is also a decision to seek to weaken or prevent the development of any international structures that might provide an alternative to military force. As long as decisions are made by military force, the U.S., which spends now over $400 billion a year on the military, has a decided advantage. This amount is more than the military budgets of the next 25 nations combined. Russia, the nation with the next-largest military budget spends about $60 billion on its military each year. (Source: Center for Defense Information and FCNL.) For over a year, it has been the stated policy of the Bush Administration to seek "full spectrum dominance"—to be able to do whatever the U.S. wants anyplace in the world without fear of retaliation by its opponents. That is one reason the attacks of 9/11, using commercial aircraft as missiles against civilian targets, were such a shock to the government.

There are, of course, consequences to such military buildup. Other nations feel they have to respond in kind. The European Union, friends and allies of the U.S., confronted by a unilateralist U.S., has decided it must develop a European military capacity capable of acting without U.S. involvement, in situations where the U.S. has no interest. Japan and Germany are, for the first time since World War II, sending troops outside their borders, in what some citizens of these countries regard as an unconstitutional policy. China, believing itself to be a potential target of the U.S., is increasing military spending by 17 percent.

Conflicts in those parts of the world where the U.S. has an interest in oil or military bases are intensifying. And every military dictator and despot is now using the catch phrase of "terrorism" to expand military operations, crush dissent, limit human rights, and carry out atrocities—

all in the name of fighting terror. Open our eyes! Look and see!

India and Pakistan still stand poised for conflict, and each side now has nuclear weapons. Indonesia's military, which only a few months ago was a pariah in the world because of the atrocities in East Timor, has now been given a green light to crush "terrorism," with grievous consequences for the dissident movement in Aceh. This summer I met a young man from Aceh at the Peace Brigades International conference, and I worry about him and his family. The Israeli-Palestinian conflict has worsened in recent months and at times descends into war. It is hard to tell if the recent UN resolution on Palestine has come soon enough or will be implemented. Certainly many on both sides have died. Naming North Korea and Iran as part of an "axis of evil" set back, perhaps for decades, the diplomatic work and the work by nongovernmental organizations, including AFSC, that have tried to bring those nations back into the international community. In the Americas, the war in Colombia is escalating dangerously with peace talks broken off and a new offensive underway. It is already spreading into neighboring countries. I worry about the Peace Brigades team and the Mennonite community in Colombia. I pray for the safety of the Peace Team delegation that Val Liveoak is preparing to take into Colombia.

War Does Not Work

This, of course, is the way of war. Once started, wars are almost impossible to control. They tend to spread. There are always unintended consequences. We cannot know where the path we are now on will lead. What we do know is that hatred and greed always breed violence, and that violence always begets violence.

Pacifism has been called naive and unpatriotic. But I ask you, which is the greater naiveté—to believe that the frustrating but productive path of using and strengthening international law is the path of safety, or to believe that a never-ending worldwide war against loosely defined terrorism fought with weapons of mass destruction will make us safe and secure in our gated communities?

The path of war is always, as history proves, the more naive. War almost never works. Even when it seems to, for a short time, or after a long struggle, it is with a horrific cost of life, and property, and treasure, and the fouling of the Earth, and the killing of its creatures. Almost always, similar ends could have been achieved through negotiation or international law and peacekeeping, with far less cost.

In the end, even when war seems to work, as in World War II for the Allies, it is because of the quality of the peace that followed. In World War I, the soldiers were just as brave, but the peace was an excuse for revenge, and it led in a generation to Hitler and another, greater war.

For some months as I have been preparing my talk, I have been drawn to the prophet Habakkuk. It is a very small book—only three chapters. In the first chapter Habakkuk complains to God, as only Hebrew prophets can, that injustice and violence are everywhere. How long, the prophet asks God, before you will act? I thought I was supposed to use that chapter as my text tonight, and I couldn't understand why it wasn't working. But I discovered I was supposed to use chapter two, God's response to the prophet's complaint. I want to read part of it to you:

> I will stand at my watch post, and station myself on the rampart;
> I will keep watch to see what he will say to me, and what he will
> answer concerning my complaint.
> Then the Lord answered me and said:
> Write the vision; make it plain on tablets, so that a runner may
> read it.
> For there is still a vision for the appointed time; it speaks of the end,
> and does not lie.
> If it seems to tarry, wait for it; it will surely come, it will not delay.
> Look at the proud!
> Their spirit is not right in them, but the righteous live by their faith.
> Moreover, wealth is treacherous; the arrogant do not endure.
> They open their throats wide as Sheol; like Death they never
> have enough.
> They gather all nations for themselves, and collect all peoples as
> their own.
>
> —*Hab. 2:1-8 (NRSV)*

I think the message is very clear. Those who live by greed and violence—and that characterizes us more than we want to admit—will find our own violence turned against us. The path of war will be disastrous for the U.S. as well as for the many peoples who live in lands labeled "terrorist."

I have a close friend who has served in the White House and National

Security Council in two previous administrations. She told me she is frightened of the whirlwind this country is sowing. If you travel in Europe, or the Middle East, or Asia, or Africa, or almost anywhere outside the U.S., you will find many experienced statesmen frightened about the forces this war is unleashing. It is a frightening time, and I have said nothing about the damage already done at home—not just in New York and Washington, but also to our psyches; to our democracy, with the shocking attack on civil liberties and democracy; to the immigrants and refugees among us; and to our economy, as we transfer more tens of billions to the Pentagon and the wealthy.

Faith in Violence

What propels us toward war? Why do we rush toward battle in the belief that combat and killing will make us safe? We could talk about the economic, military, and cultural roots of the conflict—and these are important to understand. But tonight I want to talk about belief. Again Habakkuk, this time in chapter one, gives us insight.

Speaking of the Chaldean armies of his time, Habakkuk complains: "Dread and fearsome are they; their justice and dignity proceed from themselves." (1:7)

In verse 1:11: ". . . Their own might is their god."

And verses 1:15-16: ". . . He [the Chaldeans] brings all of them [the people] up with a hook; he drags them out with his net. He gathers them in his seine. Therefore he sacrifices to his net and makes offerings to his seine, for by them his portion is lavish and his food is rich."

Habakkuk complains that the Chaldeans have come to worship themselves, their own power, and their weapons of war, allegorically described as hook, seine, and net.

I believe this is what we face. We also live in a time when the nations and those in positions of privilege have come to worship their own power and the military forces which they use to ". . . claim dwellings not their own."

Walter Wink, a theologian and author, wrote a remarkable book, *Engaging the Powers*, which gives insight on the role of active nonviolence in the world around us. Wink points out that for many centuries the culture in which we all live has been founded in the belief in combat as the way that goodness overcomes evil. This belief, dating back at least to ancient Babylon, is the undercurrent of our myths. The ritual story is always the same: the hero is attacked by evil and almost overcome, but in the end, good prevails through strength and skill in combat and slays the evil enemy.

This myth pervades our own culture in the West. Whether Gary Cooper in the western movie *High Noon*, or Superman, or with a darker veneer of the outlaw-heroes of current times, this myth of what Wink terms the belief in "redemption through violence" becomes the underlying structure of our culture and actions.

Make no mistake. This is a system of religious faith, often blind faith, in the effectiveness of military force or the threat of force—which is sometimes mistaken for a peaceful alternative. So pervasive is this myth that we speak of military force as "the last resort" as if it would, though costly, be guaranteed to work. In reality, while one military force may defeat another, a war rarely achieves any other aims. Once it starts, defeating the enemy becomes the only war aim, and the original goals are forgotten.

Faith in militarism also shows up in the questions not asked. We do not inquire why almost $400 billion for the U.S. military—about seven times that spent by any other nation—didn't make us safe. We do not ask this. We only assume we need to spend more—sacrificing our cities, our environment, the education and training of our children and youth, the health of our people—to do so. Like the Chaldeans of ancient times, the nations and institutions of our time have come to worship themselves and to make sacrifice to our weapons and our military structures as though they were gods.

Faith in God

Luke and Matthew tell the story of Jesus' temptation in the desert when he was preparing for his ministry. According to these Gospels, there were three temptations. In one, Jesus was shown all the nations of the world. The tempter, Satan, offered Jesus dominion and power over them all. Satan urged Jesus to think of the good he could do with such power, if only Jesus would worship Satan. The Gospels tell us that Jesus rejected this temptation, saying, "Worship the Lord your God, and serve only Him."

In my mind, this is what the Peace Testimony is really about. What do we worship and trust? What do we understand to be the real base of power and change in the world? How does God want us to treat one another?

In turning away from realpolitik, Jesus pointed to power—God's power—that is real and lasting, and he rejected the illusion of power that lay in the nations of that time. After all, where now are the Chaldeans of Habakkuk's time? Unless we are professors of history we do not even know who they were. So too have many empires come and gone—the Greeks of Alexander's time, the Romans, the Mayan and Aztec Empires, the Spanish conquistadors, and the British Empire on which it was said the sun never set. All have come and gone. Most of us carry in our blood the inheritance of both the conquerors and the people who were conquered. Perhaps in our DNA we carry the ancient memories of many conquerors and many of the once vanquished. The stories are dimly remembered if at all.

Jesus left the desert and began a ministry of preaching and living the power of God's love for the sick, the poor, and the people who had made mistakes in their life but wanted to make amends. He seemed to pay little attention to those in power. The message of that ministry is perhaps best summarized in the Sermon on the Mount, one of the most remarkable and radical prescriptions for living. In it we are told to love our enemies, to do good to those who hurt us, and to love one another.

As early Christians, and later early Friends, studied these teachings and the life that Jesus lived, they came to believe that God had clearly shown us that we were not to kill one another. The Gospel is full of teachings about forgiveness and the power of love. The Gospels and the Epistles that follow do not teach hate or violence or human vengeance. We should remember that all of the world's principal religions teach these same principles. Universalist Friends tend to emphasize the Light within, rather than the Sermon on the Mount, but the teaching about how to live is the same. God has spoken to us in many faiths and many cultures with the same message of love and compassion to one another and of love, obedience, and faithfulness to God.

The Gospels and other sacred writings give a different view of what power is—a different view of what human beings are capable of if we dare to trust in the power of God to transform us and the situations of our lives. It calls us to worship not the institutions of this world, but to worship God and to live in faith and harmony with one another.

Early Quakers, reading the Gospel, found in it a vision of a different kind of power than the armies then contending in the English Civil War. One of the earliest statements against power was from George Fox, who had been asked to accept a commission in the militia. In those days, many people believed that if the good people could gain control of government, England could be a holy commonwealth. All that was needed was military success over the corrupt government of the time. Sounds familiar, doesn't it? In our time, we see many opposing forces each strong in the belief that God's kingdom can be achieved through military power—whether a crusade or a jihad.

Fox turned down the commission, explaining that he ". . . lived in the virtue of that life and power that takes away the occasion of all wars"; that he ". . . was come into the covenant of peace which was before wars and strife were." The power that takes away the occasion of war, the peace that existed before wars and strife were, is the power and peace of the Spirit of the love of God. That is the love that has the power to overcome hate and violence. That is the power of love that can transform even the situation in which we find ourselves today. That is the power of love that sustains the witness for peace through many centuries, and despite persecution. That is the power of love and witness that outlasts all the empires, and all the armies.

What We As Quakers Can Do

How shall we as Quakers sustain ourselves as a people of peace in the midst of worldwide war? By living in that covenant of peace which was before wars and strife were . . . by living in the virtue of that life and power that takes away the occasion of all war. It is not our Quakerism, or our pacifism, or our knowledge, or skill, or emotion that overcomes hate and violence. We shall surely fail if we become proud of our virtue and traditions and become vain in our witness. We shall fail if we think the power that may move through us is our own. The power is not ours, it is God's.

This is the foundation of what we must do in our Testimony of Peace in this time of war. The foundation is faith in the power of God's love to transform us and our society and to bring justice to the poor and the oppressed. Our task is to act, as best we understand what we are led to do, in obedience to that power. Our meetings and Friends churches, if they have grown lazy in their faith, need to "get ready." The time is now.

I cannot claim wisdom as to how God will have us act. I have some suggestions of things we can usefully do now.

First, we can make sure that our young adults are counseled about conscientious objection. We are already in a time of persecution of COs and war tax resisters. Young men who do not register for Selective Service in the U.S.—and there is no way to indicate conscientious objection on the form itself—lose student loans, federal employment opportunities, and, in some states, driver's licenses. Young men must think about their registration for Selective Service, and be sure to be on record with the meeting or Friends church as COs in the event of the draft's reinstatement. Meetings and churches also need to counsel young men and women who are not Quakers but who need our help thinking through the realities of military service. We should be helping young people who are poor to find alternatives to military service as a path of advancement and education. There are a number of Friends organizations with good information on youth, militarism, and conscientious objection. Counseling young people on this topic also lends reality to the meeting's discussion of the war because the youth at risk are our own children.

Second, we can begin the work of nonviolent resistance. Militarism and injustice may seem very strong, and they are, but nonviolence is "a force more powerful." One of the dangers of the myth of the power of violence is that it robs us of the memories of effective nonviolent resistance. How can we say that bullies and unscrupulous people cannot be defeated when we have the successful examples of Mahatma Gandhi; of the Solidarity movement in Poland against Soviet domination; of the Danish resistance to Hitler's Germany that saved thousands of Jews; of the end of legal racial segregation in the United States with Dr. Martin Luther King Jr.'s inspired leadership; of the astonishing, peaceful transfer of power in apartheid South Africa and the equally amazing Truth and Reconciliation Commission that followed; of the "people power" movement in the Philippines that toppled Marcos's corrupt and brutal regime; of the nonviolent people-power movements in Eastern Europe that brought down the Iron Curtain and the Berlin Wall; of the popular demonstrations in Chile that ended Pinochet's rule; and many, many more stories of active, disciplined, nonviolent change?

A first step in the formation of a nonviolent movement in the United States against this war may begin on April 20 with a student-led mobilization in Washington. The mobilization will, for the first time, begin to bring together the Colombia Mobilization, an antiwar demonstration, and concerns about the global economy. All have pledged nonviolence. Let us hope the police and other authorities also are nonviolent.

Third, we in the U.S. can ask the prayers, help, and support of Friends throughout the world. We are not used to asking for such help, but we need it. Some of you Friends in other countries are living through or have lived through violent struggles or wars in your own countries and have much to share with us about what it means to be faithful in difficult times. You can also help U.S. Quakers to "see ourselves as others see us." Most people in the U.S. do not know what our country is doing in your lands. We need to learn, and where appropriate, we need to have the strength to try to change it. You can help us. Friends should also remember that we have much to learn from those who are poor and from people of color in our own country. Here, too, we can benefit from the prayers and insights of those whose experience of life in this country may be different from our own.

Fourth, the "historic peace churches" of Friends, Mennonites, and Brethren have an opportunity to articulate a new vision of a peaceful world that does not rely on military force to solve problems. This is partly the story of the road not taken on September 12. It is also sharing the vision of how nations, nongovernmental organizations, and people of faith can work together to build the institutions that can prevent most armed conflict. There is much to be learned from experience and the literature. This is at least a whole other speech! It is in fact the one I intended to give, but instead the Spirit needed us to remember that war is a terrible thing, and that our Peace Testimony is realistic, not naive.

Finally, let us put on the whole armor of God. The forces of culture, wealth, nationalism, and fear against which we contend are very powerful. Our protection is the power of the love of God to sustain us through what may be the dark days ahead.

Mary Lord is a member of Adelphi (Md.) Meeting. This address was delivered to the annual meeting of Friends World Committee for Consultation, Section of the Americas, in Philadelphia, Pa., on Friday, March 15, 2002.

Viewpoint: Can Friends Come Together in the Search for Peace?

I am writing this because I was very moved by the articles of Mary Lord and Arthur Rifkin in the July 2002 issue of FRIENDS JOURNAL.

On September 11, 2001, my wife Margery and I lived close enough to the disaster at the Twin Towers to be able to see it. We watched people coming over the 59th Street Bridge from Manhattan. Many thousands, walking like refugees, clothing covered with dust and debris, trying to find a way to get home and away from the smoke and the fire. We gave first aid to a neighbor, a young man who hurt his leg running from the disaster. In the days that followed we could see the fire, smell the acrid smoke; it seemed that it would never go away. We cried and mourned and lit candles for those we knew who had lost someone at the Trade Towers.

I felt I had to do something besides attend peace vigils and candlelight services, so I volunteered at the only restaurant that, just a few blocks from Ground Zero, was feeding the rescue workers, firemen, policemen and women, Red Cross workers, state troopers, and members of the National Guard. I worked shifts of six to eight hours to help, with other volunteers, with the feeding of at least 3,600 people a day, 24 hours a day, every day. All the food was donated. You cannot imagine what these people looked like, covered with dirt and debris, tired, many working 12-hour shifts. This "hands-on" work helped me cope with my own inner turmoil.

I am a Quaker and a pacifist, and I came to my convictions from a different direction than most. In World War II, I was an Air Force gunner flying out of England. On our 18th mission over Germany, my crew and I were shot down and I became a prisoner of war. Wounded, beaten, almost executed, and imprisoned in a Stalagluft, I found out very quickly what the consequence of being a combatant in war is all about. To this day I have never gone to visit Ground Zero. I do not need to see the area of destruction. In my lifetime, I have seen enough. Living near London in 1944–45 after the blitz and during the V1-V2 rocket attacks, I watched the people go about their daily lives, with streets, houses, and stores all destroyed. As a POW, I walked through the cities of Frankfurt, Nuremberg, Regensberg, and others. Not one whole building was standing as a result of the Allied bombing raids. The people walked about like robots, with nothing to do and no place to go except hide when air raid sirens went off. I watched them, mostly women and children, standing in a line that stretched for miles waiting with pails for water at a common spigot. With all of these memories, how do I find a way to respond to the Peace Testimony? One had to be in New York on September 11 or tested in combat to know what it feels like to see the hell of humankind's inhumanity.

It is now that I need my Quaker extended family more than ever to help me in this personal turmoil. With great excitement and anticipation I am looking forward to the Friends World Committee for Consultation Conference in January 2003. I would like to see all the branches of Quakerism unite to face this crisis of our time—the threat of global war and terrorism. I need to see our Peace Testimony made relevant for the 21st century. I want to hear the stories of others about their search for peace. I want to know more about our history as it pertains to this search. I want my Quaker family to find a response that is an affirmation both for the living and the dead and that will free us from the scourge of war and terrorism. Friends must declare that we can no longer endure hatred and fear. This will mean taking risks in a search for peace, but in the end we may have a more trustful world and a better living faith. The future of the Religious Society of Friends in the 21st century depends on finding new ways for others to hear our message. Is there still a "great people waiting to be gathered" as George Fox thought at the top of Pendle Hill? I believe this is a time for a new social and spiritual revolution so that we are not irrelevant in the marketplace of religious ideas and action.

As the writer/poet Norman Corwin said at the end of World War II, ". . . and press into the final seal a sign that peace will come for longer than posterity can see ahead, and that human beings unto their fellow human beings shall be a friend forever." I know that this will not be easy. The peacemakers have always steadfastly refused to give up. I fervently hope that the conference in 2003 will be a start on this journey. I also hope that we are not too late.

We need to listen to the prophecy of Joel, so often repeated since his day. It still rings with hope for those who believe in the eternal power of the Spirit over the hearts and minds of men and women: "and it shall come to pass afterward, that I will pour out my spirit upon all flesh; and your sons and your daughters shall prophesy, and your old men shall dream dreams, and your young men shall see visions." (Joel 2:28-29)

—*George Rubin, Medford, N.J.*

George Rubin, of Medford, N.J., is a member of Manhassett (N.Y.) Meeting, now attending Medford (N.J.) Meeting. A former clerk of New York Yearly Meeting, he is a member of the American Friends Service Committee Corporation and previously served on the Executive and Personnel Committees for Friends World Committee for Consultation.

Tokyo

I saw in her eyes
her dead sons
killed in the war.
Our glances held
for just a moment
while we recognized
each other—
enemy mothers—
she, selling me a spool of
thread
to mend my sons' clothes
and I,
trying to control my sadness
and my trembling hands.

—*T.V. Wiley*

T.V. Wiley is a member of Sandy Spring (Md.) Meeting.

Queries

If I found myself living in a brutal environment, could I still look for and speak to that of God in all people and in all creation?

What ways do I find to speak out against the loss of freedom of information, movement, speech, and religion?

Do I speak out against national policies that devalue some people or some part of creation?

In what ways have I found solidarity with oppressed people, at home and abroad?

How can I take steps to become a humble servant of creation rather than a destroyer of it?

Return to the top of the list and ask the Queries in the plural, searching with others to see how your monthly meeting, committee, or community might answer the questions.

Response from a Journalist

Journalists are trained to see a "story" and write about it immediately. Scott Simon's years of experience in radio and television and his reputation as a sensitive and balanced commentator make him a valuable and popular guest in many public venues. Since he says quite plainly, "I happen to be a Quaker" and because he was active in opposing the Vietnam War, his comments become connected in people's minds with Quakers and the pacifist position. He articulates arguments Friends face among their peers within and without the meeting, and he does it in language that often challenges readers. The article's provocative prose, framed in the language of today's press, struck resounding chords in readers of FRIENDS JOURNAL.

The letters that followed Scott Simon's article were numerous and probing. They serve as excellent texts for Friends to ponder, for they speak directly of the immediate reactions and problems we face when we find ourselves, and our ideas, swiftly and decisively, under attack.

The poem by Ken Thompson, "No More Trenches," is like a quiet prayer after the sometimes hectic discussion. The reader hears ricocheting echoes of earlier wars and poems and hopes. One senses the sadness, the horror, and the seeming intractability of war, both in its making and in its resolving, such as it is. At the end, there is only hope.

Reflections on the Events of September Eleventh

by Scott Simon

I am grateful for the opportunity to speak with you at what is so clearly an urgent time. With your permission, I will depart from the line of remarks I had initially sketched out and address myself explicitly to the events of this war.

I can certainly be expansive on the subject of broadcasting, and how we are—or are not—meeting our responsibilities. But those observations would now be small-minded. The fact is, during the recent weeks of crisis all major broadcasters—not only including, but specifically the much-maligned commercial broadcasters—have met those responsibilities with professionalism and devotion. This week, they have only my admiration.

I suspect that what I have to say today about war and peace will not please a good many of you. They are certainly not the remarks you might expect from the person you invited several months ago. I don't want you to feel compelled to offer courteous applause for remarks with which you may vigorously disagree. I am grateful for the chance just to be heard in this forum; that is as much courtesy as I can expect. So let me suggest that my remarks be received simply with silence.

There is nothing good to be said about tragedy or terror. But miseries can distill a sense of utter clarity—remind us of who we are; whom we love; and what is worth giving our lives for.

When Jeremy Glick of Hewitt, New Jersey, called his wife, Lyzbeth, during the last moments of United Flight 93 he said:

"I love you. Don't be sad. Take care of our daughter. Whatever you do is okay with me."

The depth of his love compressed, and clear as a diamond.

Over the past ten days, the pain of loss and fear of terror may have caused many Americans to admit to themselves how much they really love their country. Love it not blindly, but with unblinking awareness.

They love that frivolous America that proclaims pride in 31 flavors of ice cream—but also the solemn mission of having a gaudy Times Square assortment of all the world's peoples within its borders.

They love the America that can be shallow, giddy, and greedy—but also funny, delightful, and generous.

America can abound with silly, malicious, and even dangerous ideas— because people here are free to express any damn-fool idea that comes to them.

America can be bigoted and inhospitable—but it also takes strangers from all over the world into its arms.

America has now been targeted by a few blind souls who are willing to kill thousands—and themselves—to make this nation bleed. But far more people from around the world have already been willing to die— over-packed into holds of ships and trucks—just to have a small chance to live here.

It's not that Americans don't want their country to change, in a thousand ways, from making good medical care available to all Americans, to abolishing the designated hitter rule. But the blast at our emblems last week has made many Americans see their nation as that place in the world where change is still most possible.

Patriotism has often been the last refuge of scoundrels—and we've had those scoundrels. But what hiding place is open to those who twist their faith into a weapon to run through innocent people?

Do we really want to live in the kind of world such blind souls would make for us? In the end, the choice may be that harsh: to live in a world that revolves around fear—or in America, with all its faults.

Now I say this knowing that we have our own American mullahs; and by this I don't mean—in fact, I specifically do not mean—American Muslims who have recently been the object of harassment and threats. I am not of a mind to be obscure about this: I mean specifically the Reverends Jerry Falwell and Pat Robertson. Please permit me to repeat the thrust of some remarks I delivered this past weekend. In a way, I am grateful for this duo: they renewed my capacity to be shocked at a time I thought my sense of shock had been exhausted.

Right after the terrorist strikes in New York and here in Washington, when America was wounded and confused, the Reverend Falwell was a guest on Pat Robertson's 700 Club. He said that God Almighty, angered by America's abortion rights, gay rights, and secularism in the schools, had permitted terrorists to slay the World Trade Center and smite the Pentagon:

"What we saw on Tuesday," said Mr. Falwell, "could be minuscule if in fact God continues to lift the curtain and allow the enemies of

America to give us probably what we deserve."

Mr. Robertson joined in, saying, "Jerry, that's my feeling. I think we've just seen the antechamber to terror. We haven't even begun to see what they can do to the major population."

Then Mr. Falwell concluded, "I really believe that the pagans, and the abortionists, and the feminists, and the gays and lesbians who are actively trying to make that an alternative lifestyle, the ACLU, People for the American Way—all of them who have tried to secularize America—I point the finger in their face and say, you helped this happen."

Last week, both the reverends issued apologies. Mr. Falwell called his own remarks "insensitive, uncalled for, and unnecessary"—everything but wrong.

Also last week, it was reported that Mark Bingham, a San Francisco public relations executive, may well have been one of the passengers who so bravely resisted the hijackers of American Airlines Flight 93, which crashed into an unpopulated field, instead of another national monument.

Mr. Bingham was 31. He played on a local gay rugby team, and hoped to compete in next year's Gay Games in Sydney, Australia.

I don't know if Mark Bingham was religious. But it seems to me that he lived a life that celebrated the preciousness of this world's infinite variety, while the Reverends Robertson and Falwell, and the mullahs of the Taliban, see a God who smiles with approval on murder and destruction.

Let me put it in the bald terms in which many Americans may be thinking right now: if your plane were hijacked, who would you rather sit next to? Righteous reverends who will sit back and say, "This is God's punishment for gay Teletubbies?" Or the gay rugby player who lays down his life to save others?

And by the way: which person seems closer to God?

One of the unforeseen effects of being in journalism is that your firsthand exposure to the issues of the world sometimes has the consequence of shaking your deepest personal convictions. I happen to be a Quaker; I suspect that may have something to do with me being invited to speak here today. I covered conflicts in Central America and the Caribbean, the Middle East and Africa. None of them shook my belief that pacifism offers the world a way to foment change without the violence that has pained and poisoned our history.

Gandhi and Nehru's nonviolent revolution gave India a skilled and sturdy democracy, rather than another violent religious tyranny. Nelson Mandela's willingness to employ deliberate and peaceful protest against the brutalities of apartheid made today's South Africa an inspiration to the world of the power of reconciliation and hope. Martin Luther King Jr.'s campaign to bring down American segregation; Corazon Aquino's People Power revolution in the Philippines—pacifism has had its heroes, its martyrs, its losses, and its victories.

My pacifism was not absolute. About half the draft-age Quakers and Mennonites in North America enlisted during World War II, on the idea that whatever solutions nonviolence had to offer the world, it was without a response to Adolf Hitler. I hope I would have been among those who enlisted.

And then, in the 1990s, I covered the Balkans. And I had to confront, in flesh and blood, the real-life flaw—I am inclined to say literally fatal flaw—of pacifism: all the best people could be killed by all the worst ones. Bosnia, we might remind ourselves, had the ambition of being the Costa Rica of the Balkans, an unarmed democracy that would shine out to the world. Its surrounding adversaries were not impressed or deterred by this aspiration.

Slobodan Milosevic will now stand trial before the world—but only after a quarter of a million people in Bosnia and Kosovo have been killed. Forgive me if I do not count his delivery for trial as a victory for international law, and therefore a model to now be emulated. In fact, I am appalled by the fact that much of the evidence presented against him at trial will almost undoubtedly be derived from U.S. intelligence information. That evidence will be used to try to convict Slobodan Milosevic after he has committed murder—because America lacked the will to use its military might to prevent those murders.

So I speak as a Quaker of not particularly good standing. I still am willing to give first consideration to peaceful alternatives. But I am not willing to lose lives for the sake of ideological consistency. As Mahatma Gandhi himself once said—and, like Lincoln, the Mahatma is wonderful for providing quotations that permit you to prove almost any point you choose—"I would rather be inconsistent than wrong."

It seems to me that in confronting the forces that attacked the World Trade Center and the Pentagon, the United States has no sane alternative but to wage war; and wage it with unflinching resolution.

Notice I don't say reprisal or revenge. What I mean is self-defense—

protecting the United States from further attack by destroying those who would launch them.

There is a certain quarter of opinion in the United States—we certainly hear from them at National Public Radio—who, perhaps still in shock, seem to believe that the attacks against New York and Washington were natural disasters: horrible, spontaneous whirlwinds that struck once, and will not recur.

This is wrong. It is even inexcusably foolish. The United States has been targeted for destruction. We know now that more hijackings were likely planned for September 11th. Other agents were at least exploring the possibilities of other kinds of attacks, including sending crop-dusters over cities with poisonous chemicals. If you dismissed these kinds of scenarios as Hollywood folderol before, it is just not informed to do so now. There is an ongoing violent campaign aimed at bringing down the United States. How many more skyscrapers and national monuments— and the people in them—how many more citizens are we willing to lose?

There are some quarters of world opinion who believe that simply delivering those who plotted the attack to international justice should suffice. But this is not the nature of the danger we confront—literally, physically, in this very city—which is present, persistent, and current. Simply arresting those who executed the attacks in New York and Washington will not deter other assaults that we must assume are proceeding right now.

There are some quarters of opinion who say, just this bluntly, that Americans somehow invited this attack upon ourselves—for sins that range from slavery to the policies of the CIA.

The people who make these arguments usually consider themselves at the polar opposite of the Reverend Jerry Falwell and the Reverend Pat Robertson. But are they? They say that those who died in New York and Washington have only their country to blame for their deaths. By ignoring the extensive advancement America has made towards becoming a just society, they make it seem as if sins that are centuries and decades old can never be overcome by progress.

Some of our finest minds have become so skilled at playing this parlor game of moral relativism that they make little in American life seem worthwhile. They insist, in so many ways, that the United States cannot criticize the Taliban for enslaving women in the 21st century because we once had slavery ourselves—a century and a half ago. They suggest that the United States does not have the moral standing to oppose terrorism because we once supported the Shah of Iran.

But what price would those who urge reconciliation pay for peace? Should we surrender Manhattan Island? Iowa, Utah, or Hollywood? Relocate Israel, piece by piece, to Ohio, New Jersey, or Florida—to fatten the vote for Pat Buchanan? Should we impose a unitary religious state on these shores, throw American women out of school and work, and rob all other religious groups of any rights so that we will have the kind of society that our attackers will accept?

To reconcile ourselves in any way with the blind souls who flew against New York and Washington—and who have other targets within their sights now—is to hand our own lives over into wickedness.

I'm glad to see reporting now that asks, "Why do they hate us?" We need to hear the complaints of those who experience U.S. foreign policy, sometimes at the blunt end. But I would not want our increasing erudition to distract us from the answer that applies to those who are now physically attacking the United States: they hate us because they are psychotics. They should be taken no more seriously as political theorists than Charles Manson or Timothy McVeigh.

I have been impressed by President Bush's determination to make the rights of Muslim Americans—and American respect for Muslim nations—an essential part of U.S. policy. This is vastly different from the actions that were inflicted against Japanese Americans during World War II. The difference between the damage that good liberals of their time, Earl Warren, Franklin Roosevelt, and Hugo Black, imposed on an ethnic minority in 1941, and what conservatives of this time, George W. Bush, Rudolph Giuliani, and John Ashcroft, have specifically avoided doing, radiantly represents America's ability to improve itself.

Over the past ten years, every time the United States has committed itself to a military deployment—explicitly in the Gulf War, then in Somalia, and over the skies of Bosnia and Kosovo—it has been in the defense of Muslim peoples. At the same time, tens of thousands of Muslim students and other immigrants have been accepted into the United States. American Muslims now number close to 6,000,000.

We still suffer the stain of racial and ethnic bigotry. But this largely peaceful incorporation of Islam into American life should be a source of pride that is not belittled by the actions of a few cranks and bigots. Surely we have the means to defeat them, too.

I can conjure a score of reasons why this war should not be fought. The terrorists who struck are ruthless, and undaunted even by their own deaths. The war will kill people—Americans, and those from other nations: sacred and irreplaceable souls all. The war will be lengthy, costly, and fail to culminate with an unambiguous surrender in a small-town courthouse. Just when we may begin to feel a sense of safety returning—another strike may occur. The war may restrict some of the liberties—to travel and communicate freely—that define us; liberties that, I would add, have already been badly abused by those who carried out these attacks.

And yet: to back away from this war would be to live the rest of our lives, not just a few years, with skyscrapers and bridges exploding, people dying by terrorist bombs, chemical attacks, and the successive devices of sharp and ruthless minds, to live out our futures with our liberties shrinking as our losses and fears expand.

I think that peace activists can sometimes commit the same error in judgment as generals: they prepare to fight the last war, not the next one. The conflict before us now does not involve American power intruding in places where it has interest. It's about American power intervening to save lives in a circumstance in which only American power can be effective.

We are living in a time when we must remind ourselves of the imperfections of analogies. But let me press ahead with one that has recently been on my mind.

In 1933, the Oxford Student Union conducted a famous debate over whether it was moral for Britons to fight for king and country. The exquisite intellects of that leading university reviewed the many ways in which British colonialism exploited and oppressed the world. They cited the ways in which vengeful demands made of Germany in the wake of the end of World War I had helped encourage the kind of nationalism that may have kindled the rise of fascism. They saw no moral difference between Western colonialism and world fascism. The Oxford Union ended that debate with this famous proclamation: "Resolved, that we will in no circumstances fight for king and country."

Von Ribbentrop sent back the good news to Germany's new chancellor, Adolf Hitler: the West will not fight for its own survival. Its finest minds will justify a silent surrender.

The best educated young people of their time could not tell the difference between the deficiencies of their own nation, in which liberty and democracy occupied cornerstones, and a dictatorship founded on racism, tyranny, and fear.

But Mahatma Gandhi knew the difference. He spent World War II in a prison in Poona and sat on his hands and spun cloth, rather than to raise a hand in revolt against England when it was most vulnerable. He knew that, in the end, a world that was spun by German and Japanese fascism offered no hope to the oppressed of this planet. And in fact, at the close of World War II, Britain divested itself of empire: exhausted by its own defense, to be sure, but also ennobled by defending its own best ideals.

Have thoughtful, moral Americans in the 21st century become so extremely sensitive to the sins and shortcomings of the United States, so comfortable with the lack of resolution that moral relativism promotes, that we do not see the blessing that has been put into our hands to protect: an incomparably diverse and democratic nation?

Friends do not need any lectures about risking their lives to stop wickedness. Quakers resisted slavery by smuggling out slaves when even Abraham Lincoln tried to appease the Confederacy. But those of us who have been pacifists might consider that it has been our blessing to live in a nation in which other citizens have been willing to risk their lives to defend our dissent.

When George Orwell returned to England after fighting against fascism in the Spanish Civil War, he felt uneasy over finding his country so comfortable—so close to fascism. His country, he said, with its fat Sunday newspapers and thick orange jam—"all sleeping the deep, deep sleep," he wrote, "from which I sometimes fear that we shall never wake till we are jerked out of it by the roar of bombs."

On September 11, Americans, with our 40 different kinds of coffee drinks and diet pills, heard that roar. And that blast awakened a gratitude to live in a country worth loving—worth defending.

Scott Simon, host of National Public Radio's Weekend Edition, is a former member of Friends Meeting of Washington (D.C.) and of Northside Meeting in Chicago, Ill. He spent many hours covering the terrorist strike at the World Trade Center. This article is based on a talk given on September 25 in Washington, D.C., as the annual Parker Lecture sponsored by the United Church of Christ; audio version is available at <www.ucc.org>. Scott Simon is the author of a novel, Pretty Birds, *about two teenage girls during the siege of Sarajevo.*

Forum: Diversity of Opinion Appreciated

As three conscientious objectors from the Vietnam era, and as members of Friends Meeting of Austin (Tex.), we are writing to thank you for the article by Scott Simon, "Reflections on the Events of September Eleventh" (*FJ* Dec. 2001), regarding pacifism and the challenges of responding to those events. While each of us may or may not agree with every point Scott Simon makes, his article encourages Quaker discourse, and reminds us that very sincere Quakers can differ in what each perceives as appropriate action.

He raises many concerns that are not often or easily expressed in meeting for worship, sometimes for fear of seeming "un-Quakerly." Pacifism is so much easier to discuss abstractly than to implement specifically. It is easy to forget that so much of Quakerism's relevance comes from eschewing dogma in favor of application of our testimonies to each new situation.

Scott Simon's article is filled with many real-world examples that challenge our individual commitment as Quakers. It is so often easier to write generally about Quaker principles than to explore real-world situations that reflect those principles in action. As with the person who said he "loved humanity, it's just people I have trouble with," it is similarly easy to say, "I love the Quaker testimonies, it's just their implementation that I have trouble with."

Your publishing Simon's article helps to make certain that a variety of Quaker voices are heard, including those that are less comfortably or clearly certain of what ought to be done. Such diversity of opinion within FRIENDS JOURNAL is appreciated.

—Joe Farley, Ted Dix, Ben Kuipers, Austin, Tex.

Forum: Reactions to Violence Vary

I have been and am a devoted fan of Scott Simon. I try never to miss his segment of Weekend Edition on National Public Radio. FRIENDS JOURNAL is to be commended for publishing the article (*FJ* Dec. 2001) based on the address he gave in Washington, D.C. just two weeks after the assaults of September 11.

Surely one clue to Scott Simon's change of heart in respect to pacifism derives from his firsthand experiences of being at Ground Zero in New York immediately following the attacks. Anyone who heard his broadcast three months later about the Rockaway community on Long Island will understand the depth of his empathies. "One of the unforeseen effects of being in journalism," he notes, "is that your firsthand exposure to the issues of the world sometimes has the consequence of shaking your deepest personal convictions."

A reaction quite opposite to his is found among some who served on the front lines in World Wars I and II and in Vietnam. Their experiences led them to peace activism, if not to absolute pacifism. The realities of war shook their personal convictions.

The bottom line in Scott Simon's statement is that "the United States has no sane alternative but to wage war and wage it with unflinching resolution." Yes, and the resolution passed by Congress, with only Barbara Lee dissenting, gave President Bush authority to attack anyone involved in the September 11 assaults—anywhere, in any country. It was this same unflinching resolution that led the United States and its allies in the Second World War to insist on unconditional surrender, paving the way for obliteration bombing of German cities and the dropping of atomic bombs on Japan.

It is regrettably understandable that the U.S., which spends over $400 billion for military purposes—one-half of the federal government's discretionary budget—chooses to rely largely on that force to counter the September 11 assaults. But this response deflects us from grasping why the acts of a tiny number of extremists strike a resonant chord in many Muslim nations.

The sad fact is that they see the U.S., the only superpower in the world, as the Great Satan undermining their cultures, striving to sustain our opulent, materialistic lifestyle. They also see the U.S. supporting repressive and corrupt Gulf governments. It is out of the soil of oppression and poverty, allied with a warped interpretation of Islam, that terrorism grows.

The focus of the Quaker Peace Testimony is rightly the issue of war itself. Only when a vast number of people in the U.S. come to the conviction that war and preparations for war, like terrorism, are inherently evil, will our beloved country be able to move toward radically different foreign policies.

The poetic author of Deuteronomy put an exasperated plea into the mouth of God: "I have set before you life and I have set before you death, and I have begged you to choose life for the sake of your children."

—*Larry Miller*, New Britain, Pa.

Forum: What is the Moral High Ground?

Thank you for printing Scott Simon's "Reflections on the Events of September Eleventh" (*FJ* Dec. 2001). I applaud him for speaking the truth as he sees it at the risk of offending good people. (It is easy for me to say that, since I agree with most of what he says; I confess I would have a harder time being so charitable toward opinions with which I disagree).

I would dearly love to call myself a pacifist. I admire the work Friends have done in preventing wars and in repairing the ravages of war. But I have a very hard time with the absolutism of our Peace Testimony. There are other groups who call themselves pacifists, which do not altogether rule out military action. Martin Luther King Jr. said that he would have "set aside" his pacifism during World War II "in the face of such evil."

"Violence only begets more violence," we say. Certainly that's often true. But is it always? If a sniper in a tower is firing on crowds in the street, is it wrong to shoot and kill the sniper before he kills more people? Did the group who tried and failed to assassinate Hitler do wrong? Should the passengers who overpowered the hijackers on United Flight 93 have sat on their hands? On the other hand, it seems to me that to respond in any conciliatory way to the September 11 attackers would reward a horrific act of violence, and whatever is rewarded is encouraged: this too, then, begets violence. ("So this is what it takes to get America's attention!")

"No more victims," we cry. Yet surely we know there will be more victims, whether we bomb Afghanistan without mercy or whether we do nothing and wait for al-Qaida to strike again. I certainly do not mean to imply that Afghan victims are preferable to U.S. victims; just that we seem unwilling to acknowledge unpleasant realities.

If there is such a thing as a just war, then we can address the question of what criteria determine whether or not a particular war is just. If violence can be the right response in extreme circumstances, what are the boundaries of permissible violence? If war and violence are never justified, then we are spared the trouble of thinking further, or of making hard choices between greater and lesser evils. Is this the moral high ground? I am not so sure.

—*Edna Dam*, Vashon, Wash.

Forum: Are Only Peaceful Means Acceptable in All Cases?

Thank you for printing Scott Simon's "Reflections on the Events of September 11" (*FJ* Dec. 2001). I remember seeing a similar version online, where another Friend had responded in horror (it seemed to me), writing that someone needed to respond to this! It seemed to me that Scott Simon's ideas were being labeled as crazy and needed to be beaten down.

I believe in striving for peace.

However, it is not wise to ignore the fact that violent people cannot be deterred by nonviolent means except in a few cases. For us to believe that only peaceful means are acceptable moral responses in all cases flies in the face of observable facts. I would not stand peacefully by while my family was being harmed, even if it meant that I would need to use lethal force. So why should I expect my government to be any different? I can easily see that I and my government could react badly, but I believe that both are capable of reasonable responses. Not acting in some cases causes problems just like reacting badly. Irresponsibility can be the result of not responding.

So thanks for printing what seems to me to be an "opposing" view. I am convinced that peace is our goal; but in this world our responses will not always be peaceful. The military is not always wrong. Peace activists are not always saints. It is a crazy, mixed-up world. We need thoughtful and careful responses, not bumper-sticker philosophy.

—*Daniel Coston*, Fayetteville, Ark.

Forum: What is Continuing Revelation for Us Now?

Having read parts of the December 2001 issue, I feel compelled to write. The kernel of my thought occurred prior to this reading, but I am now in a position of needing to speak (with trembling and quaking).

Scott Simon dared to express the complexity of living in this modern world in a time of fear, pain, and distrust. Our history as a country is a mixed bag: great ideals with imperfect execution. At a point in crisis, all of this comes into view with a need for appropriate response and action.

I am very aware of the pacifist roots of our Religious Society, and I am also aware of the one tenet that is unique to Friends: the fact that the "truth" is always being revealed. I personally have struggled with the dilemma of what to do, given the attack on the World Trade Center. The reconciliation is an uneasy one in my own mind, but it is my sense that Scott Simon is writing, with discernment, about the issues involved and has arrived at a conclusion very similar to my own. I know from ministry in my meeting that this does not sit easily on the shoulders of those who do not believe in war at any cost. Personally, this view and potential action, does not negate "that of God" in everyone for me. To stand up and, not with a spirit of revenge, to intervene before the terrorism escalates killing even more "innocent victims" is essential.

One of the problematic areas for me continues to be with the probable "imperfect" actions of those in positions of power in our government and military. I worry about their process of discernment even under the most ideal circumstances, much less under the imperfect circumstances in which we find ourselves. I suggest that we hold in the Light those in power, those who are struggling with a wish to act out their pain and anger inappropriately, those who perpetrated this crisis, and all of the peoples of the world who struggle with their pain over this dreadful situation.

—*Sharon Bosley,* San Jose, Calif.

Forum: Religious Pacifism Encompasses That of God in All

I write in response to the article by Scott Simon (*FJ* Dec. 2001). As a journalist, he points out that while he covered the conflicts in Central America, the Caribbean, the Middle East, and Africa, his pacifism was not shaken. Now, because our country has been attacked, his beliefs have fallen to the wayside. Being juxtaposed between the articles by Carol Reilly Urner and John Paul Lederach, along with the poem by Phil Lord, one is prompted to think about the fallacy of Scott Simon's support of the U.S. war plans on September 25. His pacifism appears to be something he supports only when it is comfortable to do so—that is, when it applies to the victims of other conflicts, but not those in our country. As a Quaker, my religious pacifism encompasses our central theological belief of that of God in every person, with no exceptions. War-making is always a sinful activity because it denies the divine in our so-called enemies.

Scott Simon supports his argument with the specious statement that "half of the draft-age Quakers and Mennonites in North America enlisted in World War II, on the idea that whatever solutions nonviolence had to offer the world, it was without a response to Adolf Hitler." He does not identify his source of information, nor does he make any mention of whether these "enlistees" were combatants. Was this an intentional oversight to support his argument? I checked with Center for Conscience and War (formerly NISBCO) and the folks there say that Simon's statement is wrong. Approximately half of these groups did not enlist, although they did accept military service when drafted. His statement is not justified since he ignores that these were primarily veterans who registered as 1AO and thus were among the 25,000 noncombatants.

He goes on to assert that pacifism's "fatal flaw" doomed Bosnia's effort to become the Costa Rica of the Balkans. The comparison is an ill fit, at best. Costa Rica was not threatened by its neighbors, nor did it have similar ethnic problems. Perhaps Bosnia and Herzegovina can try demilitarization again in the future, with the help of the UN, as that region stabilizes.

Simon notes that the terrorists "hate us because they are psychotics." That may be. But to summarily dismiss them as not to be taken seriously is dangerous. Osama bin Laden and al-Qaida are an organized crime network, and should be dealt with as such. To equate them with a foreign military power against which to retaliate is a mindset that could easily lead us down a spiral of endless violence. The suggestions given in John Paul Lederach's article ("The Challenge of Terror: A Traveling Essay," *FJ* Dec. 2001) are much more thoughtful and reasonable than blindly going to war to "defend" (i.e. killing for) our country.

Scott Simon stated that he was impressed with President Bush's statements regarding the treatment of Muslim Americans. I was as well on September 25. But since that time, with the passage of the USA

Patriot Act, the signing of the executive order regarding the assignment of suspected terrorists to military tribunals, along with the secretive detention of immigrants through racial and religious profiling conducted by the Justice Department and the Immigration and Naturalization Service, one sees that Bush's actions belie his words.

Scott Simon "can conjure" but not see "a score of reasons why this war should not be fought." I wonder if he knew of Lederach's essay, which was written on September 16. If not, would his words have changed? I doubt it because throughout the article he belittles pacifists as if we are passive in the face of violence, terrorism, and war. Reading about the Urners, and knowing of the work of such groups as American Friends Service Committee, Christian Peacemaker Teams, Fellowship of Reconciliation, Mennonite Central Committee, and Peace Brigades International contradicts that premise entirely.

A violent, war-making response to terrorism is expedient, but does not solve the problem. Eliminating the cause of terrorism and pursuing justice for everyone is the hard, but necessary, path to follow.

—*Daniel G. Cole*, Middletown, Md.

Forum: We Need to Ask Hard Questions

I was deeply troubled by Scott Simon's article "Reflection on the Events of September Eleventh" (*FJ* Dec. 2001). He is a shrewd journalist who is expert at pushing the right buttons. I was struck by his unquestioning acceptance that we are "at war" and reduction of our choice to a "world such blind souls would make for us, . . . or America, with all its faults." That's close to saying "America, right or wrong." Moreover, he is disingenuous (I can't believe he is that naive) to portray people, hiding in the holds of ships to enter this country, as admirers of our way of life. Most immigrants I have met are here escaping hunger and destitution, not because of cultural admiration. The "31 flavors of ice cream" was a gruesome touch, when one recalls that two-thirds of the world goes to bed hungry every night.

But the clincher came for me when he said, "I covered conflicts in Central America and the Caribbean, the Middle East, and Africa." Then he is no stranger to Guatemala, El Salvador, and Nicaragua, where the Catholic Church and human rights groups have documented that from

1975 to 1985 more than 450,000 innocent, defenseless civilians were killed by death squads and military forces, led by officers trained at the School of the Americas at Fort Benning, Georgia. I would like to read his comments on that.

Before these atrocities there was Iran in 1953, Cuba in 1959–60, Congo in 1960, Brazil in 1964, Indonesia in 1965, Vietnam in 1961–73, Chile in 1973, the Philippines in 1960–80, Iraq from 1991 to the present. In every one of the countries mentioned, our government supported the dictators who ran them at least some of the time, and the CIA armed, trained, and financed their armed forces. The CIA trained the police departments of those countries and many more on how to torture without killing the victim. No one is better at the "down and dirty" than we are when we want to be. The "commercial broadcasters," who Scott Simon claims are so responsible and professional today, have kept that history a secret from most people in the U.S. for 40 years.

The painful truth that Scott Simon misses is that many in the world who hate us are not psychotic, although this condition may apply to bin Laden. As observers of our civilization, via television, they perceive how driven we are by money, as a suffocating cornucopia of individual wealth and power is constantly displayed on the screen. The destitute of the world, who survive on less than a few dollars a day, have intuited correctly that our obscene consumption is in direct proportion to their wretched poverty.

We consider ourselves generous, but tolerate hunger and homelessness in our own country while consuming 40 percent of the world's natural resources. That amounts to the generosity of a millionaire who drops a quarter in a tin cup. We consider ourselves just, but execute prisoners without benefit of a fair trial. We say we are alarmed about the environment, but turn our backs on the Kyoto Protocol, despite being the leading source of greenhouse gas emissions that cause global warming. We consider ourselves law abiding, but refuse to join the International Court of Justice. We think our strength is the only virtue that matters, our power to retaliate and crush the designated enemy.

It is difficult to love, like, or respect what our nation has become. We appear to believe that the goods of this world are infinite, are set aside for us, and are completely capable of satisfying the desires of the human heart. In reality, no amount of wealth will ever bring about a decent, loving, and just world, any more than will all the "intelligent" weapons currently in our arsenal.

Scott Simon's article is based on the assumption that God is sometimes wrong and that we have to put things right. Thus, kill we must. That is nothing more than the glorification of the "I" in ourselves over the existence of God. For my part, I choose the spirit and power of love, no matter how righteous, well-intentioned, and moderate the sword claims to be. Nothing can justify the attacks of September 11, but flag-waving, blind patriotism, and the suspension of civil rights cannot resolve it. We need to ask some hard questions about who we are and how we have treated the world.

—Roy Herrera Jr., Kissimmee, Fla.

Forum: Let's Understand Motivations

I really appreciated the honesty with which Scott Simon explored his thoughts and reflections about 9/11 (*FJ* Dec. 2001). This is such a complex issue that it deserves just such in-depth examination. However, I was startled to read his statement, "The conflict before us now does not involve American power intruding in places where it has interest." As British writer John Pilger wrote in the newspaper the U.K. *Mirror* on 10/29/01, the oil and gas reserves in the Caspian basin are the greatest source of untapped fossil fuel on Earth, and it is a geopolitical fact that only if the pipeline runs through Afghanistan can the U.S. hope to control it. That is why we need to control Afghanistan. To quote Mr. Pilger: "When the Taliban took Kabul in 1996, Washington said nothing. Why? Because Taliban leaders were soon on their way to Houston, Texas, to be entertained by executives of the oil company, UNOCAL. With secret U.S. government approval, the company offered them a generous cut of the profits of the oil and gas pumped through a pipeline that the Americans wanted to build from Soviet central Asia through Afghanistan."

A U.S. diplomat said: "The Taliban will probably develop like the Saudis did." He explained that Afghanistan would become a U.S. oil colony, there would be huge profits for the West, no democracy, and the legal persecution of women. "We can live with that," he said. Although the deal fell through, it remains an urgent priority of the administration of George W. Bush, which is steeped in the oil industry.

So, not surprisingly, U.S. Secretary of State Colin Powell is now referring to "moderate" Taliban, who will join a U.S.-sponsored "loose federation" to run Afghanistan. The "war on terrorism" is a cover for this: a means of achieving U.S. strategic aims that lie behind the flag-waving façade of great power.

I know this reality does not decree whether one follows pacifist or nonpacifist responses to the attacks on the U.S., but we must understand the reality with which we are dealing in order to take the most informed approach.

—*Margaret Lobenstine,* Belchertown, Mass.

To FRIENDS JOURNAL Readers: A Response

by Scott Simon

I am grateful to have been able to follow the debate over my remarks that were printed in FRIENDS JOURNAL ("Reflections on the Events of September 11," December 2001). I might add that portions of my remarks, which were abstracted from a speech I gave shortly after the terrorist attacks to a United Church of Christ convention in Washington, D.C., were also excerpted in *The Advocate* and *Soldier of Fortune,* as well as FRIENDS JOURNAL. (There cannot be many people like myself—on the mailing lists of all of those publications as well as *Martha Stewart Living.*) I took some pleasure in directing the small fee that I was owed for publication of my words by *Soldier of Fortune* to be sent to American Friends Service Committee.

I would like to offer some responses to what many readers wrote. Please understand that I respect every Friend's personal convictions and do not seek to change them. (I rather doubt that anything I say would anyway.) I'd like to think that my own change is the result of working around the world as a journalist for more than two decades, often in zones of conflict. My religious convictions have been knocked about by real life. Many of my experiences have borne out the essential truth of the Peace Testimony. But other encounters—say, in the Balkans, or the war on terrorism—have led me to see ways in which nonviolence, arguably, can abet suffering and the loss of innocent lives. As a reporter and, I hope, still a faithful person, I feel an obligation to share my thinking.

I have come to regret one phrase of my remarks in "Reflections on the Events of September 11." When I asserted that the hijackers of September 11 "hate us because they are psychotics," I was unfair—to psychotics. As several readers wrote, psychotics have a genuine mental disorder. It is often the product of a chemical or emotional imbalance. The hijackers of September 11 were mass murderers. As far as I can tell, they were in full possession of their faculties when they massacred 3,000 people.

Many people who responded to my remarks [in the FRIENDS JOURNAL Forum, Feb.–May, July 2002—eds.] made wild representations about the number of people killed by U.S. and Allied bombing in Afghanistan. I find these assertions particularly fantastic because many were advanced while I was in Afghanistan, actually reporting on the war, including civilian casualties.

I tend to hold with the judgment reached by my colleague, Mike Schuster, and the reporters of the *New York Times*: about 800 Afghan civilians were killed in the U.S.-led military campaign there. Many of those deaths are being investigated. Several have already been ruled a mistake or negligence by the U.S. military. Perhaps a few will be found to be war crimes.

Amnesty International, which I greatly admire, puts the number significantly higher, at about 3,000. I think their number lacks documentation, but I note it with respect. It is, at any rate, still well below the tens of thousands that some FRIENDS JOURNAL readers advanced with certitude.

Now 3,000 lives—or 800—are not negligible. I would not want to be among that 3,000 or 800. I would not want anyone I loved to be among that number. I would not want any stranger to be among those killed. But I would invite Friends to measure the number of civilians killed in the war to liberate Afghanistan from the grip of the Taliban alongside the number that would have been killed if the Taliban had stayed in power.

I did a story from the Kabul soccer stadium. When the Taliban was in power, thousands of people would be rounded up from the streets of Kabul and locked into that stadium each Friday afternoon. Then, 12, 18, 20, or 25 people would be marched onto the field and executed by Taliban "judges" for various religious crimes. (Perhaps it is needless to add: there were no appeals, no inquiry of a free press, and no F. Lee Bailey or ACLU to file last-minute appeals.)

Some men and women would be strung up from the goal posts.

Others had their hands or legs amputated and were left to bleed their lives out into the grass. Not even in Texas, I suspect, would you get a large crowd of spectators to willingly witness routine executions. The roundup of an audience at gunpoint to watch hangings and butchery were meant to emphasize a message that the thousands who witnessed this weekly crime were intended to bring back to their friends and families: the Taliban rule, and by blood.

If the Taliban had not been displaced, those routine, despicable murders—hundreds of people a year—would have continued. We interviewed the man who had been the chief groundskeeper at the soccer stadium and asked a question that might have struck him as coming from Martians, as much as U.S. citizens: Why did he mop up the blood shed by murderers week after week, and keep reporting for work? "What else could I do?" he asked. "I had no reason to think anything would ever change."

My crew and I also reported on mass graves in the mountains of Bamiyan province. More than 3,000 people were probably slaughtered and buried in the countryside surrounding the massive Buddha statues that the Taliban used slave labor to destroy—and then killed many of the workers. I doubt that the remaining Hazzara people would have been safe for long; certainly they lived in constant fear.

I saw the kind of world that the al-Qaida terror network and the Taliban created when they had the chance to build their own society. It is the only kind of society they accept as legitimate and holy. It was a society in which women were chattel; skeptics, doubters, and dissidents of all kinds were imprisoned; and arts, entertainment, sports, and other diversions were forbidden. Gay rights? Don't even think about it. Anyone who doubts that Afghanistan is a better place because of the Allied military intervention should ask him or herself if they would have been willing to live as a gay man or woman under the Taliban. How long would they have treasured peace when it meant their continued enslavement?

There are some Quakers who will say there is no difference between 3,000 people killed by the Taliban and 3,000 killed in Allied bombing. I know the bromides of pacifism. I used to say that kind of thing myself. But I think there's a significant difference.

If the Taliban had stayed in power and were permitted to murder thousands more, Afghanistan today would be even more blighted for having no hope of change. Perhaps 800 or 3,000 innocent civilians died in the military campaign to depose the Taliban. But their families and friends now have a country in which half the people in school are women, half the people in the workforce are women, there is a free press, freedom of worship, freedom not to worship, and a free political system (a political system so free that President Hamid Karzai opposes any U.S. invasion of Iraq). Yes, some warlords are gaining power. Yes, hunger and poverty still stalk the land. But there is also joy, music, culture, and a hope of change that had been crushed before the world was aroused by the events of September 2001 to depose the Taliban.

I have an analogy that is conveniently available in my own family. As some readers may know, my wife is from Normandy. A number of her aunts, uncles, and cousins who grew up during World War II were adolescents at the time of the Allied invasion. They have vivid memories of the British bombing that was ordered to break British and Canadian troops out of the thickly hedged French countryside in which the invasion got ground down. Many of them can recall family friends who died when they got caught up in that bombing. They still grieve when they recall those frightening times. But that grief and loss do not mean that they wish they had spent the rest of their lives under Nazi occupation. They did not expect that brutes would be displaced without bloodshed.

A number of respondents also argued that since U.S. policymakers had, at one point, ignored the crimes of the Taliban, it is inconsistent and hypocritical for the United States to depose them now. This is a fair debater's point, but it is not necessarily a good guide for policy. It was a mistake to overlook the crimes of the Taliban in the mid-1990s (as it was a mistake to countenance the crimes of Saddam Hussein in the early 1980s). That mistake is only compounded, not relieved, by consistency. As Mahatma Gandhi once observed to someone who he had maddened by changing his mind, "I know more today than I did yesterday."

I am similarly unconvinced by arguments that try to diminish the moral logic of defeating the Taliban by observing that the U.S. did not intervene in Rwanda; or until it was too late to avoid mass murder in Bosnia and Kosovo. I tend to feel that the United States should have intervened in those places, too (intervention in Bosnia might have even forestalled the slaughter in Kosovo). There is no comfort or honor in seeing lives sacrificed for the sake of intellectual or moral consistency.

I believe that Afghanistan is a better, freer country because of Allied military intervention that defeated the brutal, repressive, women-enslaving, gay-bashing theocracy that ruled there and made a home for the training and export of terrorism. I believe that the breakup of some elements of the al-Qaida terror network has already led to the interruption of several ongoing plots that have saved lives—including, perhaps, the lives of people who opposed military action.

I will not be sidetracked into defending the civil liberties policies of Attorney General John Ashcroft. I will note that it is a remarkable feature of U.S. democracy that a time limit was built into the provisions of the so-called USA-Patriot Act, largely at the insistence of conservative Republicans who were alarmed at the potential for misuse in many of those laws.

I don't feel that the entire war on terrorism is discredited by those laws; any more than I feel that the Allied effort to win World War II was altogether discredited by the U.S. incarceration of innocent Japanese-Americans, the racial segregation in the U.S. military, the bombing of Dresden, or the colonialism of the British Empire—and if there are FRIENDS JOURNAL readers who do not believe that they have grown up in a better, freer world because the Allies were able to defeat the Axis powers in World War II, I doubt that there is much I can say to convince them otherwise. I do know that such a judgment does not make me eager to hear anything else they may have to say.

If you open any daily newspaper, ride a big-city subway, step into any big-city public school—or if you attend almost any big-city Quaker meeting—you still will be impressed by the strength and vigor of diversity, and the state of free expression in the United States.

Over the past year, I not only read the letters sent to FRIENDS JOURNAL, but made a number of appearances at Quaker schools and meetings. It seems to me that many of the people who were eager to confront my views were not acting in the light of the Peace Testimony so much as they were inflexible political ideologues. Some sounded as if they hadn't taken a fresh look at the world or reassessed their own thinking since Joni Mitchell's first *Greatest Hits* album.

I would not begin to try to convince FRIENDS JOURNAL readers that war is moral. I don't believe that myself. But I do believe that it may sometimes be necessary for survival.

Asia Bennett, former AFSC executive secretary, once told me, "Quakers are very good at recognizing injustice. We are not always good about recognizing evil." Her observation (even as she might disapprove of the lessons I eventually drew from her wisdom) stayed with me as I covered holocausts and their aftermaths in Bosnia, Kosovo, and Afghanistan. The people who sponsored those crimes often said they had been impelled to act by injustice. But when I looked down into mass graves, or uncovered mutilations, I saw, near as I suppose I will ever recognize it, a force I am no longer diffident about calling evil. In my judgment, too many Quakers have condoned too much violence and nonsense because its perpetrators have been shrewd enough to invoke injustice as their inspiration.

Peace activism has a history that can be as tarnished as war. While I was researching my most recent book, I found it instructive to read accounts of some of the most prominent peace activists of the 1930s:

• Charles A. Lindbergh said that Germany was rearming and expanding only to redress the injustice of the Versailles Peace Accords; the Nazis were nationalists who would be sated once they had a little satisfaction (say, Czechoslovakia). He said that Jewish interests were driving the democracies toward war.

• George Bernard Shaw said that the United Kingdom and United States did not have the moral standing to oppose Germany because British colonialism and U.S. economic imperialism were greater sources of injustice in the world.

I concluded that what saved peace advocacy from being totally discredited was the German invasion of the USSR (which forced the left to reassess its conviction that only capitalist colonialist countries were at risk), Pearl Harbor (which forced the right to reassess its certainty that it was possible to stay clear of conflict), and the atom bomb (which made urgent the need to develop peaceful alternatives).

Millions of brave people risked their lives to devise those alternatives—and they shook the world. Nonviolent resistance won Mahatma Gandhi's campaign for independence in India. Love in action, embodied by the Birmingham Children's Crusade and the march of Martin Luther King Jr. and the heroes of the U.S. civil rights movement into the crush of water cannon and police dogs, overthrew the laws of segregation that made too much of the United States a living prison. Corazón Aquino's campaign to oust dictatorship, Mitch Snyder's fasts to focus concern on homelessness—the Peace Testimony still has much to offer the world.

But peace does not always hold every answer, any more than military action. Peace advocates who excuse the crimes of al-Qaida as their response to injustice while excoriating the force the United States uses in its own defense as unjustified terrorism are putting their moral weight on the same side of the scale as murderers. Urging peace at any price will leave terrorists in place and insure more crimes of terrorism in our immediate future. And when terrorists strike they will make no distinctions between Quakers and Pentagon generals, inner-city school teachers or B-2 bomber pilots, busboys or bankers, John Ashcroft or Noam Chomsky. Pacifism can assist spilling the blood of innocents, too.

I thank FRIENDS JOURNAL readers for their responses. And again, I thank the various Quaker assemblies that not only have received me with such courtesy over this past year, but actually have sought me out to share my views that they knew to be at odds with those of their own membership.

Scott Simon, host of National Public Radio's Weekend Edition (Saturday), *is a former member of Friends Meeting of Washington, (D.C.), and of Northside Meeting in Chicago, Ill. His novel,* Pretty Birds *(Random House, 2005), has "garnered the best reviews" of his life.*

Forum: The Quaker Peace Testimony is a Testimony or Witness

Many Friends in the U.S. must be taking stock of the events since Ninth Month, 2001, and the subsequent events in Afghanistan, and must be asking how Friends can witness to their truth in light of these events. I had a chance to reflect on this when I read Scott Simon's contribution posted on the Internet on the United Church News (<www.ucc.org>). [The actual text of this speech was published as the article, "Reflections on the Events of September 11" in *FJ* Dec. 2001.— *eds.*] I am sure these comments and responses to them have no doubt been well-aired in the U.S., so I almost hesitate to reopen this issue.

I read Scott Simon's comments and was very disappointed. I was disappointed because here was a fellow Quaker witnessing against two of the most important truths in the Quaker faith: unity and Christian nonviolence. How important it is that we can share the unifying experience of hearing God's leadings together as a fellowship. Scott Simon's comments reveal something about how we have allowed "diversity" to get in the way of that experience. Doesn't the stand he has taken illustrate the end result of diversity: a watered-down witness and moral relativism?

Secondly, he refers to pacifism as "fatally flawed." As I understand it, Quakers have never believed in "pacifism." I tend to avoid the term "pacifism" and prefer the term "Christian nonviolence." There is an important difference. Pacifism is an "ism," an intellectual position taken on the basis of human thought and argument. Positions like this can be argued against and people dissuaded from them. It is then possible to agree with Scott Simon, when he said that Quakers and Mennonites joined up in World War II because they could offer no intellectual response to Hitler, if I read him properly.

Christian nonviolence arises from inward obedience to the Living Christ. Such acts of obedience do not rely on intellectual argument, but from a sense of deep, inward conviction. Although these convictions can and do often make sense intellectually, sometimes they don't. The Quaker Peace Testimony is a testimony or witness. By being obedient to it, we testify or witness that we are living in the Power of Christ, and the refusing to take up arms is a testimony that Christ is alive and can lead us into righteousness, if we are willing to obey. It is a sign of our personal, inward transformation and the fact that we are under God's leading. This is the basis of all Quaker testimonies; it is also part of what we understand as "Gospel Order."

The original 1660 declaration, which many Quakers of several traditions use, clearly states that it is "the spirit of Christ by which we are led." Early Friends took up this position because they believed that Christ was leading them into it, not because they thought it was a good idea. I've always lived in the hope that Friends hold to our testimonies for those reasons.

—*Allistair Lomax,* Fritchley, Derbyshire, UK

Forum: Who Shall Judge?

Thank you for once again publishing an article by Scott Simon (*FJ* May 2003) that challenges us pacifists to sort out our beliefs about war and peace.

War kills people and destroys things; it is immoral. But, according to Scott Simon, war is sometimes necessary to alleviate human suffering and end brutality that is worse than war. His justification of war in his view seems to hinge on two factors, one seemingly quantifiable and hence objective factor, and one rather murky factor.

The quantifiable criterion is a comparison of the number of people likely to be killed in war versus how many would be murdered if the current perpetrators of evil were not forcibly stopped. This might seem to be a reasonable kind of criterion, yet the vast discrepancies in quoted numbers of civilians killed in the Afghanistan war, which Scott Simon refers to in the article, are one indication of how tricky such counts can be, not to mention the utter unpredictability of future casualities and murders.

The other criterion in Scott Simon's defense of war is the degree of stomach-turning brutality, of repression, and of the unmitigated inhumanity perpetrated by regimes like the Taliban and that of Saddam Hussein. The implication is that there is some threshold of evil above which such a regime warrants its destruction by force, justifying invasion by other countries, and that the elimination of this evil outweighs the suffering brought about by war against it.

But how can this judgment be made, this weighing of the scales, and by whom? Who can presume to know whether choosing to go ahead and kill people and destroy things right now will do more good for humanity—or more harm—in the long run? And what moral authority is it that can rightly determine which malevolent regimes have exceeded that threshold of evil repression and brutality, thus inviting invasion? As a peace advocate I believe that rarely, if ever, do considerations of saving lives and overcoming evil outweigh the immorality of war itself, and that judgments about numbers of killings, judgments on the brutality of tyrannical regimes, judgments about the future, cannot rightly be made by anybody.

In the world of realpolitik where our wars are made, such questions of morality may well be peripheral. It was President George W. Bush who made the momentous decisions to unleash U.S. military might against Afghanistan and Iraq. Betraying myself now as what Scott Simon would call an "inflexible political ideologue," I have to say I believe that the Bush administration's drive to war had just about nothing to do with humane considerations of easing suffering and eliminating evil. But they do use these arguments to great effect in the media, including National Public Radio.

—Zandra Moberg, Philadelphia, Pa.

Forum: Faith Relative to "Real" Life

Scott Simon chose to identify himself as a Quaker (*FJ* Dec. 2001). He certainly did not have to; he had a microphone in any case. By identifying himself as a Quaker before going on to justify violence he was making a point, and I believe he must have realized that it was a dramatic one.

Simply put, the point is, "This time it's different." This time even the pacifists will have to put aside their pacifism because of the horror of September 11, 2001. It should have come as no surprise to him that his comments were picked up by *Soldier of Fortune*. This was music to the ears of those who are interested in justifying military action.

Because Scott Simon chose to identify himself as a Quaker, it is fair to ask some Quakerly questions.

The Peace Testimony is one of our oldest and most revered testimonies. It is arguably what we are most identified with by the outside world. It is no small thing, then, to publicly identify yourself with the Quakers and then speak against the Peace Testimony.

We believe in the ability of each individual to discern the will of God. However, there is a process to this discernment.

Scott Simon says that his religious convictions have been "knocked about by real life." He talks about his travels to areas of conflict, implying an authority that many Friends would not share. Is there any validity to this? Is it surprising that his religious convictions were "knocked about by real life?" Who has not had their religious convictions knocked about by real life?

What do Friends do when "real" life conflicts with their religious convictions? They talk to others in their meeting. They ask for clearness and discernment. They take the time to religiously follow practice.

We worship together in meetings. The other people in the room are there for a reason. It is not unusual for a seeker to be in conflict with a testimony, and it could be that even after a process of prayer and clearness that person could still be conflicted. However, my experience has been that this process helps not only the person, but also the community come to a better understanding and resolution of the conflict.

Without this process, without recognizing and valuing each other in our religious search, we can become easily lost to the voices of our egos. Truth will be found in humility and in faith.

There is no plane ticket to any destination that will endow a member with a special connection to the Truth. We need each other, and we need to attach more value to our testimonies than Scott Simon has demonstrated. My hope is that he will find that other members have something of value to share with him.

—*Scott R. Penniman,* Springhouse, Pa.

Forum: "Just War" Theory?

In justifying U.S. military action in response to the events of September 11 on the grounds of self defense and the rightness of the Western cause, Scott Simon (*FJ* Dec. 2001) propounds a version of just war theory. That position stands in stark contrast to the 1660 Declaration by the Religious Society of Friends to King Charles II of England: "We utterly deny all outward wars and strife, and fightings with outward weapons, for any end, or under any pretense whatsoever." That declaration is the basis of the Quaker Peace Testimony. As such, we are free to disagree with it as individuals, but not as Quakers. I presume that Friend Simon recognizes this fact when he states that he is "a Quaker of not particularly good standing."

What, then, is the Quakerly response? Friend Simon states that he prefers peaceful alternatives, but that "I am not willing to lose lives for the sake of ideological consistency." If one looks at the issue ideologically, one would probably come to the same conclusion that he does, namely that Quakers and other pacifists should support U.S. military involvement because of the danger that "we" will lose. This line of reasoning conflates "we" as Quakers with "we" as U.S. citizens. Endorsing the Peace Testimony does not mean that Quakers should ask their own government to lay down its arms while everyone else does battle. It is a testimony that Quakers are called to deliver not to one side or another at some particular time, but to the whole world at all times. This has nothing to do with ideology, and everything to do with faith.

Elsewhere in the same issue (p.5), Paul Buckley writes, "Pacifism is easy if there are no enemies." The implications of this point for all Quakers are profound indeed. Pacifism was not easy in 1660, and it is not easy now. It requires the faith to see beyond the dangers and potential setbacks inherent in any specific conflict. That faith is of the sort advocated by Dr. Martin Luther King Jr. when he told the world, "Right temporarily defeated is stronger than evil triumphant." It may well entail temporary defeats, because it is not oriented toward having the "good guys" come out on top until the next conflict—and in our deeply flawed world there is always a next conflict. Rather, it asks us to have the faith to look beyond this or that temporary defeat in favor of living, as George Fox put it, "in the virtue of that life and power that takes away the occasion of all wars." The Peace Testimony is not oriented toward short-term successes, or even toward long-term ones. It is a testimony with an eye to eternity.

—*David Shiner,* Knollwood, Ill.

Forum: There's Hope in the Quaker Vision

Scott Simon's article (*FJ* May 2003) presents a challenge to Friends. I struggled with a response.

One evening, several months ago, I was too tired to do anything productive, so I turned on the TV and got hooked on an old Western, starring Clint Eastwood. His wife is killed and he is left with a child. He sets out by himself to find the four suspect killers who are the bandit bad guys. He takes the law into his own hands, kills off the bad guys one by one, is given a hero's welcome when he returns to town, and gets a beautiful woman besides. Walter Wink has called this the "myth [false belief] of redemptive violence." This is a dominant theme in U.S. society, including our foreign policy.

Scott Simon presents Afghanistan as a very enticing example. The Taliban was a brutally repressive, murderous regime. The U.S. comes along, takes the law into its own hands, defeats the Taliban with very few civilian or military deaths, and the world is a better place as a result: Afghanistan is now a free country. Women are no longer suppressed and there is freedom of religion and even politics. Also, we are safer because of the breakup of some of the al-Qaida terror network. It sounds so good: redemptive violence at its best. How do I respond?

Scott Simon makes no mention of the religious aspect of our Peace Testimony. I came to believe war was wrong before I joined the Religious Society of Friends. I could not understand how the fundamentalist Christian church in which I was raised could support war and claim to believe the teachings and life example of Jesus. Jesus lived in a country occupied by a military that was brutal and repressive. He rejected violence as a solution. He preached and lived an alternative approach. Early Quakers appealed to this power of Christ as the reason for rejecting violence. They referred to the "spirit of Christ by which we are guided" and quoted Isaiah and Micah: "Nation shall not lift up sword against nation, neither shall they learn war any more." (Isa. 2:4, Mic. 4:3)

Simon appeals to the practical, not the religious. What about the practical? There are questions about Afghanistan he does not address: refugees, the destroyed infrastructure, and the torture and murder of hundreds of imprisoned Taliban soldiers (article in *The Guardian*, 3/25/03). Afghanistan is a desperately poor country. Simon makes a brief allusion to this. For example, it has a high infant mortality rate, and of those children dying, at least in one province, one-third die of malnutrition and one-third from measles. Refugees, poverty, and the destroyed infrastructure were present before the U.S. war, but all are made worse by that war. It is too soon to tell how the future in Afghanistan will evolve. It is also too early to know if terrorism has been reduced and the world is safer, as Scott Simon claims.

He says, quoting Asia Bennett, that Quakers are good at recognizing injustice but not evil. This is clever but not true. I would counter that the U.S. is good at identifying evil in others but not good at identifying or admitting the evil of our own governmental actions. Our military and CIA have been instrumental either covertly or overtly in establishing and/ or supporting the Shah of Iran, Saddam Hussein in Iraq, Augusto Pinochet in Chile, Anastasio Somoza in Nicaragua, the death squads in Guatemala and El Salvador, and more. We continue to give armaments to countries that have repressive regimes. Scott Simon dismisses past U.S. support of the Taliban. He quotes Gandhi, saying that circumstances change and we all change our minds. But what about past U.S. support of Osama bin Laden? The U.S. funded and helped recruit and train his forces even in U.S. cities (See Gabriel Kolko, *Another Century of War*, pp. 48–49).

Violence in the U.S. is a serious problem, called an epidemic by the American Medical Association. All one has to do is read the paper every night. We have aggrieved workers killing fellow workers, and students killing other students and teachers. The killers, in their view, have just causes. Redemptive violence is repeated. The causes of violence in the U.S. are complex but certainly, at least subliminally, citizens could think they are justified in following the example set forth by our government: violence for a just cause is all right.

Scott Simon ends by referring to "Peace advocates who excuse the crimes of al-Qaida as their response to injustice. . . ." and that "Urging peace at any price will leave terrorists in place and insure more crimes of terrorism." Both are untrue. Peace advocates I know do neither. The truth is that the U.S. has exported violence, war, and arms for decades, and on September 11, 2001, the terrorism came back to our shores to haunt us. It is scary. I am scared. As I write, the nation has just again been put on high alert. The solution is not more of the same, as Scott Simon advocates. More violence as in Afghanistan and Iraq will not stop terrorism. We are the strongest military nation in the world and have never been less safe. Why can't we seem to grasp the need for a change in direction? Somewhere, sometime, we have to stand up and say, "No more."

We need to use the many alternatives already out there and use our enormous resources to find new alternatives to violence as a solution instead of more war. Simon gives little hope for any change in the military— and violence-dominated world. I see a lot of hope in the Quaker peace vision, application of the teachings of Jesus, and the use of the many alternatives to violence already known.

—*Rich Van Dellen*, Rochester, Minn.

No More Trenches

I

I pray for Peace

That there be
no more trenches
for the living,
nor for the dead.

No more tracer fire,
veiling the stars
like bright, beaded curtains.

No more lungs gassed, collapsed,
burned to black.

Not another rising, lightning tangled,
smoking plume
to mediate
the Earth's yellow Sun.

II

Poppies and unknowns and walls . . .
There never was a war to end all wars.
War does not keep its promise.
Fields
have been ploughed and sewn
with silent graves
    arranged in
      neat even
      parallel lines,
But still
the dead cannot yield Peace
to the living.

III

Peace is in the Light.
Candled in the heart, it is borne
on the unswept flame
    and in God's silent keeping.
It is an untangled Love,
separated from the hand.

It is the gift of trust and
unselfishness
that leads the living,
    the knowing,
To hold
    the Light
over no man's land,

So that we may
dig no more trenches,
for the living, nor for the dead.

—*Ken Thompson*

Ken Thompson lives in Ocean View, N.J.

Queries

Can I read and consider prayerfully ideas, concepts, information, or opinions with which I disagree?

Do I consider the writer's full argument or does one word or concept make me dismiss the writer or the writing?

Do I set aside time to learn about the issues of the day and about what other Quakers are saying about them? What are the best sources for me to learn about international history and politics to be an informed citizen?

What can I learn about the definitions of and concepts around "just war"?

If I read or hear facts, figures, claims, suspicions, etc., when and how should I speak to others of them?

Am I careful in my use of language as I speak? In my choice of words? In my tone?

What does the term Christian nonviolence mean to me? How does my understanding of it help me think about contemporary issues?

What do I know about Friends' historical responses to paying taxes for war? Am I opposed to paying for war? If so, what steps could I take to tell others about my objections? If not, can I explain to others my reasons?

Do I support others who witness to war tax resistance today? Should my meeting, like many others have already done, consider a minute concerning paying for war and a minute for supporting tax resisters in our meeting?

What do I know of the wars of the United States in the past that may influence the way I talk and feel about war today? Do I explore my knowledge with others?

Am I careful not merely to acknowledge but to understand our cultural dishonesties?

Time to Heal:
Grieving, Meditating,
Reflecting, Praying

G rief may have been the most profound feeling that engulfed many of us as we took in the enormity of the devastation left by the attacks in the United States in 2001. We grieved as we saw the loss of life and heard tales of the immediate bravery and ongoing perseverance of many of those who suffered directly. We grieved with the workers who tirelessly strove to bring the chaos into some semblance of order. We grieved for the families and friends of those in the many photos posted in Manhattan on remembrance boards. We felt grief for the perpetrators of the attack, men who were convinced that they must destroy. We felt grief for the shortcomings of national and international systems, and grief for the reactions that we feared would only deepen the chaos and hurt more people.

George Lakey, a Quaker with a long history of witness and teaching, knew almost immediately that we needed "to grieve deeply and to set aside time for praying and searching," and that we needed to do it not only alone but collectively. He calls us to worship, to centering, to hope. Notice the tone, calm but firm, and the sensible advice that rose from his faith as most of us were still floundering to find our footing.

John Blum's experience at Ground Zero expresses grief in an immediate way. He allows those of us at a distance from Oklahoma City or New York City or Washington or Pennsylvania to mourn with those who felt the grief most keenly, the immediate survivors of those who died. Grieving with others was a necessary step on the path Friends found themselves on as the calls for revenge gathered momentum.

In "Essay on War," Cameron McWhirter gives voice both to our confusion and to his grounding in seeking and worshipping. "The answer, for each of us and for us as a collective body, will come in frank discussions amongst ourselves and in coming together in the sacred silence of meeting." Then, he says, we would be ready to face "the hard questions."In the letter that follows, Mike Murray answers the questions posed in "Essay on War" in his own words, giving us one model of someone who is willing to step forward and engage the discussion.

In his slim, provocative book *A Light to Live By*, Rex Ambler reminds us that George Fox advised people of his day that "the first step to peace is to stand still in the light." In *Friends for 300 Years*, Howard Brinton reminds us that Fox wasn't the first to give this advice. The Psalmist told us to "Wait on the Lord . . . and he shall strengthen thine heart" (Ps. 27:14). We sorely needed to feel a healing balm that might open our minds and hearts to ways to move forward.

In the three meditative pieces that follow, the writers share with readers the quiet epiphanies that they found in their everyday connections after the attacks. For Robin Mello, it was a telephone call to her father. For Pamela Haines a chance meeting with a book. For Marcelle Martin standing in a peace vigil. Their stories encourage us to trust our own reaching out in quiet, timely ways.

Terrorism and the Practical Idealist

by George Lakey

When I encountered Quakerism for the first time as a young man, I was struck by the sheer boldness of early Friends in following the Light. I tried to imagine, for example, an argument between a Quaker who had decided to take his family to farm in the new colony of Pennsylvania and his non-Friend neighbor:

But surely you're not going to that wild place without a gun? The savages will kill you! Even if you're willing to risk that possibility for yourself, will you let your scruples get your family slaughtered?

With historical hindsight, we now know that the nonviolent Quakers were the safest people on the frontier. It turned out they were very practical idealists. At the time, however, they must have been amazingly brave—or faithful to their calling.

As a Quaker attender I was also introduced to Gandhi, another practical idealist, who was determined to put "the ploughshare of normative principle into the hard soil of political reality," as Martin Buber put it. These days we might say Gandhi thought outside the box. He said about himself that he was "a politician trying to be a saint."

Gandhi confronted nonviolently the largest empire the world had ever known, not to mention countless evils in his own backyard. Even during World War II he launched a nationwide offensive against British rule (the 1942 "Quit India" campaign) and sent associates to the part of India where the Japanese would most likely invade, to begin to organize villagers for nonviolent resistance to threatened Japanese invasion.

No one could say Gandhi was an idealist removed from the power struggles of his time. As an activist, I've read Gandhi over and over to inspire me to out-of-the-box thinking. These days I ask, what might he, the father of his nation, have advised U.S. power holders who carry responsibility for our nation in the wake of September 11?

He surely would have advised national leaders to assist us to grieve deeply and to set aside time for praying and searching. Gandhi's style was "from the inside out"; he expected wisdom to emerge from the inner surrender to Truth, and he found that this spiritual work could be a collective process as well as individual.

I imagine he would have urged putting the response to al-Qaida in the framework of law enforcement rather than war. It is obvious that normal conditions for law enforcement don't exist for this case, and he might see that as both a challenge and an opportunity. Gandhi's genius as a visionary leader was to make his immediate actions point toward the emergence of something-not-yet-realized. He was one of the most effective nation-builders the world has seen, in a subcontinent rife with bewildering diversities and hostilities, because he believed in the consistency of ends and means.

Not unlike William Penn in this way, Gandhi's brilliance lay in a two-fold strategy: first, to be able to perceive the possibility of a new emergent order in the midst of chaos; and second, to refuse to undermine that possibility by means that make the emergence impossible.

This strategy is what most marks the difference between political innovators and the leaders who run their people off cliffs by operating within conventional wisdom. Gandhi knew that without a vision the people perish. And he insisted on the means/ends linkage; he saw means or methods of action as ingredients that largely determine the future. He had no faith that figs will grow from thistles.

Gandhi, like another amazing nation-builder, Nelson Mandela, liked to operate politically from the moral high ground. He would surely have pointed out to U.S. power holders that a window appeared in September in which the U.S. held the moral high ground—an unusual circumstance as those of us who get out and about in the world will know. That's precisely the moment for visionary initiative, for rallying the anti-terror energy and creating structures of accountability that enable law enforcement to proceed. Begin, as Gandhi and Jesus preferred, with ourselves: join the treaty for the international criminal court, join the land mines agreement (land mines may be the most murderous of terrorist instruments, and the U.S. wants to keep making and using them), join the Kyoto agreement on pollution, forgive Third World debts, fundamentally revise our approach to the Middle East, and on and on. Gandhi liked to bring humor to the table, so he would probably have a twinkle in his eye as he'd point out to U.S. power holders that we can't be both one of the world's greatest impediments to community and also expect global community to be there when it's convenient for us.

Even as we would be getting our own house in order, becoming an accountable state among states, new kinds of collaboration would become possible for bringing criminals to justice, including al-Qaida.

In addition to seizing the opportunity for immediate initiatives toward global structures of accountability, Gandhi would surely advise a response to Afghanistan along these lines: "Those of us with family members and friends killed on September 11 know the harsh pain of loss. We wouldn't want others to have to go through the suffering of the needless loss of their loved ones. Yet we are newly aware that famine and decades of war confront millions of Afghans with the possibility of starving this winter. We realize that previous U.S. governments played a role in causing this crisis, both by what we have done and also by what we have left undone. Let's forge a new relationship that's not about the Cold War, not about oil, but about the interdependence that provides the only path to security for all our peoples. We begin today to work with the UN and international nongovernmental organizations to be sure you can eat this winter. We propose the creation of a peace zone throughout Afghanistan, where the focus is on food, shelter, healthcare, and infrastructure. We want to make sure those who died on September 11 did not die in vain: it is time the world learns that 'the security of each lies in the security of all.'"

The Terrorist's Strategy

When terror is used as an instrument of mobilization, which is how movements against colonialism often used it, the basic dynamic is obvious: I kill, you retaliate disproportionately and move to protect your privileged friends, the people who lean toward my cause but haven't been active are propelled into motion, my movement grows.

In Vietnam the National Liberation Front used terror for this goal: as an instrument for mobilization. A favorite tactic, for example, was to kill the village chief; the government's army then comes and wipes out the village in retaliation, and people in adjoining villages, having seen the government's disproportionate violence, then join the National Liberation Front. For years the power holders in France, and later in the U.S., made the same, predictable response to terror: violent retaliation, until each in turn was thrown out of Vietnam.

Osama bin Laden clearly wanted to mobilize a vast movement, and like so many before him, he knew that terror can help to do this. Again, the success of terror depends on the reaction of the opponent, a condition the U.S. power holders are dutifully satisfying. As in Vietnam for the National Liberation Front, the violent behavior of the U.S. could turn out to have been a giant recruiter for al-Qaida.

Given the self-defeating character of massive violent retaliation, creating a nonviolent alternative does not seem to me as big a risk as even those early Quakers took coming to Pennsylvania.

Strategy for Quakers

I notice that some of today's advocates of violent retaliation take a tough-minded tone: "The U.S. must be strong and do whatever it takes."

My challenge would be: How tough are you? Are you really willing to do whatever it takes? What about getting out of the box, giving up the dominator role, addressing poverty, and supporting the growth of world community rather than empire?

As someone who loves my country, I am not delighted to call attention to its character as an empire. The great British historian Arnold Toynbee, however, was even 40 years ago gently suggesting that many in the U.S. acknowledge its imperial character. U.S. power holders have military bases circling the globe, from which violence is repeatedly threatened and used, when nations or groups do something that doesn't fit our game plan. Business practices backed by the military are used to increase U.S. wealth at the expense of already-poor countries. The way the U.S. uses power to dominate is not actually related to the American people's value of democracy, since the U.S. power holders frequently support dictatorships (as in Saudi Arabia and apartheid South Africa) while overthrowing democratic governments (as in Guatemala or Chile). In my most objective moments, I'm forced to concede that these are the behaviors of an empire.

To those, therefore, who urge Quakers to support military action because we need to use "any means necessary," I would challenge them to extend their own argument and ask whether—if they found that imperial behavior by the U.S. invites terror—they would be willing to give up that behavior, or urge the power holders to do so.

"Everything has changed," I hear, and maybe the power holders can make a creative leap and give up empire. Human security is a basic need; perhaps it could prevail over power and greed.

Then again, maybe those who run our nation will continue to rely on violence and the protection of privilege. The airline bailout passed by both parties in Congress was chilling: at a moment of national crisis when flags were being waved in support of "togetherness," the Congress protected those with million-dollar salaries while doing nothing for the 100,000 employees laid off.

If the power holders continue to cling to empire, I propose that a representative group of U.S. Friends gather to consider how to ground ourselves as Quakers who are willing to let go of empire while remaining U.S. citizens. It is first of all a spiritual challenge, with many ramifications for our lives as citizens. We might call it "the Woolman Project" after a Friend who pointed the way.

The Religious Society of Friends was born before anyone thought of the U.S. empire, and I expect we'll survive the empire's demise. How to accomplish that? We'll need each other.

George Lakey is a member of Central Philadelphia (Pa.) Meeting, under whose care he is performing a ministry of nonviolence. He is director of Training for Change (<www.trainingforchange.org>) and is coauthor of Grassroots and Nonprofit Leadership: A Guide for Organizations in Changing Times.

A Quaker at Ground Zero

by John Blum

The Family Assistance Center (FAC) described below was located in a historic railroad terminal/museum at Liberty State Park in Jersey City, New Jersey, on the Hudson River and up from the Statue of Liberty. Shortly after September 11, it was established to help New Jersey families in the difficult and painful process of reporting missing loved ones, preparing various state and federal paperwork (including death certificates), and somehow beginning that frightening and often elusive state of mind called "closure." Initially, mental health services were offered by National Organization of Victims Assistance (NOVA) volunteers, and later supplemented by professional mental health volunteers (I was one of these), as well as representatives from various religious organizations. It was an awesome task—almost 4,000 families lost loved ones in the disaster, about 40 percent of whom were New Jersey residents. The FAC operated seven days a week, from 9 A.M. to 9 P.M. A similar center was established on Manhattan Island for New York residents. What follows is an excerpt from my journal of this experience.

It was the day after Thanksgiving and I had signed up to accompany families on the ferry ride to Ground Zero. With feelings of anticipatory anxiety, I checked in at the counseling trailer and went over to staff orientation. Upon entering, each of us received a handwritten card created by school children from around the country. Mine came from "Christine, Grade 8," address unknown, who wrote in large colorful ink marker letters, "Be Proud to be an American!! Come Together as Americans!!"— all against a backdrop of a teenage girl wearing USA clothing, a bubble message next to her head showing the World Trade Center twin towers and "Be back soon!" The cards were ours to keep.

The orientation began with two state officials describing their Ground Zero visits, followed by detailed instructions for us:

> We are not here to give answers or offer solutions. We are here to be present and offer support during a very difficult period of grief and mourning. You will be assigned a family to be with before, during, and after the ferry ride. Please do not lose sight of them, but don't follow them too closely unless they ask you to or you feel that they need your immediate presence. Remember, this is their time, not yours. Since construction equipment is still in use, you will be given hardhats, goggles, and dust masks. Please make sure that you and your families wear the hats at all times. Also, please wear your "Companion" name tags so that you will be distinguished from family members. Remember, we will be entering a crime scene. While on the viewing platform, no photographic or any other recording devices are permitted. Unfortunately, there is no law prohibiting onlookers in New York from taking pictures of you or your families during the walk. Police officers will ask onlookers not to take pictures, but if they do it anyway, please stand in between them and the families. Be prepared for any kind of emotional responses from your families. Please respect how each family member chooses to use his or her time on this journey. Any questions?

I looked around. No questions.

Off I went to meet my "family." I noticed a group of six casually dressed adults, three couples in their mid-30s or so. The NOVA worker waved me over. I approached and introduced myself, doing my best to make eye contact with each person. One by one, they introduced themselves, shaking hands, some firmly with businesslike eye contact, others gently with wounded and red eyes. I nervously joked, "If I remember all of your names by day's end, I will have earned my keep." I then removed my badge, wrote "John" below "Companion," and re-attached it. "At least I'll know who I am." We smiled nervously at each other and proceeded to the remembrance wall.

"Is this your first time here?" I asked. "Yes," was the uniform response. Before I could ask anything else, they split up, with one of the women announcing, "There's supposed to be a whole wall just for him." I stayed in the background. As I watched, I tried to get a sense of their moods and feelings. The three women seemed restrained, the three men more solemn and distracted. "Here it is," someone said. Everyone gathered around. On a wall that was shared with other victims, the upper right corner was separated with a hand-drawn, curving black line. They were looking up at a few family photographs, a funeral service program, and a "Nittany Lion" decal, all stapled in place. One man finally turned to me and said, "Tom was my brother, this is my wife, and these are his two sisters and their husbands," pointing to the others huddled around the wall. "I'm very sorry for your loss," I replied. "Thank you," he answered softly and turned back to the wall. I later found out that Tom had perished in the South Tower, leaving behind a pregnant wife and five young children. A few weeks earlier, his widow and his father came to the FAC to process the death certificate and had gone by ferry to Ground Zero to pay their respects.

I tried to slip back into anonymity. No one wrote anything at that time, all eventually drifting away, wandering among the other walls. Later, in their own time and privacy, perhaps inspired by other family messages, I watched each sibling approach with black marker in hand and write, pausing between words—thoughtfully searching, treating this moment as if it was the only chance to leave a message for their deceased brother. I thought to myself: What would I write if I were standing at my loved one's only memorial, a piece of shared white wallboard with pictures and handwritten messages? Where would I begin?

Eventually, we all gathered again.

"We have time for lunch, if anyone is interested," I offered. They looked at each other, noncommittal. "We'll be gone for about two hours," I added, "and it's strongly suggested we all eat something." "Let's go, then," one sister replied, and all agreed.

The family dining area was already filling with other families and their companions but luckily we found a table large enough for all seven of us.

We chatted nervously as we ate, but later I was able to hear more personal stories about their brother and some "good and funny family stories." What courage and grace, I thought. At 12:30 PM, I made my announcement about the details regarding the ferry ride (hardhats, goggles, dust masks, no cameras). We made restroom stops and proceeded to the general orientation. We were introduced to the volunteer chaplain on duty, a rabbi who would be conducting the interfaith memorial service on the viewing platform at Ground Zero. A one-page "WTC Damage Assessment" map was distributed detailing the buildings that had collapsed or were destroyed, partially collapsed, or suffered major damage. Many family members were having difficulty looking at their maps. The reality of this visit was becoming evident, for here was the blueprint of the last known locations of their loved ones. With the orientation over, we boarded four New Jersey Transit buses lined up along the curb. A uniformed New Jersey State trooper sat up front, and two paramedics with medical gear rode in back. (I was reminded how grief and stress can trigger all sorts of physical problems, including, in extreme cases, stroke and heart attack.) I quietly said a prayer as the buses left for the ferry dock, winding through the streets of Jersey City, preceded and followed by state police cars with red lights flashing.

It was a bright, clear, and unusually warm November day, a nice day for a ferry ride to Manhattan Island—too nice, given these grim circumstances. Once aboard, each family member was offered a teddy bear and a single carnation to keep. No one turned them down, even the most macho of men. We sat on the open upper deck. Looking around, I noticed how diverse this group was—multiethnic, senior citizens, a woman who required a golf cart to get around, and a girl about ten years old with her mother. I glanced over at the state police officers riding with us. As they sat rigid and golem-like, I realized they weren't just chaperones or there for crowd control—they were there to protect us from any possible harm, maybe even another terrorist attack. What a high profile target, I thought, a boatload of grieving families on their way to visit the remains of their loved ones. So this is what we've come to; God help us all, I thought.

The Hudson River was very calm. Replete with our hardhats, goggles, dust masks, paramedics, state police escorts, teddy bears, and carnations, we disembarked and began our walk toward the World Trade Center complex. Families huddled in the center of the column, flanked on both sides by their companions and New Jersey state police officers, joined almost immediately by New York correctional officers. The two-block walk was through New York City streets that were temporarily closed to vehicular traffic and partially roped off. Many New Yorkers were out on this warm and sunny day, the day after Thanksgiving. It seemed many were not expecting to see this peculiar parade of people. As we turned a corner, the smell hit me: acrid and burning, like smoldering ash mixed with hot dust. I will always remember it as the smell of death. The crowds along both sides of the street were thicker, with people watching silently, an occasional camera being raised to capture this solemn procession, quickly lowered respectfully when approached by a police officer requesting, "No photographs, please." Losing track of my family, I stepped off to one side and scanned, then saw them moving along quietly. I looked at the throngs of onlookers, the voyeurs, and felt resentment building up in me. How dare they glare at us like we're some kind of cheap entertainment! But as I looked closer, I didn't see morbid excitement or curious wonder in their faces—nothing like what one sometimes sees driving by a car accident. I saw pain. I saw red eyes and waves of grief and sympathy. These New Yorkers knew exactly what they were watching, and they were sensing the bitter and overwhelming pain of these strangers from across the river. This wasn't a television show; it was real, up close and personal, in your face. Still, I perceived a healing energy in their eyes and in the air, through the city sounds and burning stench. One man, visibly moved, leaned over the rope toward a Red Cross worker standing next to me and said, "Good job."

We came to a large, chain-link gate that opened onto a plywood walkway. We had arrived at Ground Zero. We marched single file onto the viewing deck, into the noise and smell of what had been the World Trade Center complex. The gate closed behind us. This wooden viewing platform had been constructed at one corner, a perch overlooking the entire area of devastation, like the view from home plate in a baseball diamond. Families worked their way up front, with police, staff, and companions staying in back. I stood next to a small memorial wall covered with the names of over 60 countries that lost nationals in this disaster—earlier in the month, United Nations dignitaries and President Bush had come to this platform to view the site firsthand and dedicate this memorial wall. Around the wall, flowers and teddy bears covered the ground; handwritten messages were scrawled on any available spaces. The smell and noise were intense, almost overwhelming. The site looked like an open construction pit, with large cranes prying and probing in efforts to stabilize and clean up. The building directly across from us was gouged out, its entire facade scraped away by the violence of the collapsing buildings. Other buildings were covered with black canvas or plastic sheeting to prevent more debris from falling. Water cannons were sweeping the area, looking for "hot spots" of heat and smoke. One crane pulled up a slab of concrete, immediately releasing a plume of fresh smoke from underneath. The two nearest water cannons converged on the exposed area and quickly doused the smoldering ground. It's been about two-and-a-half months, I thought, and it's still burning. In the far left corner of the destruction, two iron girders formed the shape of a Christian cross. We were told that, during the early days of the recovery work, this cross was unearthed exactly as it was now, created by the falling and twisted iron, impaling itself straight up at that spot. It had become a symbol and shrine for the rescue and recovery workers. Next to me, a woman reading the UN memorial wall began to sob hysterically, prompting her companion and another Red Cross worker to approach and give comfort. Many others were wiping their eyes and holding on to each other. My family was up front, against the rail, quiet but fixated on what was their brother's grave.

After 15 minutes, the rabbi moved to the center of the platform. We all huddled around her as she loudly and movingly gave the memorial service. Although I could barely hear her through the noise, it didn't matter. I was already deep in prayer, looking over the remains of thousands of people, all victims of horrific violence, some rushing to get out, some rushing to get in, some who had jumped from windows in desperation, some on the ground caught up in the falling debris and burning jet fuel. This was a holy place, a sacred place, a cemetery.

The service over, we left the platform, walking down the ramp and back onto the streets of New York. Being one of the first out, I stood off to the side to help with crowd control, keeping an eye on my family. More onlookers thronged along our route as we left the viewing area. I looked behind me and saw the little girl and her mother coming down, wearing their hardhats, holding hands, carrying their teddy bears and carnations. My heart ached. I had forgotten about her. I glanced over at an elderly woman standing with other onlookers by the rope barricade. Someone's grandmother, I thought. She caught sight of the little girl and quickly covered her mouth with her hand, suppressing a moan, tears streaming down her cheeks.

Back on the ferry, we all were quiet and distracted. About halfway across the river I looked back, along with many others, to face the city for one last look and prayer. As we left the ferry, we placed our hardhats and goggles in large boxes for the next trip of grieving passengers. The buses and police escorts returned us to the FAC where, upon disembarking, my family lingered outside of the entrance near a flagpole. I gently approached and asked, "How's everyone doing?"

"All right, considering," one brother answered.

"You're all welcome to go inside and get some refreshments and we can talk a bit, if you feel up to it," I suggested.

They looked at each other. "No," one responded, "I think we'll just head back. We have a long ride ahead of us. Thanks anyway."

"You're welcome." I paused, then added, looking each of them in the eyes, "I just want to tell you all that I'm very honored that you permitted me to be a part of this difficult journey with you."

"Thanks for being there for us," a sister replied.

"Could you do us a big favor?" a brother quickly added. "Would you take our picture?" As I stepped back to capture the entire scene, they huddled together, arms around each other, a U.S. flag flying above their heads, Manhattan Island behind. I took two shots and returned the camera. Remembering again how grief can affect concentration and coordination, I asked, "Who's driving?"

Puzzled, they looked at each other. "Why, I am," the older brother replied.

"Please drive carefully," I added, and waved them off as they walked toward the parking lot.

I missed the "debriefing" session, a required group event for all staff to discuss each other's feelings about the day. Instead, I found myself relieved that it was over—that I hadn't been intrusive or pushy, that I didn't break down.

The next thing I knew, I was standing at the remembrance wall, reading what Tom's siblings had written earlier. I forced a deep breath (one of many this day) and walked back to the counseling trailer. There I talked about some my experiences and feelings to the remaining counselors on duty. Perhaps I was in shock, perhaps denial. It all seemed too surreal, like a bad dream.

I left to go home. Driving alone down the turnpike, I realized why the debriefing was so important as I struggled to keep my attention on this fast and busy roadway. With every American flag I saw, every "God Bless America," every "United We Stand," my eyes welled up, and I gently and quietly moaned in my own private grief.

John Blum is a certified and licensed mental health and substance abuse clinician. He is a member of Rancocas (N.J.) Meeting and lives in Moorestown, New Jersey. Names have been changed to preserve confidentiality. This excerpt is part of a larger journal, available free of charge by contacting the author at <johnjblum@yahoo.com>.

Essay on War

by Cameron McWhirter

At the onset of the American Revolution, a group of New Jersey and Pennsylvania Quakers issued a four-page broadside declaring that Quakers should not participate in the rebellion against King George III because Friends oppose violence and because political change should be left up to God.

These Quakers gathered for one meeting and wrote that they affirmed "our just and necessary subordination to the king, and those who are lawfully placed in authority under him."

Thomas Paine, the son of a Quaker, assailed the group in a responding pamphlet. By passively supporting the king, he argued, they quickly chose sides in the coming conflict while pretending to sit on the sidelines. They were supporting violence by an aggressor, just not actually doing any fighting. His simple message: don't be hypocrites.

"We do not complain against you because ye are Quakers, but because ye pretend to be and are not Quakers," he wrote.

Paine's diatribe raised hard questions for our faith, questions that have never really gone away. They arise every time human-engineered calamities upset civilization's apple cart: slavery, the Civil War, World War I, World War II, Vietnam, on and on. How do Quakers, the practical mystics, involve themselves in the messy affairs of human relations without becoming... involved? How do we avoid becoming hypocrites?

After September 11, we are faced with yet another challenge, one that calls on all of us once again to carefully examine our faith, principles, and actions. Essays by Scott Simon and others have brought out in print moral wrangling that has beset many meetings and individual Friends since the terrorist attacks. Many Friends see this confusion as disconcerting, as exhibiting a weakness of our faith.

I disagree. I see our ambiguity as an essential, if uncomfortable, process of a true Religious Society trying to discern God's will. To think that we, as a collective body and as individuals, would have an immediate uniform response to what happened on September 11 flies in the face of our valued ideal of waiting in silence for direction from God.

Figuring out how to not be Paine's hypocrites will take time. As Friends, we know that answers to complex problems always take time. Eventually, however, they come. The Quaker opposition to slavery was a long and difficult internal process for Friends. Deciding how to oppose the Vietnam War was long and painful.

After September 11, some Friends were disappointed at the knee-jerk response of some traditional Quaker organizations that offered pat answers about nonviolence while making vague references to "bringing those responsible to justice." Justice, that oft misused and abused word, was not defined.

Janet Rothery, in the January issue of *The Friends Quarterly*, wrote an essay entitled "Spiritual Humility." She argued that "when we get actively involved in lobbying and direct action we are tied into a political world of one-sidedness, which weakens our spiritual role as mediators working for just and long-lasting outcomes."

Our spiritual role today requires that we take a long look at ourselves and what our pacifism truly means. This goal cannot be accomplished by impromptu meetings in a Philadelphia or Washington, D.C., office.

I believe our faith, at its heart, is about wrestling with difficult questions. Here are some that I have been mulling over:

Is pacifism defined as non-participation in violence or active opposition to violence?

Is a Friend who believes that military action is necessary to preserve innocent lives not a "good" Quaker?

How does a Friend who opposes all military action stop innocent people from being killed?

How many Quakers, seeing how the Taliban regime treated women, opposed its military collapse?

If you were on a hijacked airplane, would you kill a hijacker to save the other passengers and yourself?

Are you benefiting now, as you read this article, from the work of the

U.S. military?

Having worked in war-torn Bosnia, Eritrea, and Ethiopia, I know what war can inflict, and I know that I never want to participate in it. But those same places also taught me that innocents get crushed unless defended. Would I have picked up a Kalashnikov to fight the Bosnian Serb militia as it randomly fired rockets into Sarajevo? Would I have joined Eritrean rebels battling Ethiopia's Mengistu dictatorship if soldiers had destroyed my village?

My answer: I thank God that I did not have to make those hard choices, and I will not condemn those who chose violence.

We know how Jesus responded to violence, because we have his words: "Forgive them Father for they know not what they do." But what would we honestly do?

The early Quakers have been held up as the ultimate pacifists. They would not fight either for the king or Parliament during the English Civil War. But in truth, Fox and other early Quakers issued their famous declaration of 1660 against war, in large part, to publicly declare that the Quakers were not involved in plots to overthrow the king.

A chief purpose of the pamphlet was to remove "the ground of jealousy and suspicion from magistrates and people concerning wars and fightings."

Leave Quakers alone, the pamphlet argued, we aren't political. Practical mystics indeed: they sat on the sidelines. Quakers did not march outside Windsor Castle with peace signs; they did not withhold taxes to the Crown.

Would those Quakers qualify as pacifists by our modern standards? Is stepping to the sidelines even possible in today's complicated world?

Quakers today must not become Paine's hypocrites, comfortably protesting war while smugly ensconced in homes kept warm by capitalism and kept safe by the military.

To avoid hypocrisy, they should not abandon pacifism. They should seek to understand it—what it means practically at this time in history.

What does our Peace Testimony mean after September 11? I truly don't know. One day I think all military force must be opposed. The next day I think some policing force is necessary. The next day I opt for the sidelines. The ranging emotions and internal debates are draining. And this confusion is plaguing many in my meeting and in meetings across the country.

I know that one day the answer will come. I answer Thomas Paine's complaint this way: I will be honest about my ambiguous feelings and about my desire for an answer. In the meantime, I will try to help the innocents caught up in this mess as best I can.

I believe that we must put aside comfortable platitudes and let the confusion caused by September 11 pour through us, through our meetings.

The answer, for each of us and for us as a collective body, will come in frank discussions amongst ourselves and in coming together in the sacred silence of meeting. We must wait patiently for the answers that continuously and amazingly are born from that silence.

Cameron McWhirter is a news editor at FRIENDS JOURNAL and a political reporter for the Detroit News. He is a member of Birmingham (Mich.) Meeting.

Forum: God Before War Means God Instead of War

I was disappointed by Cameron McWhirter's "Essay on War" in the September FRIENDS JOURNAL. For him, the terror attacks of September 11, 2001, pose formidable challenges to the advocacy of peace, as though the dead of September 11 were original in their innocent victimization. He counsels a type of anxious patience during which we should refrain from platitudes, restrain our witness, and broadcast our confusion before waiting in silence upon the Lord. He refers us to the "long and difficult internal process" by which Quakers eventually came to oppose slavery.

But Cameron McWhirter's counsel itself comes close to platitude. It is a handy salve for confused consciences, and a ready justification for unnecessary, and perhaps immoral, delay. It's disgraceful that Friends needed a century to condemn slavery. We share that disgrace when we hesitate to condemn the evil of modern war.

"Waiting in silence for direction from God," to use Cameron McWhirter's words, does not occur in a moral vacuum. We're not obligated to remain inert until fresh inspiration arrives to shove us along. Each of us has traveled with the Light into our silent assemblies. Our Religious Society has searched the Light for 350 years. Even as we wait in humble silence for greater understanding, we maintain a living testimony of truth for the world.

But Friend McWhirter confesses a reluctance to proclaim the Peace Testimony while "wrestling with difficult questions." His questions are fair, born in his experience of violence in Bosnia and Ethiopia as well as the horror and aftermath of September 11. They center on how innocent life may be protected, and they convey a whiff of suspicion that most pacifists are culpable by omission in the murder of unprotected innocents. It's important that we attempt to answer these questions.

Is pacifism defined as nonparticipation in violence?

Yes.

Is a Friend who believes that military action is necessary to preserve innocent lives not a "good" Quaker?

Many good Friends don't reject violence categorically. Like William Penn, they carry on, wearing their swords as long as they can.

How does a Friend who opposes all military action stop innocent people from being killed?

By placing herself, when the opportunity arises, between the innocent person and the would-be killer. By working to establish institutions which interfere in this way on a larger scale. By working to disestablish institutions of violence, greed, and nationalism. By rejecting the hubristic notion that she is responsible for stopping all murder.

How many Quakers, seeing how the Taliban regime treated women, opposed its military collapse?

It's doubtful that many Quakers opposed the collapse of the Taliban regime. It's equally doubtful that many Quakers would have killed to effect gender liberation in Afghanistan. Many Quakers did take up arms against slavery and against Hitler. We understand their motivation and don't condemn them. Neither do we honor their willingness to kill.

If you were on a hijacked airplane would you kill a hijacker to save the other passengers and yourself?

You might and you might not. Perhaps you would not have to kill in order to save lives. In any event, adrenaline would go a long way in determining your response.

Are you benefiting now, as you read this article, from the work of the U.S. military?

Where can we move on this Earth where no army claims to protect us? Because we're relatively safe, must we be willing to support killing in order to remain safe? Or might we risk our own safety to promote the nonviolent security of all?

There are other, better answers to these questions, but even the most comprehensive and persuasive answers don't open the door of faith or cement the validity of the Peace Testimony. The experience of God, of God's goodness, and of God's care for all of us is the ground of peace. That experience emerges in our lives even as we carry our various swords and struggle to greater understanding.

After World War II, soldiers-turned-monks filled the monasteries of Europe and North America. Quaker GIs returned to the silent assemblies they had often neglected before the war, new champions of the old Peace Testimony. Would that people everywhere would reverse that process now. God before war means God instead of war, which is another way of stating our Peace Testimony, the truth that imperfect Friends should never hesitate to proclaim.

—*Mike Murray*, Ashland, Mo.

Forum: Reflections on the September Attack on the United States

Recent events have challenged my faith, in particular, my belief in pacifism. My inner turmoil can never compare to the suffering of those who have been personally affected by these events.

One friend, with whom I've talked, is trying to resolve her belief in the Quaker Peace Testimony with her love for her family members who are active members of the military. I have always rationalized that we each will answer to God and our conscience when faced with violent alternatives to life's situations, and that we should always work for peaceful resolutions to conflicts. I always figured and hoped that God would guide me in the right direction.

I don't have any grand answers for world peace. I only know that I will continue to pray for it, and that from that I hope answers will come. I've written the following note to my friend, which I hope might be helpful to others:

I've thought a lot about the Peace Testimony and how to live it during this time. I am not sure I can tell anyone how they should live it because, like many people, I am conflicted by my own reactions to the recent tragedies. Here are some suggestions for prayer:

Pray for peace and justice, because we won't be able to have one without the other.

Pray for forgiveness for those whose actions led us to this conflict, and for those who will react violently to it—no matter who they are.

Pray for patience with those who let their anger, fear, or pride drive their actions.

Pray for courage to speak and act with truth and kindness in every situation we encounter—no matter how unpopular it may be.

Pray for wisdom as we try to live in a reality where many matters are out of our control.

Pray for the vision to see clearly how we can personally make a difference in this world—no matter how small it may seem.

Pray for the chains of hatred and blood lust to be lifted from the hearts of all peoples.

Pray for real learning to take place so that we can solve our differences peacefully—no matter how difficult they are.

Pray for faith that will guide us to find more answers than questions in our searching.

Pray for the resolve never to give up trying to build a better world—no matter how discouraged we may be.

Pray for creative thoughts and innovations to find peaceful solutions to violent conflicts.

Pray for healing to take place in our hearts, minds, and souls—no matter how many scars we may have.

Pray for love to warm our hearts against the pain of sadness, confusion, and helplessness.

Pray for hope to rise up and inspire us to live more fully, and to find joy in our lives again—no matter where we find it.

—*Dana Kester-McCabe,* Salisbury, Md.

Forum: Why Can We Not See Ourselves?

What is terrorism? Who is a terrorist? When a suicide bomber brings explosion and agony to a city street, the media are there. The world sees it on TV and is filled with horror and sympathy. When weapons of massive destruction, sent from great distances, rain down on civilians, this is certainly one of the most devastating forms of terrorism, but few people are there to record it. There are no TV pictures to bring reality, response, and compassion. Land mines are an everlasting source of terror all over the world, so easily spread, almost impossibly dangerous to remove.

Unlike most of the nations of the world, our nation has never been attacked and reduced to rubble by continuous bombing, or experienced thousands dead with power, water, infrastructure, hospitals, schools, farmlands, factories, all sources of income all demolished. Is this why our nation, really kindly of heart, seems so incredibly slow in really letting its right hand become deeply aware of what its left hand is doing?

—*Barbara C. St. John*, Lexington, Mass.

My Father's Peace

by Robin Mello

I am a member of the baby-boom generation, born after the GIs and G-gals came home from the Second World War and settled into civilian prosperity and peace. I grew up knowing that there was only one war, World War II. It was "The War" that we heard about at family gatherings, remembered on Memorial Day, saw depicted on television, and played at in the sandlot. It was a "war to end all wars"—but didn't.

Growing up in suburbia in the late 1950s and early 1960s, I had no personal understanding of war until the year I turned five. My father, Richard Mello, then an art teacher, was granted a sabbatical. With the funds and time given him, he decided to study how art was taught in schools overseas.

We traveled as a family to Italy, settling in a small village just outside of Verona where my father's relatives had lived for untold generations. Here, my parents left us in the care of Rosetta and Luigi, our adult cousins, while they went off exploring on their own.

Living on this farm was like stepping back in time. Cousin Luigi still plowed his fields with oxen, and Rosetta did the laundry by hand at the communal village tubs near the river. I was learning Italian quickly, and before a month had passed, I was communicating in a strange patois of English mixed with the village's Roman dialect, and I understood much more than I could express.

After dinner was over and the work of the day was complete, neighbors, friends, and family would gather around the kitchen table to talk. It was then that I heard about "The War." These stories were not about triumph and victory, nor were they nostalgic reminiscences of rationed food and rubber drives, as in the United States. These memories were full of fear, terror, anger, and sorrow. I heard how armies marched back and forth through the town taking whatever they wanted. My cousins talked of the rape of the land and its people, and in my childish way I began to understand that in war there is no such thing as a real victory—that those who survive have the horrific and difficult task of picking up the pieces, burying the dead, and building anew.

Our family returned to the States, and as I grew up I eventually heard more war stories—this time from my father's perspective. I learned that my father was desperate to join up after the devastation at Pearl Harbor, but at the draft office he was declared "legally blind" on account of a congenital cataract, rated "4F," told that the army didn't want him, and summarily sent away.

This wasn't the first time his eyesight had been a barrier. At the beginning of his school career, the teachers labeled him "slow" and "stupid." Luckily, an observant teacher thought to check his eyes, and my father, who is now an artist by profession—whose world is rooted in images—was given a pair of glasses. Suddenly the world came into focus! His "learning problem" disappeared.

In spite of his "bad eye," he kept trying to enlist until finally, as my father tells it, "the army didn't care who they took as long as you were a warm body." He requested immediate induction, was sent to basic training, and then shipped off to Italy as part of the army of occupation. The transport ship landed at the port of Livorno. From there, troops were sent to Pisa, home of the famous leaning tower, and as soon as they had leave, my father and his cronies made for town.

In 1946, the city was left decimated by repeated bombings and artillery fire. Its basilica and abbey were reduced to rubble, and the great frescoes that had been part of their plaster walls had disintegrated into small pea-sized chips. Making their way through this destruction, they reached the tower of Pisa—at which point, my father reports with a wry grin, they raced to the top.

The next day, leaving the devastation of Pisa behind, the company was trucked into Florence—the city of my father's revelation. The streets were empty. Motor traffic was nonexistent and the populace had fled, so my father had an uninterrupted, almost private, view of the city's master-pieces, including the Cathedral, Uffizi Museum, Giotto's Tower, and the

Pitti Palace. He met the works of Michelangelo and Leonardo in person. He roamed the foothills and looked down on the eternal landscape of Dante. He had arrived in an artist's paradise at a time when the world was experiencing hell. His vision soared and his mind's eye expanded. He was transformed by a passion for creation and design.

After his tour of duty was over, he was shipped home, but he vowed to return someday. The magnificence and grandeur that was Florence stayed with him. The war that oppressed countless millions had, in this way, liberated my father. In addition, some far-thinking politicians had taken the phrase "men shall study war no more" seriously enough to send a generation of soldiers to college. The GI bill gave thousands of veterans an opportunity to study, and my father used his money to attend the Museum School at Tufts University. He eventually graduated, became an artist, married my mother, and fathered my sister and me.

My father's artwork, with its strong images, was woven into my family's everyday world. We took for granted the smell of oil paint that permeated the house, and the long hours of silence when my father would disappear into his studio—with only a transistor radio for company. When my friends would report that their parents fought over where to put the new swing set, I would counter with a description of my parents' argument over where and how to hang a painting. When other families took camping trips, we went to museums. At least once a month we'd make the long trip into New York City to see a new Picasso exhibit or a Pollock opening. Through countless galleries of impressionists and modernists we'd follow my father, watching him watch the artwork. He never talked much at home, and in the museum he was even more restrained. We came to think of museums as sacred spaces.

Sometimes one of us would be brave enough to break the hallowed silence and ask: "Dad, what is that supposed to be?" His perennial answers were: "What do you think?" "What do you see?" and "How do you feel about that?"

We were always encouraged to interpret for ourselves: to construct our own understanding, our own emotional and artistic vision. Of course, this was frustrating as a child. It wasn't until I grew up that I really began to appreciate the lessons my father taught us during those Saturday after-noons wandering the galleries. To this day his voice stays inside my head, telling me, "Look! See! Feel! Know! Imagine! Be!" I know now why he was considered such an extraordinary teacher: he encouraged his students to know and value themselves as creative and viable human beings. He modeled what he preached, patiently painting—trying to get "it" perfect and right.

I hadn't thought about any of this in a very long time when memories came flooding back on September 11. Once again I confronted war on a personal level as the towers in New York City came crashing down beside the Hudson River. My father's stories of Florence, and my recollections of Rosetta's and Luigi's painful tales all flashed through my mind. As I sat in my office trying to get a grip on my own emotions and desperately trying to figure out what I would say to my afternoon class, I realized that I needed to talk to someone with history: a survivor, someone who was older, a peacemaker who could put these events into context. So I called my dad.

My father lives half of each year in Italy now—having achieved that dream formed long ago when he was a young soldier. He has retired to the Chianti hills in order to paint full time. Aside from his yearly trips back home to be with family, especially the grandchildren, he spends most of his time creating images of the Tuscan countryside. My father also makes olive oil and a little wine. Each morning he eats fresh Tuscan bread spread with honey from the local abbey, made by bees whose stock goes back to the 16th century. My father's world gives me a larger perspective on things, as it is more timeless and time-honored than my own.

I called him on the phone after an unsuccessful attempt at getting through to my sister in Brooklyn; all of New York City seemed to have been cut off from the rest of the world. I needed to hear his voice, needed to tell him I loved him. I also needed his guidance, as he is the best teacher I have ever known. I wanted to know how it was possible, in times of crisis, not to lose yourself in the agony of the world around you. What was the secret to surviving hard times?

He didn't really have an answer to my questions; his response was more like a cosmic shrug: "Just sit tight, stay safe, it will resolve itself, it's how the world goes." For some reason this practical, fatalistic view calmed me down.

As the television flashed images of the World Trade Towers imploding, I prayed that my family in New York City was safe, and I drifted off into memory, recalling a trip my dad and I had taken to Pisa together two years ago. We went back to the port where my father had landed as a young soldier and walked through the palazzo, now reconstructed to its former glory. Of course, we went to the museum too, walking silently in its sacred air. In one of the galleries was a large, elaborate fresco. Originally titled "Heaven and Hell," it had been painstakingly restored—brought back to life out of the bombed-out rubble. Photographs of the restoration process covered one entire wall. With tweezers, toothpicks, magnifying glasses, and tiny brushes, artists and craftsmen had picked up the pieces of war-crushed art bit by bit and glued them back onto the reconstructed walls. The work had taken decades, and now, were it not for the photo essay, one would never have known that a bomb had destroyed the painting, or that the ancient walls that supported it had ever been harmed.

I stood in that gallery, watching my father looking at the mural that he once had climbed over when it was a pile of rubble. Its title was "The Inferno." Glaring devils and avenging angels danced around our heads; men and women screamed in agony and underwent tortures of the vilest kind. It was a medieval warning of what humans can perpetrate upon themselves. The artist had given succeeding generations a glimpse into a gruesome and yet thrilling medieval judgment day. I found it ironic that this image, one of ultimate Armageddon, was destroyed by the world's most destructive armies and then rescued by the world's most patient artists. But, after all, as my father had shown me, that is what artists do.

That is what art is for: to mirror our own experience back to us, encouraging us to expand our universe; and to challenge our perceptions so we are compelled to delve into our own beliefs and see them from a new perspective—to persevere; to Look! See! Feel! Know! Imagine! Be!

Surrounded by the images of this ancient hell, I also thought about our modern one: of hunger, homelessness, poverty, and oppression. Times had not changed much, at least in terms of human suffering, since the fresco had first been created. And I began to understand why my father chose to paint the things of this world that are eternal, like the ancient olive trees, grape vines, Etruscan hills, rock foundations, fortresses, and walls—all of which have outlasted numerous wars, famines, earthquakes, droughts, and floods.

He looks for things that last, are strong and intense, or things that eternally renew no matter who sits in power or whose face is minted on the currency. He embraces life fully and intensely, teaching and connecting to those around him, painting the faces and images that are dear to him, celebrating the life of the landscape, acknowledging the power of the earth and sky. Like the artisans who reconstructed Pisa's frescoes he explores life through his paintbrush and pen, in small stages, intimately and painstakingly working on an infinite theme.

I am deeply grateful for my father and his vision of the world, especially in this year when global turmoil, war, and hatred have come closer and closer to my home. Now I see clearly that what we need are more teachers like him. We need their peace and vision and the courage to remember what "real war" is, that it cannot be ignored, and will cause real destruction.

For we cannot, like children playing games, simply erase the things we do not like or ignore the people we don't want to include. We cannot simply hang a flag out our window and think that the crisis will disappear. It doesn't work that way. Peace works, instead, the way my father creates a painting, piece by piece and bit by bit, patient and intense. We need to respect the peacemakers, like my father, who teach us that survival is not about destruction, but rather about vision—about building and sustaining life and honoring the things that are eternal. My father's lesson, if we have the courage to learn it, is that we look inside ourselves to see, feel, think, imagine, and that we keep strong to the realization that the pen, paintbrush, and creative heart are always mightier than the sword.

Robin Mello, an assistant professor at University of Wisconsin-Milwaukee, is a professional storyteller who is interested in how stories influence our lives. She has written Animal Tales, a storyplay, and an article, "Cinderella Meets Ulysses," in the Journal of Language Arts. *She is a member of Friends Meeting at Cambridge (Mass.), sojourning at Madison (Wis.) Meeting.*

Reflection: Imagining the Impossible

by Pamela Haines

When I came upon a book about a nonviolent Islamic warrior from the Afghan border (*Nonviolent Soldier of Islam*, by Eknath Easwaran), I knew that I needed to read his story. Pakistan had been our family's home during my father's sabbatical year of teaching at the University of Peshawar in the 1960s, and I have felt connected to the region ever since. It's been a private connection. I never met anyone who had been there, and it seemed as far away and forgotten as a place could be.

Yet I remember everything—the hard-baked earth, the mountains that rose without warning to the northwest, the buses painted in psychedelic colors and festooned with bells and beads, the blank walls of mud that hid all the life of the houses within, the Old City with its bazaar overflowing with people and goods, the tailors squatting on the ground with their sewing machines. We were told not to bother learning the national language since everybody in Peshawar spoke Pashto instead. The women were enveloped in burkas, and the men stared—at 12, I was of marriageable age.

When the United States started to bomb Afghanistan a year ago, my little frontier border town that no one had ever heard of became front-page news. Every story, every place name evoked memories and images. I could see the mountains and the mud-walled villages. I could picture the fighting in the hills, the refugee camps. The people were real.

The women had been kind, but the men had scared me. They were fierce. They made their own rifles up in the hill villages. They stared through you. It was not hard to imagine how easily their passion might be sparked by a sense of injustice. I knew these Pashtuns were warriors. I grieved at their violence, but was not surprised.

What surprised me, what rocked me to my foundations, was Abdul Ghaffer Khan. How could Islam, the Northwest Frontier of British India, and a nonviolent army exist in the same universe? Yet there he was in the book, a quiet giant of a man, looking calmly off into the mountains side by side with Gandhi. All I knew of British colonialism in that area had come from the romance of Kipling's poetry. I had no idea how harsh the repression had been up on the frontier where the British were doubly afraid, faced with warlike locals and the specter of Russia bearing down from the north. I had no idea that it was British strategy to incite the Pashtuns to violence, then use that violence as an excuse for massive military intervention.

Abdul Ghaffer Khan, the son of a village head and a good Muslim, wanted to serve his people. He set up schools in the villages of the Northwest Frontier, a seditious activity that cost him almost ten years in colonial jails in the 1920s and '30s. Inspired by Gandhi, he organized a nonviolent army of 100,000 Pashtuns to lift up the local people and stand against the injustices of colonialism. These warriors became, in turn, an inspiration to Gandhi and all India. They were key players in the struggle for independence from Britain. Their militance and fierce willingness to face death proved that nonviolence was not just for the meek and mild.

Anyone could join Ghaffer Khan's army, so long as he took the oath:

"I am a servant of God; and as God needs no service, but serving his creation is serving him, I promise to serve humanity in the name of God. I promise to refrain from violence and from taking revenge. I promise to forgive those who oppress me or treat me with cruelty. I promise to refrain from taking part in feuds and quarrels and from creating enmity." Ghaffer Khan was matter-of-fact about the Islamic imperative to nonviolence; he took it for granted. In his great love for his people, he drew the very best out of them—and they showed it to the world.

But how many saw? I lived in the city where colonial troops killed hundreds of these unarmed and completely nonviolent warriors in a deadly and prolonged fusillade one January afternoon in 1930. I lived among the people who had confirmed Gandhi in his belief that true nonviolence comes not from weakness but from strength—and I never knew. I wonder, if someone had told me, if I could have imagined it.

Now I live in a world where Islamic militance is equated with violence, and where Christians, Jews, and Muslims alike equate destruction and retribution with strength. We are suffering from a colossal and dangerous ignorance and failure of the imagination—all of us. If we are to survive, we must cultivate our ability to imagine—and live into—the "impossible."

Pamela Haines is a member of Central Philadelphia (Pa.) Meeting.

Witness: Going for the Gold

by Marcelle Martin

In the time since September 11, I have often come to Philadelphia's Independence Mall peace vigil feeling very tired and not eager to talk with people. It has seemed to me there were already too many words flying around and usually I just wanted to stand quietly and try to pray.

Some statements heard at the vigil this fall and winter have stayed with me. One middle-aged man rode his bicycle up close to our line one afternoon and declared: "Pacifism equals slavery. Think about it." He didn't stay to hear our thoughts.

Another man, speaking in a strong accent, asked me if my message would have been the same if I had been living in Nazi Germany. I said I hoped that even there I would have had the courage to stand against what was happening.

"I'm Jewish," he told me. "I would have hoped you'd fight." He walked away quickly, but Bo, another vigiler, followed to talk with him. Bo shared a Scripture passage that was guiding his own stance against war and tried to explain that if we take up evil in order to fight evil, then darkness wins. The conversation I had with Bo about that afterward helped to steady me in those days.

During another week's vigil two men stopped to ask questions and one expressed the opinion that prayer is futile when there are so many evil people in the world. Taking a deep breath, I remembered to feel my connection to the ground beneath my feet, ground on which I'd been praying regularly for about two and a half years.

"I think prayer has an effect," I said with conviction.

"Well, it can't hurt," he conceded.

Like him, others have suggested that the dark situation in the world today is evidence that prayer is ineffective. I've come to believe that if people around the world had not been and were not praying, our planetary situation would be much more dire than it is. I'm also convinced that if more people prayed more frequently and with faith, then we could be living in harmony.

At this week's vigil, on February 10, 2002, I felt unexpectedly joyful. The night before I'd watched some Olympic figure skating. One year when I'd been watching a fierce competition between skillful and dedicated performers who were unhappy to receive silver and bronze medals, I'd heard this phrase in my sleep: "God gives gold for free." I understood it to mean that God bestows divine love and divine gifts not only on "winners" but on everyone, and not as a reward for hard work, but as a free gift.

Enjoying unexpected joy and peace at the vigil that day, those words kept coming back to me: "God gives gold for free."

Usually I don't step up to interact with people unless someone walks up to our literature table, but this day I was drawn toward several people who stayed at a distance. A four-year-old girl stared at us with great curiosity. I held out a button as I approached her.

"Peace be with you," I told her, reading the words on the button as I put it into her hand. She repeated the words back to me, her brown eyes big and alert.

"God bless you," I said.

"God bless you, too!" she exclaimed, and I felt I was talking to a solemn angel.

I watched as her parents examined the button and her father pinned it to her coat. She turned to show me, and then we waved good-bye to each other.

Our vigil line grew to nine people. The peace and joy I felt continued to shine inside me, in spite of drizzling rain. Late in the hour I noticed a man who was reading our signs from a distance, dressed in black from fingertips to toes. I walked over to offer him a flyer and button, which he accepted.

He wanted to know who we were, if we were Christians, and whether we were fundamentalists. He told me he was a pacifist, too, although not a Christian. He said he lived in the suburbs and that everybody he knows thinks his views against bombing are crazy. We talked a long while. I wondered if I was allowing myself to be distracted from my task of prayer. At the same time, as I looked into his eyes, I felt as if I was sensing the place from which his argument against war was coming. Early Quakers might have called it the seed or the witness, or the divine light within. Perhaps by looking into his eyes I could nourish that seed or help that spark of light grow brighter. I sensed his hunger to be illuminated by that light.

"You're listening to me!" he exclaimed with astonishment. "Nobody does that. Usually I talk to myself." He dropped a hint about God entering his life recently. When I asked about that, he told me he'd been an atheist most of his life but had begun to believe there might be a God. "But I don't believe in Jesus!" he insisted hastily, afraid that making space for God might open the door to lots of notions he firmly rejected.

The bells rang five o'clock, signaling the end of the vigil. I told him that my prayer for him was that he would come to have more direct experience of God.

"I've never had an angel talk to me," he responded, and I smiled, thinking that maybe he was wrong about that. The light I'd seen in his eyes stayed in my mind a long time, prompting me to continue to pray for him. Later I decided that perhaps my conversation with him had not been a distraction from prayer, but another way to pray for God's gold to shine in all and for peace to prevail.

Marcelle Martin is a member of Chestnut Hill Meeting in Philadelphia, Pa.

My Grandma Knew What She Was Doing

Your war is packaged neatly
as a pre-cut chicken—select
facts stacked under headlines,
pale as breasts in plastic wrap—
but Grandma set me straight.

When I was ten she yanked
the biggest Leghorn from the coop.
She made me hold her squawking
on the maple stump and chopped
her head off.

Blood gushed hotly on my hand,
her feet clawed air, her limpness
quivered. I felt sick to death.
But Grandma made me hold her
upside down and dip her
in the boiling pot, pluck out
her feathers, split her open.

There inside, her eggs lay
forming. There her heart
was knotted down. I had to
tear them out, her lungs,
intestines—save the liver—
rinse and cut her up, prying
my knife between her joints
so like my own two knees.

I had to dry and salt and flour
each piece and fry them
in the spitting iron skillet.
Pile them on the heated platter.
bring them in to Grandpa
at the dinner table. Eat.

My grandma knew what she was doing.
Never, never will I see
a packaged chicken blind again.
Or buy your Grade A federally-
inspected bloodless war.

—Helen Weaver Horn

Helen Weaver Horn is a member of Athens (Ohio) Meeting.

Queries

In my creative imagination, can I experience something of the anguish of a person angry enough to destroy others? Of persons who see their lives "reduced to rubble"? Of politicians caught between their convictions and the political will around them?

When we gather in shared worship where there is a need for healing, do we invite those present to name concerns either in writing or orally? Do we attend to each concern in silence, holding it in the Light?

How do I engage in quiet worship or service to others as I wait for that still small voice to show me the way forward?

Do I know what our *Faith and Practice* says about Friends' rejection of war? Have I read the appropriate passages to our children and discussed them? Have I discussed the statements in *Faith and Practice* on war with other Friends and friends?

Have I read the Bill of Rights so that I know the basis of rights in our nation? Have I shared these with the children?

Have I read the Patriot Act so that I know whereof I speak if I address the issues surrounding it?

What do I understand as the differences between being naive and being wrong-headed?

Do I allow myself to be infatuated with the stimulation and emotion of marches and demonstrations? Or am I able to participate in them in the spirit of witnessing for peace and justice?

Learning: Complex Truths

In the September 2003 issue of FRIENDS JOURNAL, readers are reminded that "Truth is complex." It is many-sided, but illuminated only on some planes. Its shape is perhaps irregular. It appears slightly different in different lights. It won't hold still. If we contemplate it quietly, absorbing its shape and apparent changes, however, we may begin to hear its sound, much as we might hear a deep, simple wind chime or a buoy bobbing in the fog. We have to rely on others, though, to build a buoy and to set its parts in relationship so the soundings convey some part of the truth, for most of us don't have the experience to do so ourselves.

In his short contribution to "Viewpoint," Cliff Marrs, an experienced London Friend, sets a tone for recognizing that the issues facing us in the world are complex. The three articles that follow take us more deeply into issues that we should know about but that we are not likely to find in such clearly stated terms in the mainstream media. Each author brings us information based on many years of working in an international field. Furthermore, the information is set in the context of Quaker thought and life today.

Charlie Clements brings us a perspective that reflects his background in the U.S. military, and his broad experience in peace and public health work. Having been faithful to each aspect of his life's experience makes his remarks especially valuable. At the same time, one hears his commitment to the work to which he has been led in his final statement: "Do not be daunted by the enormity of the world's grief. Do justly, now. Love mercy, now. Walk humbly, now. You are not obligated to complete the work, but neither are you free to abandon it."

Paul Barker bases his conclusions about the effects of military actions and his examples of practical alternatives on two decades of international relief work in the Middle East. His advice, specific to Afghanistan, offers us ways to talk in our communities about alternatives and gives us a model for thinking about the effects of military or humanitarian actions in any place.

Malcolm Bell has been deeply involved in the work of the Religious Task Force on Central America and Mexico. He knows much about the work of the Archdiocese of Guatemala and UN commissions to find the truth about torture in Guatemala. He also knows that "much of the public doesn't care to . . . [know about] . . . U.S. participation in state terrorism and genocide." He admits that it is highly unlikely that the United States would appoint a truth commission to examine its role in perpetrating and encouraging others to perpetrate torture. Nevertheless, the United States urgently needs such a truth commission. Friends need to ask if we "largely go along impassively with the idea of U.S. exceptionalism." Do we assume that to ask for a truth commission is unnecessary, or un-American, or impossible in the United States?

Edward Snyder, with long experience in working with government and with Quakers, challenges us to define our current position on pacifism thereby giving ourselves a standard for our actions. After worship, and attention to others' thoughts on the issues, it is time for each of us and for us collectively to articulate our best understanding of pacifists' beliefs today and of the beliefs of Quakers who hold to the Peace Testimony. The letters that follow Snyder begin to do that.

Michael Dawson calls us again to enter into an experience imaginatively, this time into an experience of knowing where we stand and standing there firmly, truthfully, but gently. His statistics about the numbers of Friends who have joined war can be and have been questioned. Signing up and serving, for instance, has not always meant that men and women have decided to kill. Recall those, for instance, who sign up for ambulance corps and other non-combatant positions. We can debate the merits of such decisions, but we should do it, he warns us, with a "voice of love."

At the end of the section is a quiet reminiscence of one family's odyssey through the journey of living as a conscientious objector in middle America during the 1940s. Lyle Tatum offers no advice, no admonitions, just his story of living faithfully.

Forum: 9/11/02: A Day of Remembrance?

The commemorative events on the first anniversary of 9/11 make it seem likely that that date will evolve into another annual day of remembrance for the fallen. But the victims commemorated on 9/11/02 were a minority of those who lost their lives on 9/11/01. In addition to the 3,000 who died from terrorism in the rich world, more than 72,500 died from poverty-related preventable diseases in the poor world. (UNFPA's "The State of the World Population 2001" report says that annually dirty water and poor sanitation kill approximately 12.6 million people, with air pollution accounting for a further 5.2 million, and tuberculosis another 3 million. UNAIDS notes 3 million deaths from AIDS each year. According to the Malaria Vaccine Initiative in Maryland, malaria causes 2.7 million fatalities per annum—75 percent of whom are African children under the age of five. These figures total 26,500,000 and convert to an average of 72,500 per day. This figure does not include deaths from other widespread poverty-related preventable diseases such as hepatitis, respiratory infection, and bilharzia.)

Those who were actually remembered on 9/11/02 had names—as the roll call of the dead so vividly demonstrated—and photographs and videos show us their faces; they were individuals we can identify. The tens of thousands of others who died on 9/11 did not appear on our TVs or in our newspapers; they died invisibly and remain nameless and faceless to us, each one a mere statistic, but they were parents, siblings, friends, etc. to those who shared their struggle for survival. What all the victims of 9/11 have in common is that their deaths were the result of choices: the former by the suicide attackers, the latter by the economic policies pushed by the multinationals and adopted by the G8 through their bankers—the World Bank and International Monetary Fund—and their trading cartels via the World Trade Organization.

By insisting on the removal of food subsidies and the replacement of dietary staples for cash crops for export (to generate currency to service loan repayments), and by the introduction of prohibitive hospital "user" fees, the use of expensive patented medicines instead of cheaper generic ones, the privatization of water supplies (which invariably cause consumer costs to spiral, often beyond the means of the poor), and diminishing aid budgets, these bodies decide that we should not share our food with the hungry, our medicines with the sick, or try to ensure clean water for the thirsty. (See Matt. 25:31-46)

Kwesi Owusu monitors the G8 and other global institutions on behalf of Jubilee Plus. In the months preceding the Genoa summit, she "watched the world's richest men and their hired merchants of spin talk themselves out of any vestige of real concern for the plight of the poor." In 1975 the UN set the target for rich countries—to donate 0.7 percent of their Gross National Product (GNP) to aid. By the early 1990s, the average was 0.33 percent; this has now fallen to 0.22 percent. The world's richest nation, the U.S., is also its meanest donor—giving just 0.11 percent of GNP. The only nations to reach the UN target are Denmark, Norway, Sweden, Luxembourg, and Holland.

Billions of dollars have been spent in response to the 9/11 attack. By 9/13, the U.S. Congress had appropriated $40 billion for its war on terrorism. In February 2002, President Bush increased the U.S. military spending budget by $48 billion, to $380 billion. The prospect is that billions more will be spent on a war against weapons of mass destruction. But what about combating poverty-related preventable diseases of mass destruction? Diseases that are preventable do not have to be tolerated but can be eradicated. According to the UNFPA report: "An estimated 60 percent of the global burden of disease from acute respiratory infection, 90 percent from diarrheal disease, 50 percent from chronic respiratory conditions, and 90 percent from malaria could be avoided by simple environmental interventions." *The Economist* reports that "16 million people die each year from easily preventable diseases." These evaluations support the claim of the South African AIDS campaigner Zackie Achmarr that "poor people die only because they are poor." James Wolfensohn, president of the World Bank, seems to agree: "People in poor countries . . . live on the edge. When you are living on a dollar a day [as 1.2 billion people do] it's a question of life and death."

The 2001 Commission on Macroeconomics and Health report for the World Health Organizations calculates that an investment of $27 billion per annum on the war against poverty-related preventable diseases—0.1 percent of the collective Gross Domestic Product of the G8 (or $25 per citizen—the cost of a Harry Potter video)—would save 8 million lives each year; yet little is done. At their last meeting in Canada last year, the super-rich G8 could find just $1 billion of new money to aid Africa (the same amount they spend each day subsidizing their farmers). While 9/11 may have been a kairos day for the rich world—the day that changed the world—for the world's poorest people, it was just another day of death. Tragically, it did not change their world. Action to alleviate the causes of their deaths has been minimal; over 72,500 have died every day since.

The multibillion-dollar response to the attacks of 9/11 and the failure to respond adequately to poverty-related preventable diseases highlights a double standard in the value of life. Do we really need to be reminded that there is that of God in everybody, that all human beings are equal, that all life is equally precious, and that the pain of death does not vary with context?

—*Cliff Marrs*, London, England

The Faces of "Collateral Damage"

by Charlie Clements

I am a public health physician. In January [2003] I participated in a ten-day emergency mission to Iraq, sponsored by the Brooklyn-based Center for Economic and Social Rights. Our task was to assess the potential consequences to Iraqi civilians of a war on Iraq. As a graduate of the U.S. Air Force Academy and a Vietnam veteran, I have some understanding of the potential consequences of the air war we are about to unleash on Iraq as a prelude to an invasion by U.S. troops. The Pentagon will refer to the innocent victims of this assault as "collateral damage," but I've seen their faces, and I think they should have another name. One that occurs to me is "children," since half the population of Iraq is under 18 years old.

Our delegation was composed of six experts in water, sanitation, emergency health services, public health, and food security. We were given access throughout Iraq to clinics, hospitals, food distribution centers, water and sanitation facilities, and electrical generating plants, as well as granted interviews with Iraqi officials, staff of international agencies, civilians, and diplomatic personnel. We had our own translators.

In many ways, the population of Iraq has been reduced to the status of refugees. Nearly 60 percent of Iraqis, almost 14 million people, depend entirely on a government-provided food ration that, by international standards, represents the minimum for human sustenance. They have a very high infant mortality caused by communicable and waterborne diseases. They experience severe problems with their potable water, sanitation, and electrical infrastructures. The health care system can barely cope with the existing disease burden and there are shortages of medicines. Unemployment is at least 50 percent, and those such as physicians who are employed may only make $8–$10 per month. There are limited opportunities for education. There is a pervasive sense of despair and uncertainty regarding the future.

The war has yet to start, but we found the Kerbala Pediatric Hospital that we visited already filled beyond capacity, each bed filled with two or three mothers with their ill children. The pediatrician explained that there were only 28 beds for the 54 patients, so at night many of the mothers would shift onto the floor. Most of the children had the telltale signs of malnutrition—thin skin stretched over protruding bellies, eyes that seemed far too large for their small faces, hair with streaks that Western women often pay for at the hairdresser.

We walked up to a bed where a mother was rocking her tiny, crying three-year-old daughter. The pediatrician said the mother had traveled 200 km because she heard the hospital had a supply of Pentostam, the medicine needed to treat kala azar, or leishmaniasis, as we call it. The pediatrician had not told her yet that there is none. He turned to me and said in English, "It would be kinder to shoot the girl here rather than let her return home to the lingering death that awaits her." Our interpreter, by instinct, translated the doctor's comments into Arabic, and the mother's eyes began to overflow with tears.

Leishmaniasis, we learned from the pediatrician, is reemerging because Iraq is not allowed to import the pesticides that once controlled the sand fly, which transmits the disease. Malaria is also reemerging because mosquito control is no longer possible in parts of Iraq. The incidence of water-borne diseases like typhoid is 1,000 percent of what it was just prior to the Gulf War—2,200 cases in 1990 and more than 27,000 in 2001, according to UNICEF.

After saying good-byes at the Pediatric Hospital, we walked across the highway to the Kerbala water treatment plant. There the woman engineer told us much of the diarrheal disease is caused by poorly treated water, because Iraqis are not allowed to import the spare parts for water treatment plants or the chemicals like chlorine and aluminum sulfate necessary to produce clean water. We would see that only about 8 of the 32 electrical motors that turn the large paddles in the flocculation chambers used for settling solids were still functional; the rest had been cannibalized for parts. There was insufficient chlorine, so the two-step disinfection procedure had been reduced to only a single step.

Later, it was not a surprise when WHO and UNICEF staff explained that 40 percent of water samples in Iraq didn't meet standards for potable water, either for bacteria counts or total dissolved solids. We know what happens when bacteria counts are high. The average Iraqi child has 14 episodes of diarrhea a year now, compared to around three before the Gulf War. That is part of the reason that 70 percent of deaths of Iraqi children result either from diarrheal-related diseases or respiratory infections. The diarrheal diseases weaken their immune systems and make them more susceptible to colds that turn into pneumonias. Malnourished children are more vulnerable to both. The facility's chief engineer said that because the sewage treatment plant in South Baghdad is often inoperable due to lack of maintenance and spare parts, most of the city's wastewater was diverted directly into waterways connected to the Tigris and Euphrates Rivers. We then knew why UNICEF estimates that 500,000 tons of raw sewage are dumped into Iraqi waterways daily. These are the same waterways that are the sources of both potable and industrial water.

What are the consequences of all this? They were rather accurately predicted in a previously classified 1991 Defense Intelligence Agency document that discussed the sanctions imposed on Iraq after it invaded Kuwait. It suggested that if the importation of chemicals were blocked, the already poorly functioning water treatment system in Iraq would soon grind to a halt, disabling most industries that depended upon clean water, specifically mentioning electrical generation, pharmaceuticals, food processing, and petrochemicals. It also predicted that, "Failing to secure supplies will result in a shortage of pure drinking water for much of the population. This could lead to increased incidences, if not epidemics, of such diseases as cholera, hepatitis, and typhoid." This is precisely what has happened. UNICEF estimates that the excess child mortality in Iraq over the past decade has been more than 500,000 children. These children, too, must be counted as "collateral damage" from the Gulf War.

As people watched so-called "smart bombs" zero in on military targets on CNN during the Gulf War, we weren't shown the images of electrical generating plants that were hit on average eight to ten times. Without spare parts these plants have yet to recover fully, and some only operate at 50 percent of capacity causing daily electrical outages for up to 14 hours in some Iraqi cities.

How many civilians will die in the next war? That is difficult to predict with any certainty. Most researchers agree that 10,000 civilians perished in the Gulf War, primarily during the bombing campaign. That figure will surely climb because the U.S. government has threatened that more than 3,000 precision guided munitions will strike Iraq during the first 48 hours of the war. The tactic of a missile exploding every minute during the initial days of a war has been given a name: "shock and awe." The U.S. Department of Defense (DOD) has leaked its war plan to "shock and awe" the Iraqis, specifically striking targets such as the Republican Guards, intelligence and security forces, as well as command and control centers. These are largely located in urban areas where 70 percent of Iraq's 22 million civilians also live.

If the U.S. launches a war against Iraq today, our leaders know that, unlike after the Gulf War, we will not only have to govern the country but will have to rebuild it. For this reason, the DOD would probably refrain from targeting the water, sanitation facilities, and electrical generating plants this time around. (It won't have to, because it can paralyze the electrical grid with wind-dispersed graphite filaments.)

At the same time the electricity-dependent public health infrastructure such as water treatment, sewage pumping, and sewage treatment plants would come to a halt. Already in Baghdad we stepped gingerly through neighborhoods where sewage was backed up into the streets because an aging pump station failed. What will happen when all pumps fail at once and emergency generators can only supply sufficient power for 10 percent of normal capacity?

Iraq is not like Afghanistan, where people have long ago learned to fend for themselves. Iraq is highly urbanized, and the bulk of its population depends entirely upon a "food basket" provided by the government under the UN-monitored Food for Oil program. The 2,200 calories currently provided per adult are what refugee experts define as the minimum needed for human sustenance. The program, which uses surface transportation for distribution, will be suspended when U.S. forces interdict roads, rails, and bridges to prevent the Iraqi army from movement and re-supply.

Just as there are no spare parts in the country, there is little spare food in cupboards and no spare fat on the bodies of so many children who are already malnourished. Half the population is unemployed, and many families have sold their possessions over the last decade to get by. If war comes, the prospects for avoiding a humanitarian catastrophe are grim. In a country where half the population is under the age of 18, can the U.S. make war on Saddam Hussein and not the children of Iraq?

Iraq once had a modern healthcare system that is now barely functioning. What will happen when the backup generators in hospitals slowly go silent because diesel fuel deliveries stop? What will happen in the operating rooms, dialysis units, and blood banks? Iraqi health professionals answered these questions for us. After a woman physician replied to our many ominous queries in a steady and professional manner, a member of our delegation thanked her and said, "You are very strong." She responded, "We have endured a decade of war with Iran and a decade of sanctions and bombing." And then, losing her composure, she began to cry, adding, "We are neither strong nor brave. We do what we have to do to survive." There is palpable fear in Iraq, and it can be felt everywhere you have a quiet conversation.

The previously mentioned declassified Defense Intelligence Agency document, conversations with UN officials in Iraq, and the experience of several international organizations operating in Iraq reveal there has been a dark side to the enforcement of sanctions. Until last year, every item that was imported into Iraq had to be individually approved by the Sanctions Committee. Made up of representatives of some 20 countries, votes were by secret ballot and one negative vote was sufficient to block a request. Recently, a widely used antibiotic that could also be used to treat anthrax was blocked by the Sanctions Committee. Chlorine and aluminum sulfate used in the treatment of water were blocked as "dual use" (capable of both civilian and military use). Stainless steel essential for the screens in wastewater plants has been blocked for years. After enormous pressure was brought to bear by the international community, UN Resolution 1409 was authorized by the Security Council in 2001, providing a list of items that can be imported without going through the months and sometimes years of scrutiny of the Sanctions Committee.

An Austrian physician who read an essay of mine circulating on the Internet, wrote: "Our humanitarian project was blocked by the U.S. objection inside the Sanctions Committee for one year. They considered our medical machines as dual use, although the UN weapons inspectors were involved and they confirmed that not one of our instruments is to be considered as dual use. With our project we are supporting children who suffer from leukemia or cancer."

If the constant litany that visiting delegations in Iraq hear are to be believed, then the sanctions are the root of all evil there today. The truth isn't so black and white—little is, in Iraq. Visitors can see beautiful mosques and gorgeous presidential palaces being built in many places. Ba'athist Party bureaucrats and the military don't suffer the deprivations of ordinary people. Saddam Hussein rules with an iron fist and tolerates no dissent. Statues of him are everywhere and people display posters of him as evidence of their patriotism. The office of one mid-level director in a regional electric department took the prize with seven.

It is almost impossible to know what Iraqis really think because there is a government "minder" present for all visits. In a taxi or on the streets at night, people will ask where we are from and will invariably welcome us when they discover we are from the United States. As much as some Iraqis would like Saddam removed, in private one doesn't sense that they would welcome a U.S.-led war as the means. The Iraqis are a proud people, aware of their place in the history of civilization. Walking through an ornate arch that connects two parts of a market, I was told it was built in 1200 C.E. Several blocks later, I comment upon another building and am told it dates from 3000 B.C.E. Babylon itself is not far outside Baghdad where one of the seven wonders of the ancient world, the "hanging gardens," is now being restored.

The region no longer seems to fear Saddam Hussein. Most believe he has largely been disarmed and his army is no longer a threat. While the *New York Times* talks about the coalition the U.S. is trying to build, Arab newspapers report on the meeting of the foreign ministers of Iraq's neighbors—Iran, Saudi Arabia, Turkey, Jordan, Syria—to discuss how war can be avoided. These countries all fear the economic consequences of a war. Turkey lost an estimated $25 billion in the Gulf War and has so far refused the $26 billion aid package that the U.S. is dangling in exchange for use of the country as a staging area. They all say that contrary to international law they will not permit the millions of refugees to cross their borders as they did in the Gulf War.

Many think that Osama bin Laden would welcome a U.S. attack on Iraq because nothing could help the cause of al-Qaida more. They fear that television images of Iraqis fighting GIs street to street in Baghdad could inflame both the smoldering fundamentalist sentiment as well as the anti-Americanism of ordinary people across the region. We, too, should fear the hatred and resentment that could be unleashed. It could haunt us for decades to come in every corner of the world.

A subject that is infrequently mentioned in the commentaries on this looming war is the impact on economies—local, regional, and global. Our allies largely paid for the Gulf War. Without such friends this time around, the U.S. administration's legal team has determined we can charge the Iraqis using their oil revenues to finance the war against them. If Saddam torches his oil fields as he has promised to do (and did in Kuwait), then it could take even longer than the estimated five years to rehabilitate them. A Saudi oil official has said that if that happens, oil prices could rise to $100 per barrel. The last time that happened, it caused a global recession, from which Africa needed a decade to recover. The U.S. economy is not in a strong position to withstand a war, yet there is surprisingly little debate in the U.S. about the possible economic consequences.

Even now, Iraqi oil fields have had no spare parts for a decade and are operating at less than 50 percent of pre-Gulf War capacity. Already, the Food for Oil program is billions of dollars behind in critically needed items that have been authorized but not yet supplied such as food, medicine, spare parts for water treatment plants, and electrical generators. Almost half the proceeds are used for war reparations to Kuwait and to administer the program; the other half keeps Iraq alive. The U.S. has budgeted nothing for this war, and if it expects to pay for it out of Iraqi oil revenues, it will have to further starve Iraqis to do so.

This scenario is conservative. I have not taken into account any use of weapons of mass destruction, or the possibility that the war will set loose massive civil disorder and bloodshed, as various groups within the country battle for power or revenge. I have also ignored what would happen if U.S. forces became bogged down in house-to-house fighting in Baghdad, which could easily become another Mogadishu or Jenin.

There was a lot that made me angry on this trip. I have worked in war zones before, and I have been with civilians as they were bombed by U.S.-supplied aircraft. I don't think I've experienced anything on the magnitude of the catastrophe that awaits our attack on Iraq.

On Saturday, February 15, in cities around the world, millions of people joined their voices and prayers in hopes of stopping this war. The demonstrators urged agreement with the majority of the UN Security Council that believes that the weapons inspectors are making progress and must be allowed to continue their mandate to search for and disable Iraq's weapons of mass destruction. There is widespread acknowledgment that Saddam Hussein has dragged his feet on disarming, but there is also a strong desire for the international community to fulfill its obligations under Chapter 7, Articles 41 and 42 of the United Nations Charter—to exhaust all peaceful avenues before resorting to force.

If the U.S. pursues this war without the backing of the UN Security Council, it will undermine a half century of efforts to establish a community of civilized nations where there is the rule of law. We must search for alternatives other than war to resolve these troubling issues. We must be creative in developing sanctions that don't harm the most vulnerable sectors of society—pregnant women, children, and the elderly.

I am troubled by what I have seen in Iraq. I am inspired by the millions who recently made their voices and prayers heard around the globe. I am comforted by words sent by a friend, based on the Talmud: "Do not be daunted by the enormity of the world's grief. Do justly, now. Love mercy, now. Walk humbly, now. You are not obligated to complete the work, but neither are you free to abandon it."

Charlie Clements attends Santa Fe (N. Mex.) Meeting. In 1984, American Friends Service Committee made a film about his work in El Salvador called Witness to War, *which won the Academy Award for Best Documentary Short. He is currently CEO and president of WaterWorks, a not-for-profit organization that assists communities in the southwestern United States that are without potable water and wastewater systems. He also teaches at the Bartos Institute for the Constructive Engagement of Conflict at the United World College in Montezuma, New Mexico. He is a former president of Physicians for Human Rights and served on their board for 15 years. He is a Distinguished Graduate of the U.S. Air Force Academy and a Distinguished Alumnus of University of Washington School of Public Health. For the executive summary and final report of the mission described in this article, see <www.cesr.org>.*

Queries from Afghanistan

by Paul Barker

The war between 72 nations has left all in regret.
Because they have not seen truth, they have created fairy tales.

—Hafiz

In the context of President George W. Bush's declared "War on Terrorism," what does it mean to live, as George Fox said, "in the virtue of that life and power that takes away the occasion of all wars"?

What does the Quaker Peace Testimony mean in the context of an Afghanistan that has been "liberated" from the terror of the Taliban regime by force of military arms? Indeed, what did it mean in the context of the harsh rule of the Taliban? Are there times when the awesome power of modern weaponry can be used to shake up the chess board of long entrenched "evil" regimes and allow otherwise impossible outcomes? Does the destruction of the Taliban regime in Afghanistan vindicate the use of war as a means to bring about positive change?

I have been given ample cause to ponder these and other challenging questions over the past years and, indeed, decades. Revulsion at the horrors committed by the United States in Vietnam led me to become a conscientious objector and eventually to find a spiritual home in the Religious Society of Friends. Some restless spirit has led me to a career in international relief and development, spanning five years with the Peace Corps in Iran, two years managing medical programs for Eritrean refugees in Sudan for the Lalmba Association, and now 19 years working for CARE in Egypt, Ethiopia, Northern Iraq, Palestine, and Afghanistan. It has definitely been interesting, but making sense of it through a Quaker lens is not easy. Being philosophically and morally opposed to war as a tool to solve the world's problems is the easy part. What practical alternative do we then have to offer? Must the Afghans of the world suffer under intolerable regimes forever because neither they nor the international community have the will and the wherewithal to bring peaceful change? Can it be that all that is required for the triumph of evil in the world is for good people to limit themselves to prayers, demonstrations, and calls for peace?

If any group has been impugned in Western public opinion, it must be the Taliban. Their harsh and uncompromising fundamentalist version of Islam seemed ever intent on rushing from one outlandish extreme to another. And much of what has been written is true. Women were banned from most forms of employment. Severe restrictions were placed on female education. Harsh shari'a punishments were imposed on adulteresses (death by stoning), thieves (amputation of the right hand), beard trimmers (lengthy prison terms), and other offenders of Taliban morality. They conducted massacres in some Hazara communities, and they destroyed archeological treasures, including the two giant standing Buddhas of Bamiyan. As their easy territorial gains of 1994–96 receded into history, the Taliban employed scorched-earth tactics and more sophisticated military campaigns against their entrenched opposition in the center and northeast of the country. And as the years went by, the relationship of the Taliban leadership to Osama bin Laden became closer and more protective. It is an appalling and amazing list.

But truth is complex. The Taliban arose in the chaos of mujahidin-fractured Afghanistan. Reports on abuse of women in mujahidin-ruled Afghanistan were as appalling as those later written to document Taliban excesses. Armed factions had destroyed cities. Highway robbery and extortion were crippling any chance for the recovery of the Afghan economy and society from the horrors of the Soviet war. Yet from this chaos, in a matter of only two years, the Taliban movement evolved and spread with minimal violence to control half of the country. Myths evolved about Taliban virtue and invincibility. Cities, towns, and villages peacefully came under the Taliban map as commanders succumbed to perceived inevitability and bribes. By the time the movement reached the outskirts of Kabul, their extreme views on women's rights were well known, but still many Kabulis looked forward to their arrival because at least it offered the hope of peace and stability.

The Taliban were not a monolithic group. Their leadership included some university-educated officials and some more progressive mullahs who looked for ways to temper the organization's worst excesses. There were some Taliban officials with a genuine concern for the welfare of the Afghan people. While most in the West would not agree with Taliban values, we should recognize that for better or for worse they were driven by values and an uncompromising commitment to those values. To believe that there is "that of God in every one" is to believe and to act as though the Taliban leadership is worthy of respect, to appeal to and to seek to nurture that responsible side of their being.

Agreement

In March 1996, six months prior to the Taliban seizure of Kabul, I traveled to Qandahar with three of our senior national staff to negotiate a basic agreement with the nascent Taliban movement. I had expected that this process would take a couple of months, with an initial visit to get to know the accessible members of the Taliban leadership and reach an agreement in principle. A follow-up trip in April or May might be required to actually negotiate and sign an agreement. Instead, through a period of two days of meeting, sitting on the floor, drinking tea with, and getting to know Mullah Attiqallah, then head of the Taliban Foreign Relations office, and Mullah Abbas, then mayor of Qandahar, we were able to move from our initial draft to a negotiated and signed agreement. That agreement recognized the integrity and responsibility of the two parties, the Taliban Authority and CARE Afghanistan. CARE agreed to operate with respect for the culture and traditions of Afghanistan, and the Taliban agreed to respect and support CARE's humanitarian efforts in Afghanistan, including the right to transport relief commodities over besieged frontlines to needy families in then opposition-held Kabul. We subsequently made copies of the agreement to be carried in all of our vehicles operating in Afghanistan in order to facilitate their movement through Taliban-held parts of Afghanistan. While we had numerous "hiccups" along the way with our relations with Taliban officials at the local and national levels, our staff could always refer to the basic agreement signed with the Taliban leadership in Qandahar as the basis for moving forward, and usually it would work. Even after Mullah Attiqallah had been replaced by other officials in charge of Taliban foreign relations, some officials, when presented with the signed agreement simply said, "What we have signed, we have signed."

Education of Girls

A few months prior to the Taliban seizure of Khost in the spring of 1995, CARE had helped establish ten community-based schools. Under our education philosophy, CARE would provide teacher training and educational materials for the schools, but the communities were responsible for identifying and paying the teacher and for providing an appropriate space for the schools. Before CARE would support any community school we required that at least 30 percent of the students be girls. This was an ambitious target even in pre-Taliban Afghanistan. When the Taliban gained control of Khost and the surrounding districts where the schools were placed, they were dismayed to find village schools teaching girls. They told the communities to stop doing this, but the communities all responded, "No, these are our schools and our students and we are paying for the teachers. We want our children to learn." The schools stayed open and over the ensuing six years the Community Organized Primary Education (COPE) Program expanded to 707 classrooms in seven provinces, with 465 teachers (15 percent female) and 21,000 students (46 percent female). The fundamental legitimacy of the schools was established in the communities through their Village Education Committees. Often the local Taliban mullah was selected as a member of the committee. Building on hadith (sayings of the prophet Muhammad) such as, "It is compulsory on all Muslim men and Muslim women to be educated," and "Search for learning, even if it is from China," the COPE schools were accepted by communities and mullahs throughout much of southeastern Afghanistan.

Employment of Women

The 1996 Amnesty International report on the abuse of women's rights in pre-Taliban Afghanistan is as damning as any report later written on the anti-female excesses of the Taliban regime. From the rape, plunder, and forced marriages of mujahidin-ruled Kabul to the beatings, seclusion, and forced unemployment of the Taliban years, women of Afghanistan's urban centers have endured long years of abuse. In the austerity of Taliban Kabul, the 30,000 war widows and their 150,000 dependent children ranked among Afghanistan's most destitute people. Their plight was made worse by Taliban edicts banning female employment outside the medical sector, banning female education, and banning women from directly receiving humanitarian assistance. But through the nightmarish restrictions lay the seeds of possibility. In the winters prior to the Taliban seizure of Kabul, CARE had conducted emergency distributions of food and non-food items to widows. In the Taliban years this evolved to a year-round program managed by and for women. The program grew to have a female distribution team, a female monitoring team, and a female health and sanitation education team. Ugly incidents did occur from time to time. A squad from the Department to Promote Virtue and Prevent Vice (PV2 we called it) once stopped a bus carrying CARE female staff, forced them to disembark and then beat the women with a leather strap as they got off the bus. We suspended both the widows' feeding program and a large water and sanitation program until we received assurances from the Taliban leadership that the PV2 actions did not represent official policy, and that they would not be repeated. Later the regime tried to force us to retrench all of our female staff. We appealed to Mawlavi Abdulrahman Zahed, Deputy Minister of Foreign Affairs, saying that it would be shameful for men to manage a women's relief distribution program. He concurred and at significant risk to himself approved a mechanism through which female CARE staff could continue to work. (We have more recently been pained to learn that Mawlavi Abdulrahman Zahed is among the hundreds of Taliban now being held without charges or judicial process in Guantánamo.)

Prison for Beard Trimmers

At 5:00 a.m. one summer morning in 1998 Mullah Nur ad-Din Torabi, the Taliban Minister of Justice, led a group of armed Taliban to the CARE sub-office on a hillside overlooking the Kabul-Maidanshah highway. He seized half of the office and turned its basement into a prison for men who trimmed their beards. He set up a roadblock on the highway and sent all men who showed evidence of having trimmed their beards up the hill to the CARE office/Taliban prison. One of our engineers was also imprisoned: even though his beard met the Taliban length standards, he was a Dari speaker and misunderstood the Taliban beard length question when it was put to him in Pushtu. It took us many weeks of negotiation with very senior officials in Kabul before we were finally able to get the main shura (council) in Kabul to issue a decree that the CARE office in Maidanshah should be returned to CARE, and it took yet more weeks before the Ministry of Justice acted on the decree. Principled engagement was not fast, but it did work.

Polytechnic

Also in the summer of 1998, the Ministry of Planning decreed that all nongovernmental organizations should move their Kabul offices into the severely damaged dormitories of Kabul Polytechnic. We protested at the security implications and the cost of such a move and embarked on months of negotiations and stalling tactics. Finally, in apparent frustration, the Taliban began expelling international aid agencies and sealing their offices. When we realized what was happening, the head of our widows' feeding program went to see Mullah Qari Din Mohammed, the Minister of Planning, and told him, "I don't want to discuss your plans to expel agencies from Kabul. I just want to know if we can continue our widows' feeding program." The minister thought for a few moments and agreed to her request. She asked if we could have that in writing. He told her to come back in two days, and indeed it was ready.

As these anecdotes indicate, it was possible through patience, respect, and tact to work with Taliban leaders at different levels to address some of the most egregious aspects of their policies and practices. But the policy of principled, cautious engagement was inadequate to bring about fundamental change in Afghanistan in the near future. The constructive engagement strategy was not adopted by all agencies working in Afghanistan; it was supported with limited resources; it did not directly engage all of the most senior members of the Taliban leadership; and there were strong and uncompromising ideas and forces directing the Taliban regime who were not easily amenable to persuasion. Does quiet, cautious engagement run the risk of bringing about only marginally important positive steps, but ultimately end up giving a degree of legitimacy to a despicable regime? It is an uncomfortable question. And it probably does not have a neat answer.

Ultimately, the Taliban regime in Afghanistan was toppled by a massive U.S. bombing campaign and an insurgent ground war orchestrated by Special Forces and fought by career Afghan warlords and their armies. The sense of relief that was brought by the fall of the Taliban is most strongly felt in Kabul, Hazarajat, and northeast Afghanistan—areas that had suffered the most from Taliban excesses. The results are more mixed in much of the rest of the country. The peace and security of commerce that the Taliban had brought to the 90 percent of Afghanistan under their control has now been replaced with resurgent warlordism, highway banditry, and a Taliban movement transformed into a guerilla force. The near eradication of opium poppy production under the Taliban in 2001 has now been replaced with bumper crops of poppy— 80 percent of global production. "Victory" in Afghanistan is neither complete nor assured.

And the costs of the military victory over Taliban are significant. The

$10 billion plus spent in the military campaign could be seen as a great investment if it were indeed a turning point in the elimination of global threats of terror, or if it were to lead to a stable, progressive democracy in Afghanistan. But these ends are very much in the balance, and there are other very real costs that should be weighed. I find credible the estimates that between 3,000 and 8,000 Afghan civilians were killed in U.S. bombing "mistakes," more than the total number of victims of the 9/11 attacks in the United States. And it has been estimated that the United States used between 500 and 1,000 metric tons of depleted uranium in munitions attacking bunkers, caves, tanks, and other hardened targets. The prospect of up to 1,000 metric tons of uranium oxide now dispersed over Afghan cities and mountains is a sobering prospect for this and future generations of Afghans.

There has not yet been a complete or sustainable military victory over the Taliban. The military successes against the Taliban have come at a high cost in lives and environmental pollution: inflation, rising rural insecurity, and a disappointing pace of reconstruction all call into question the benefits of the regime change ushered in by the coalition war.

The stunning U.S. military victories in recent years have sown the seeds of future tragedy. Gulf War I and the establishment of U.S. military bases in Arabia became the festering wound that led Osama bin Laden to create the al-Qaida network and focus its wrath against the United States. President Bill Clinton's August 1998 cruise missile attacks on al-Qaida bases in the southeastern mountains of Afghanistan galvanized Mullah Omar's resolve to stand by and defend the residency rights of his Arab "guests" in Afghanistan.

(The Arabs had become increasingly despised in Afghanistan, and credible reports claim that the Taliban had been on the verge of expelling Osama bin Laden prior to the missile attacks.) The military defeat of the Taliban in 2001 is now mutating into a Taliban guerilla movement against the new Afghan government and its foreign supporters. War has yet to bring peace to Afghanistan.

If the cautious, principled engagement strategies of pre-9/11/01 Afghanistan were inadequate to fundamentally change Taliban beliefs and behavior, could it have been more successful had it been supported with more generous funding, followed by more agencies, and developed as a more comprehensive strategy? Humanitarian and development assistance to Afghanistan is now running at about ten times the level of pre-9/11/01 funding—and at one tenth the cost of the "American War." Had this level of assistance been annually available and creatively used in the decade before that tragic date, far more opportunities would have been created to help the long-suffering Afghan people and to positively influence the Taliban leadership. The modestly sized, community-based education program cited above could have been expanded nationwide, engaging community and religious leaders in very practical discussions leading to the advancement of female education. Similarly modest projects that built on community structures to address basic needs for food, water, and income could have been greatly expanded and those community leaders much more empowered. Had those programs been five or ten times larger, the influence of the Taliban over Afghan lives would have been proportionately reduced. Perhaps a critical mass of new ideas and behaviors could have been planted.

One program which CARE discussed in 1998–99 but unfortunately never managed to develop and get funded was a forum for dialogue between Taliban scholars of Islamic law and scholars of international human rights. It would have been designed to explore in depth the basis of controversial Taliban positions, and to explore the commonalties and conflicts between shari'a and international human rights charters and law. In that many of the most extreme Taliban policies sprang more from Pushtun culture than Islamic teaching, such a forum would have tried to help Taliban leaders to acknowledge and deal with the non-Islamic basis of many of their beliefs. It could have been a bridge between the reclusive Taliban and a poorly informed outside world.

Especially during the present administration, the United States seems determined to force its will by preemptive use of precision-guided weapons of significant destruction and quite explicitly not by treaties, courts, and procedures of international law. The weapons and the destruction are impressive, but the long-term consequences highly questionable.

We in the humanitarian community may not have preferred the "American War" as a response to Afghanistan's problems. But it has happened and we are left with its aftermath and questions of what to do now.

I have joined other voices in calling for an international security force to help Afghanistan develop and deploy a multi-ethnic, nonfactional Afghan security force throughout the country. I do not think that peace and security can ultimately come to Afghanistan until the warlords and private militias are replaced with a professional, disciplined, multi-ethnic, nonfactional, paid security force, and in Afghanistan this will probably include an army. I do see a legitimate role in Afghanistan for a disciplined force with guns for some time. But I also believe that ultimately sustainable peace will depend on offering a better life without armed coercion for generations of people who have known little else. And that can only come through a patient and sustained effort of engagement—and a determination to seek and "see truth" in the imagery of Hafez.

Paul Barker, a member of Multnomah Meeting in Portland, Oreg., is country director for CARE International in Afghanistan. He has worked for CARE for 19 years and has attended Friends meetings and worship groups in Ramallah, Khartoum, Cairo, and Addis Ababa.

Torture a Few to Save Many?

by Malcolm Bell

Should the United States resort to torture in defending against terrorism? Suppose a man is in custody who knows where a bomb is ticking? The 9/11 attack has brought us to the unhappy point that both glib and responsible people are considering whether it may be appropriate to torture a suspect in order to save innocent people from great harm. The issue seems particularly pertinent for people who believe in peace, in nonviolent solutions, and in that of God in every torturer, victim, person who permits torture, and person who will die if the bomb goes off.

On June 25–26, 2002, the Torture Abolition and Survivors Support Coalition International (TASSC) of Washington, D.C., held a conference, "On the Question of Torture: An Exchange of Views," at Catholic University of America to consider these troubling questions. The many sponsors and endorsers included the Washington and Middle Atlantic Regional offices of American Friends Service Committee. Altogether about 200 people attended, about 50 of them survivors of torture from around the world. It was my privilege to help out as a volunteer.

TASSC International came into being in 1998. Sister Dianna Ortiz, OSU, who was a missionary from the United States who survived torture in Guatemala in 1989, is its director. Orlando Tizon, who survived torture in the Philippines, is the assistant director. TASSC began as a project of the Guatemala Human Rights Commission/USA (GHRC), and is now an independent organization.

According to Amnesty International, some 150 countries currently practice torture or ill-treatment of prisoners. Survivors are a minority, since torture kills most of its victims. Yet by conservative estimate, some 500,000 survivors live in this country alone. TASSC's mission is "to end the practice of torture wherever it occurs," though Sister Dianna and the other speakers did not try to force this position upon the attendees.

TASSC also serves importantly as a mutual support group. Members representing 41 nations spent that week together. They nurtured each other in private. They lobbied public officials. Most of them have gotten to know each other at earlier TASSC gatherings. Their common experience of having been tortured, the pain they continue to endure, and their joy in each other's company bind them together.

During each of the previous four years, TASSC held a 24-hour vigil in Lafayette Park opposite the White House on June 26, which is the day the United Nations has designated for international support for torture victims and survivors—which is ironic since a large majority of UN member nations practice torture. Following 9/11, however, such demonstrations have been banned. Since another vigil there was no longer possible, TASSC decided to have the conference instead.

Back in 1992, the GHRC put on another conference on torture. That was the first time that Sister Dianna had ever spoken in public about her ordeal. She was shaky, but powerful. The audience froze as she held up a razor blade and called it her special friend that promised the release she longed for from her nightmares, flashbacks, and pain. She has come a long way in the years since, thanks to her own determination and the help of people like Dr. Mary Fabri and many others. Two years ago, Dianna gave her razor blade away.

Dr. Fabri is the director of the Kovler Center for Survivors of Torture in Chicago. She became Dianna's therapist and accompanied her on two devastating trips back to Guatemala in 1992 and 1993 to testify in court and retrace the route of her abduction. As Dianna did that, her mind plunged her back into being repeatedly raped and burned, beset by rats, and soaked in blood spurting from another woman, so that Dr. Fabri later said she actually saw Dianna undergoing torture. The Sunday before the conference Dr. Fabri took all the survivors who had arrived by then out to dinner. She says she likes to take the survivors out every year. Later she helped to lead the conference.

The program booklet included quotes that provoked thought and suggested how darkly the issue is already looming over us:

The truth is that many Americans' safety today is in the hands of men willing to shoulder this burden [of torture]. They are not sadists or homicidal, are instead fulfilling a profound, if tragic, duty.

—Matt Miller, *Morning Edition*, April 9, 2002

I remain a prisoner of history . . . wives witnessed the live dismemberment of their husbands. Fathers were . . . forced to rape their daughters and sons were forced to rape their mothers . . . men were crucified to doors. Children were decapitated while their mothers watched.

—survivor from Bosnia

Torture is bad. . . . Keep in mind, some things are worse. And under certain circumstances, it may be the lesser of two evils. Because some evils are pretty evil.

—Tucker Carlson, CNN, "Crossfire"

Will torture go away? No, it never will. It stays with you in your body and mind, forever. You may forget for an hour or a day, or two days, but it always comes back to you. It has become a part of you as long as you live.

—survivor from Ethiopia

If you've got the ticking bomb case, the case of the terrorist who knew precisely where and when the bomb would go off, and it was the only way of saving 500 or 1,000 lives, each democratic society would, has, and will use torture.

—Professor Alan Dershowitz, Jan. 20, 2002

But if a country's . . . values rest on the dignity and human rights it guarantees, that country cannot permit torture, not even in extreme situations . . . a soldier or policeman who tortures other people in the name of his country is destroying that country, not protecting it.

—Jurgen Moltmann, theologian

The ticking bomb case that Prof. Dershowitz cited is commonly used as a reason for legalizing torture, but experience in the real world teaches that where torture occurs, many thousands endure agony, yet few, if any, ticking bombs are defused. A survivor from Greece pointed out that torture is a tool, not for hearing the truth, but for hearing what the torturers want to hear. Most victims are tortured not to obtain information, but to inflict gruesome deaths that exert social control and keep potential dissidents in line. And most torturers seem to feel they are doing a necessary and patriotic job for their country. At the time of the conference, the U.S. was not known to have tortured any terrorist suspects, though it had reportedly had some of them shipped to other countries to be tortured. A lawyer told the audience that this is just as criminal as performing the actual torture. I might add that it sounds like hiring a hit person to do your dirty work.

Ariel Dorfman, who is a Chilean poet, novelist, and playwright, gave the opening talk. "What times are these?" he asked, referring to the prevalence of torture. "What kind of a world do we live in?" He had supported the elected President of Chile, Salvador Allende, whom U.S.-backed General Augusto Pinochet violently overthrew in 1973, beginning a reign of terror that "disappeared," tortured, and killed thousands. Salvador Allende died in the coup; Ariel Dorfman was exiled.

Through the day, one survivor after another talked about torture or its effects. Some of those effects were evident in the room, as speakers wept, apologized for weeping, and continued their accounts. I was often close to tears. I knew, yet knew I could not know, the price they were paying to make their stories known. Some survivors listening to them buried their heads in their arms or left the auditorium. TASSC had thoughtfully provided two recovery rooms.

A journalist from Colombia related that after he was tortured in 1976, his partner, his friends, and all of his family except his mother rejected him. Twenty years later he was arrested for videotaping soldiers as they attacked some peaceful protesters. His son, five, saw soldiers beating him on the TV news. Later they crushed one of his testicles and burst his liver; he was not expected to live. What caused him to weep, though, was telling us about the perplexity and pain that his arrest and torture caused his children. His daughter still cries easily and sleeps with the light on.

A woman wearing a striking blue dress and turban of her Ogoni people of Nigeria told how a major company has taken $30 billion worth of oil out of their land in recent decades, ruining the land, with great harm to the people who live on it. They have no electricity or running water and must pump any gas for their vehicles by hand. What price oil? Some 3,000 of her people have been killed, 20 villages have been razed, and more thousands have been disappeared or displaced, while the security forces enjoy impunity for these crimes. She, too, wept as she told of a commander who bragged that villagers may run but they cannot escape his men's machine guns.

The statement of a Peruvian woman had to be read because the U.S. Embassy had denied her a visa. When the woman was 15, she saw the police arrest her brothers, who were 17 and 14. Then she and her mother had to identify their battered bodies, which were caked with blood and earth and wet with urine. They had been shot where the bullets would inflict pain but not death. Each was missing an eye. There was brain matter in their hair.

Wednesday began with a moving litany that featured candles, which are Dianna's trademark. About 150 of them flickered in glass cups that had paper bands around them, each bearing the name of a country that practices torture or ill treatment of prisoners. The audience held the candles. A man and a woman on the podium took turns chanting the names of the countries while the man slapped out an urgent rhythm on a drum and people played flutes behind them. After each four or five names, the audience chanted, "We remember. . . ." When the name on your candle was chanted, you stood up, until eventually we were all standing. As a Quaker, I am somewhat detached from ritual, but this was strong. It took a long time. It gave me a new sense of how many people do unimaginable things to their own people—to our own people, since Amnesty International has placed the United States on the list.

More survivors spoke. So did Rep. Jim Moran (D-Va.). Every member of Congress had been invited. Two sent statements, which were read, but he was the only one who showed up. When he mentioned the problems caused by U.S. "exceptionalism and individualism," the audience clapped. Looking taken aback, he said he hadn't expected that to be an applause line.

The survivors presented a statement of their concerns about torture and ways to oppose it. As the afternoon passed, more and more survivors asked for and were given the microphone to read poems that the conference itself had moved them to write. It was an inspired response, a fitting cap for an intense two days.

In October 2002, Orbis Books published Dianna's memoir, *The Blindfold's Eyes: My Journey from Torture to Truth.* The book is an unflinching account of what it's like to survive torture—her guilt, distrust, ghosts and demons that haunted her days and destroyed her nights, her recurring urge to seek peace in death. Yet the book, like the conference, is ultimately uplifting. Dianna, like the other survivors who spoke, has persevered. She has expanded her ministry from teaching Mayan children in a remote hamlet to leading a quest to end torture "wherever it occurs."

The enormous importance of TASSC International and its mission came home to me during this powerful conference. Survivors of torture speak with unique authority. As our government considers legalizing torture, their voices must be heard. Scattered around alone, they are like sticks unheeded and easily broken (though Dianna wasn't). But bound together by TASSC, they constitute a significant force, a stout girder in a bridge to a torture-free world. (For more about TASSC, see <www.tassc.org>).

And what of people who respect that of God in every person and espouse nonviolent solutions? Will Quakers form another girder in that bridge? It is said that one's idealism varies inversely with one's distance from the problem. The answer to the question of torture may be clearer in principle than in practice, as the answer has been for the war against terrorism—the war that spawned this question about torture in the first place.

Since Scott Simon's article in FRIENDS JOURNAL (Dec. 2001) in support of that war inspired many comments from readers, I thought it would be of interest to ask him what he thinks about using torture. He replied, "I do not believe that torture is justified. My objection is not just moral. I think there is a great deal of practical evidence . . . that evidence obtained by torture cannot be trusted. . . . In fact, [a suicide bomber] may welcome the opportunity to misinform." He went on, though, to add a caution: "If someone was captured who possessed information that could save the life of my wife or children (or for that matter Dianna Ortiz), and they refused to divulge that information while a bomb ticked away, I would be tempted to want to torture that gangster myself, rather than stay faithful to my beliefs. Anyone who is certain that their convictions would be undimmed in that situation is, I think, just not being honest with themselves."

The news since the June conference has borne out the participants' fears. On December 26, 2002, the *Washington Post* reported that American Special Forces and the CIA have tortured al-Qaida and Taliban prisoners held abroad—beating them up, confining them in tiny rooms, blindfolding them and throwing them into walls, tying them up in painful positions, gagging them and binding them to stretchers with duct tape, and depriving them of sleep—or turned them over to countries like Egypt, Morocco, and Jordan for more brutal tortures. Some U.S. officials expressed confidence that the U.S. public would agree with them that these measures are just and necessary. Though this news report seems well authenticated, it has passed almost unnoticed. It has also been reported that after U.S. citizen John Walker Lindh was captured in Afghanistan among the Taliban in December 2001, he was taped to a stretcher at times and was kept cold, hungry, sleep-deprived, and in total darkness in a steel shipping container.

The debate over torture heated up with the capture of Khalid Shaikh Mohammed, an alleged al-Qaida mastermind, in Pakistan on March 1. The CIA took him to another country where, according to a report in the *New York Times* on March 4, it used "every means at its disposal, short of what it considers outright torture, to try to crack him." It has not been disclosed what means the CIA considers to meet this criterion, or whether nationals of another country applied other means during the interrogation.

If and when terrorists strike again, the question of whether our government will legalize torture and approve even more extensive use of it seems certain to grow more pressing. The question seems likely to challenge Quakers, as it will challenge others. It is not too soon to consider the question earnestly and prayerfully.

Malcolm Bell, a member of Wilderness Meeting in Wallingford, Vt., is secretary of the International Mayan League/USA. He has written a book, The Turkey Shoot: Tracking the Attica Cover-Up, *published in 1985.*

Forum: Some Musings on "Pacifism"

The excellent contributions on the events of September 11 in the December FRIENDS JOURNAL prompt these musings on "pacifism," a word I seldom use because it is subject to so many misinterpretations and stereotypes.

Scott Simon, who describes his pacifism as "not absolute," records his full support for U.S. military action in Afghanistan. I first heard Scott Simon, a most articulate, dynamic and provocative commentator, speak in person at Friends Committee on National Legislation's 1995 annual meeting. It was clear then and certainly now that he is not a "pacifist" as usually defined. He would fight in World War II, the Balkans, and now Afghanistan. But he opposed the war in Vietnam. (Ironically, the famous Oxford Student Union debate of 1933 which he cites to support U.S. military action in Afghanistan was used repeatedly by then Secretary of State Dean Rusk to support sending U.S. troops to Vietnam.) Scott Simon is inserting some fine antiwar messages in his current National Public Radio program when covering the war in Afghanistan. But his picking and choosing which war he supports places him in the "just war" not the "pacifist" camp. Instead of associating Quakers with "moral relativism" in dealing with "psychotics," willingness to "lose lives for the sake of ideological consistency," or surrendering Manhattan Island as the price of peace, he could have examined whether this war meets the demanding criteria of a just war, which include whether the violence is proportional to the provocation and whether all peaceful alternatives had been exhausted.

Despite the fact that the Religious Society of Friends is one of the three historic peace churches in the Protestant tradition, a number of individual Friends have taken the "just war" position in wars the United States has waged. In 1971 as a lobbyist for FCNL, I and many others urged broadening the definition of conscientious objection in the draft law to include those who object to a particular war. Regrettably, that proposal for "selective conscientious objection" was defeated on the Senate floor. While the Cold War raged, many people described themselves as "nuclear pacifists" who were opposed to any use of nuclear weapons in war.

The traditional definition of pacifism is opposition to all war, the definition found in most dictionaries, the Selective Service law, and the proposed Peace Tax Fund legislation. Such pacifism can be expressed in a range of ways—from passivity, through nonresistance, to active nonviolent resistance. Individuals reach the pacifist position by many different paths. Some arrive at it on political grounds, some on humanitarian, some on economic grounds, some from family or peer pressure. But, in my view, only a deep spiritual or religious conviction, usually based on personal experience, provides a foundation firm enough to withstand the impulse to use violence when faced with terrible acts of people like Hitler, Milosevic, or Osama bin Laden. Such religious faith is often expressed by the conviction that love, compassion, and forgiveness are the quintessential attributes of God. The corollary is that every person, no matter how depraved, shares in this Spirit (that of God in every human being) and to kill that person only perpetuates the violence we oppose. One consequence, which must be faced by those taking this position, is that it may require personal sacrifice, perhaps as much as soldiers on the battlefield must face.

People who take the "absolute pacifist" position face many challenges: young men when they turn 18 and must decide whether to register for the draft; most of us when we are required to pay income taxes to support war; people who are victims of violent crimes; parents and children when confronted by bullies; politicians when they balance their personal conscience against their constituents' views. Several of your December contributors (Carol Urner, John Paul Lederach, and others) have demonstrated how they translate faith into action through the lives they have led and the risks they have taken.

The events of September 11 have challenged us all. One response, which I believe is consistent with a pacifist position, sees law and order as the best nonviolent alternative to war we humans are yet capable of. Most Friends, like William Penn as governor, are not anarchists—even while they recognize there is a "more excellent way" (1 Cor. 12:31) and that the rule of law must be infused with compassion and forgiveness as an integral part of justice.

The near universal condemnation of the September 11 attack created the platform for a huge leap forward in international law and order. Many of us felt a surge of hope as several weeks passed after September 11 while the U.S. gathered a worldwide consensus against these criminal acts, and launched a full scale political, economic, and investigative effort to find, isolate, and bring to justice those who were behind them. It seemed conceivable that the U.S. would do the unexpected, not the expected, and deny Osama bin Laden the martyrdom he sought through war. But the drive for the traditional military response proved irresistible to U.S. policymakers.

We know that the decision to go to war will have consequences. History shows that violence breeds violence. This war is teaching young people who follow Osama bin Laden and al-Qaida, as well as the youth of the U.S., that the way their leaders respond to violence is to use more violence. Moreover, the end of the global "war on terrorism" proclaimed by the President is nowhere in sight. Greatly expanded U.S. military action against Iraq is proposed. The war in Afghanistan may cause increased violence in the Palestinian-Israeli conflict. More terrorist acts in the United States are expected, even as our traditional freedoms are seriously eroded.

We cannot know what lay down the road not taken. We have it on good authority (Rom. 12:21) that evil is not overcome by evil; evil is overcome by good. We have been deprived of the energy and creative new directions that could have flowed from a nonviolent response. Yet, even in this difficult situation, we must persevere in supporting those individuals, ideas, and proposals that are compassionate, constructive, life giving, and life supporting. With nonpacifist George Washington, we can say, "Let us raise a standard to which the wise and honest can repair. The event is in the hands of God."

—*Edward F. Snyder,* Bar Harbor, Maine

Edward F. Snyder is executive secretary emeritus of FCNL, and represented FCNL from 1955 to 1990. He is a member of Acadia (Maine) Friends Meeting.

Forum: Pacifism is Logical

I read with interest the continuing responses to Friend Scott Simon's article (FJ Dec. 2001). One response, "Peace Testimony isn't logical" (*FJ* Mar. 2002 Forum) caught my attention. While I agree that the Peace Testimony is grounded upon spirituality and not logic, I disagree with the implication that pacifism is illogical. The following discussion represents my basic logical counterarguments for pacifism, which I think Friends might find interesting:

1. Pacifism is useless because a pacifist cannot defend him/herself.

A pacifist can defend him/herself. What a pacifist cannot do is become the aggressor. These are the main theories when dealing with violence: passivity, pacifism, aggression. When faced with violence (or the threat of violence), a "passivist" will nonviolently do nothing and potentially allow the violence to occur. A pacifist will attempt to prevent the violence, perhaps even going so far as to subdue the violent person while taking pains to preserve the well-being of all involved. An "aggressivist" might harm or kill the violent person in order to subdue him/her. In my opinion, only pacifism stands a chance of being wholly beneficial. A "passivist" does indirect harm by allowing violence. The "aggressivist" allows him/herself to become the aggressor by harming or killing someone who may have been only potentially violent. The pacifist attempts to follow the middle path, preventing violence or subduing the potential assailant and keeping everyone involved healthy. In this way, a person who is violent can be prevented from doing harm, and helped or placed in detention for everyone's benefit.

2. What does pacifism truly mean? Surely pacifism must be passive.

Pacifism means searching for peaceful resolutions to violent actions. There are no rules saying that pacifists must be passive. Refusal to resist violence, although passive, is not pacifist. In fact, nonresistance of violence often ends up merely aiding violence. But if I stand between an aggressor and his intended victim, am I being violent? If I refuse to let him beat someone to death by placing myself in the way to ward off blows, am I being violent? Of course not. These are inherently nonviolent actions on my part. To assume that an active response to aggression is violent is to misunderstand the meaning of the word violence. Violence is generally defined as the "unlawful use of physical force; physical force intended to injure." None of the actions mentioned in the examples above is by definition violent. They would be using lawful force not intended to injure.

3. What if 20 armed aggressors want to massacre 3,000 innocent victims?

A pacifist must work to disarm them. The point is not whether the pacifist is successful, but that he/she tries to stop violence. In the end, pacifism will prevail because it represents the most persuasive global argument. If a pacifist tries to stop a murder, he/she may not be successful, but the effort is a strong psychological weapon, which works positively on the victim, on those who hear of it, and even on the aggressor. A good example of pacifism at work is shown by the movie *Schindler's List*.

Schindler saved the lives of over 1,300 persecuted people in the heart of the Third Reich. Oskar Schindler found a way that preserved life rather than taking it—he succeeded. The Allied nations chose to take life in an attempt to preserve it, and they only succeeded in making the death toll higher.

4. Everyone knows that Hitler could never have been stopped by a pacifist response.

It was readily apparent as early as 1923 that the Nazis were a brutal, extremist group. During the 1920s the industrialized world should have refused to aid the nascent National Socialist Party. During the 1930s, restrictions should have been imposed by industry on all trade with Hitler's Germany, while ensuring that humanitarian needs were not ignored. Resumption of trade should have been predicated on human rights improvements. These measures represent an active pacifist response. Instead, corporations continued to trade with Nazi Germany up to the beginning of hostilities and sometimes well beyond. If these corporations had refused to aid the Nazis, World War II may never have happened, and Hitler and the Nazis may have remained the small time beer hall bullies that they had been in the early 1920s. Nazi Germany could have been turned from aggression by pacifist political and financial pressures. The great tragedy of WWII was that greed overcame morality throughout the capitalist world. Hitler was not unstoppable—he needed the acquiescence of the industrialized nations, and he got it.

5. Not all people will behave decently. Everything cannot be solved with nonviolence.

Nevertheless, some things can be solved nonviolently. One thing is certain: violence is no solution. The world teaches us that every day.

—Ian Cooper, Somerville, Mass.

Forum: War Is Not the Way

Scott Simon, in "Reflections on the Events of September Eleventh"(*FJ* Dec. 2001), has made an excellent case for why pacifism is unlikely to provide a solution to the problem of terrorism. Instead, he urges support for the U.S. attack on Afghanistan because none of us knows an easy way to make peace. He is disappointed with pacifism because it does not provide a blueprint for making a better world.

But pacifism is a guide for the human spirit, not a blueprint for nations. We pacifists hold a deep religious conviction that taking human life is morally wrong, for many the greatest possible wrong. We follow that religious conviction even when it leads to trouble, as is often the case. We certainly do not give up the conviction just because it is convenient to do so. There is a long history of pacifists who have been jailed for their refusal to kill.

The U.S. attack on Afghanistan is wrong because it is killing human beings. Furthermore, we in the U.S. are being led to forget that those innocent dead Afghans have loving families who are grieving just as families of the innocent victims of 9/11 have grieved. One of the greatest tragedies of war is the psychological effect on a people when the "enemy" has been identified and dehumanized. Pacifists must decide how to stand up to U.S. terrorism. I for one find that I must join those who refuse to pay a portion of federal taxes because that money is buying the bombs.

Most pacifists agree that sticking with our moral leading and refusing to kill is more likely to lead eventually to a better world. However, that is by no means certain and is certainly not a sufficient reason to take a pacifist stand.

I regret that there are pacifists who emphasize the hope that if our government would use nonviolence and negotiation all problems would readily be solved. I suspect that this shallow pacifism is a legacy of the Vietnam War, which did end when the U.S. decided to quit. In most wars the way to peace is not so simple. War, however, is a simple way to insure more deaths.

—*Irving Hollingshead,* Boyertown, Pa.

Forum: Pacifism vs. Passivism

This letter is in response to Scott Simon's article (*FJ* May 2003). He starts out by admitting that his position statement on the U.S. invasion of Afghanistan was also published in *Soldier of Fortune.* While I am thankful that he gave his payment from that magazine to the AFSC, I am curious as to why he allowed his text to be published in that forum. Was it to present himself as a "pragmatic" or "realistic" Quaker to the militaristic readers of that journal?

He then claims to respect every Friend's personal conviction, while later belittling those who recite the Peace Testimony as "inflexible political ideologues" who have not "reassessed their own thinking since Joni Mitchell's first *Greatest Hits* album." I also distinctly remember hearing him on his radio show mock the peace activists who were coming to Washington, D.C., in the spring of 2002 for a rally on the Mall. He made fun of what would be the appropriate clothes to wear and songs to sing for the rally. Scott Simon declares that he has changed his thinking about war and peace as a "result of working around the world as a journalist for more than two decades, often in zones of conflict." He no longer echoes the "bromides of pacifism." Well, during the past 33 years, my views have changed as well: from starting off as a religious pacifist who was willing to register 1-A-O if drafted, to an absolute pacifist, who sees that all wars, in my lifetime at least, have been unjust, and who sees that the militarization of the U.S. has corrupted our society.

No self-respecting pacifist would excuse the crimes of al-Qaida, the Taliban, or Saddam Hussein, nor would one argue that Afghanis or Iraqis are better off now because of our military invasions. But the ends still don't justify the means (another bromide). War is still immoral, and as the pope says, war signifies "a failure of humanity." And I must ask: will the Afghanis and Iraqis stay better off? First, a low-intensity conflict is still ongoing in Afghanistan; second, because of the lack of opportunities in Afghanistan, opium production has increased dramatically; and third, the U.S. has yet to commit much to cleaning up our mess and rebuilding Afghanistan.

Later in his article, Scott Simon disparages peace activism by focusing on Charles Lindbergh and George Bernard Shaw. I question why he chose to cite these two men who are not usually thought of a being prominent, historic peace activists. Charles Lindbergh especially was better known as a Nazi apologist. Instead, why didn't Scott Simon cite a Quaker or other prominent religious peace activist?

Scott Simon was able to oppose military responses until September 11, 2001, since the previous conflicts in Central America and elsewhere did not directly affect our country. No more; now he supports the expedient military response. The International Criminal Court was formed to deal with organized crime networks like al-Qaida, but then, the Bush administration doesn't support the ICC.

No true pacifist wants peace at any price, but instead, love at all costs.

We want peace with justice, which does not come easy or cheap. And while terrorist strikes make "no distinctions between Quakers and Pentagon generals," our bombs and cruise missiles make no distinctions between combatants and children, soldiers and wedding parties, generals and reporters, and so on.

I fully recognize the evil that exists around the world. Evil allows unchecked militarism to redirect money that could be spent to end starvation and poverty, to provide decent housing and education, to end the fear of recruitment of children into the military, and to prevent the landscape from being littered with mines or poisoned by chemical nuclear debris.

—*Daniel G. Cole,* Middletown, Md.

Forum: Our Testimony to the World?

In the aftermath of our country's encounter with its terrorist assailants, I have been sometimes dismayed by Friends' too handy condemnation of the U.S. military response, particularly so when the criticisms are accompanied by proclamations about Quakers "standing upon our Peace Testimony of 350 years." Not even we, it seems, are entirely immune to tendencies toward fundamentalism. I would like to remind Friends that our original 1660 Peace Testimony statement was much less a call for proactive peace-making than it was a declaration of the Friends' innocence in the armed uprising against the Crown. I would also point out that the wording of the testimony in our *Faith and Practice,* "We do utterly deny all outward wars and strife and fightings," omits the five very important and revealing words, "as to our own particular."

In Isaac Penington's explanation of the testimony's implications for the outside world he wrote that a people called by God to live in the Spirit of Christ can look to their Lord for their preservation, but that the Friends did not believe this necessarily applied to secular nations defending themselves against foreign invasion and that, indeed, a "great blessing may attend the sword where it is borne uprightly." Thomas Story echoed similar sentiments from Pennsylvania. Robert Barclay, whose writing still provides the theological underpinnings for a great many Quakers in the world today, wrote that the refusal to defend self is the hardest and most perfect part of Christianity because it requires the most complete denial of self and the most entire confidence in God. He contended that the present state of authority in this world, even in the Church, was far from such a state of perfection and that "therefore, while they are in that condition, we shall not say that war, undertaken upon a just occasion, is altogether unlawful to them."

I remind Friends that during the American Revolution, one-third of the military eligible Quaker males in New Jersey were disowned for war-related offenses, that 25 percent of Indiana Quakers joined the Union Army in the Civil War, that about half the draft-age Quakers in North America enlisted during World War II, that similar statistics exist for every war, even Vietnam, reflecting the divergent views within the ranks of Friends over the issue of justifiable warfare. I remind Friends that when we say we "stand upon our Peace Testimony of 350 years," we stand upon all these things and not just upon the fundamentalist rhetoric, "We do utterly deny outward wars and strife and fightings with outward weapons, for any end, or under any pretense whatsoever and this is our testimony to the whole world."

I urge Friends to reflect upon and fully comprehend the extent of conviction required to make such an absolutist statement, particularly when we feel moved to cry it out in public places. We must not gloss over the fact that beneath this "rock of peace" we would stand upon, we find ultimately a call to lay down our lives and the lives of our loved ones for the cause of peace rather than to live abetting the derangement of war.

Let us acknowledge that many of our fellow citizens honestly feel that we are at war for just and righteous causes and that they believe that losing one's life in defense of one's country and one's loved ones is a high and noble calling. If we do in fact utterly deny, for any end, under any pretense the waging of war, let us speak always in the same breath of the price we are willing to pay for that denial and let us never cease to speak of that price, lest our resolve be shaken, or perhaps more to the point, lest we outrun our measures of truth. The 1660 declaration goes on to say that it is the Spirit of Christ that commands us against war as evil. Even the Friend who is absolutely convinced that he is guided by Christ should remember that, in the Passion of Jesus Christ, no disciple—not one—was able to remain faithful unto the end.

This is by no means a call to abandon our witness to peace. It is rather a call for Friends to speak with voices of honest, heartfelt, soul-searching conviction and not with a disembodied voice from the past. It is a call to feel at a loss to know what to do when that is, in fact, the truth of one's condition; to wait calmly and silently for real opportunities to speak and be peace, always first with each other as members of our families and as members of an ostensibly like-minded religious community. Then, if we must speak of our Testimony of Peace to the rest of the world, to speak of an absolute denial of war, let us do it in a voice of love, with a sacred sense of the personal sacrifice such a testimony may well demand, not in defiance of our political adversaries with whom we may find ourselves perpetually annoyed. Let us speak not without first recognizing the fears and the courage of those countrymen whom we ask to cease engaging in what they perceive as a defense of life and freedom, so they may join us in paying the price for peace required of those who will not live by the sword but who must be prepared to die by it.

—*Michael Dawson,* Hopewell, N.J.

Vignettes of an Antiwar Vet

by Lyle Tatum

Introduction

I have written these vignettes for Susan, the little girl I had to leave behind when I went to prison during World War II. Now that she is a grandmother, it is probably time for me to tell her something about where I went.

I have never written about this experience or said much about it because of the heavy emotional involvement I have with the incidents that meant the most to me. More than 50 years after the event, I still could not read aloud to a group the vignette "Farm Machinery." Support from unexpected sources when holding an unpopular position is difficult to handle. The guard in "Tensions" would understand.

I know Susan will be glad to share this story with siblings, aunts, uncles, cousins, nieces, nephews, and others who may be interested. The new generations have a right to know more about their father/grandpa/uncle/friend who sometimes walked the road less traveled.

There may be friends who are not clear about some relationships described here. Elizabeth Lindsay Tatum, always called Bickie by me, is the wife and mother in this story. We had been married for 22 years when she died in an automobile accident in Tanzania. Florence Littell Giffin also lost her spouse in a much too early death. Flo and I have been married for 31 years.

Although in roughly chronological order, the vignettes do not make a continuous story. Each one may be read alone as a separate unit. This is just a collection of a few things I remember.

—December 1996

Farm Machinery

I was serving as superintendent of Quakerdale Farm, New Providence, Iowa, a home operated by Iowa Yearly Meeting of Friends for neglected boys. My time of availability was uncertain and limited, as I expected to go to jail for refusing to go into the army. With my approval, a new superintendent was hired, and we (Bickie, infant Susan, and I) moved to Fort Dodge, Iowa, where my parents were living. We rented an apartment, and I got a job as a painter working for the Coats Manufacturing Company.

I was one of about 20 blue-collar workers making manure loaders that fit on tractors. The loader was the invention of Mr. Coats. He was a self-made man, competent and very conservative on some issues. He was strongly antiunion, and workers signed on with that understanding. However, he would often call the men together and discuss shop matters with us.

After about three months, the date came when I thought I would be sentenced. I had a guilty feeling about never telling the men why I was leaving. On my last day there I told them my story without getting much reaction. I discovered the next day that the date of my sentencing had been postponed. I had just given up a badly needed job. I telephoned Mr. Coats and asked if I could go back to work. He said I was a good worker, and he would be glad to have me but the men would never work with a draft dodger. I then asked him to raise the question with the men and leave it up to them. He agreed.

That night I called Mr. Coats for the result. He said, "Lyle, every man in the place voted for you to return to work. Be there in the morning." My job was saved by men none of whom had more than a high school education and none of whom previously had ever heard of Quakers or conscientious objectors.

Mr. Coats did not let the matter drop at that point. He asked me if I would be willing to become a welder and continue to work there if the draft board would allow it. I told him, "Yes, I was willing to continue making farm machinery." He wrote my draft board asking them to give me an essential worker classification and told them he was training me as a welder. The draft board turned him down.

Iowa State

A grad student friend of mine, a conscientious objector, was a Methodist who later joined the Mennonites. A couple of years after I graduated he wrote to the Iowa State alumni office to ask why their news bulletin hadn't carried a story about my struggle with Selective Service. He pointed out that since I was a member of Cardinal Guild (the student governing body), was elected president of the student body, had earned my "I" as a member of the debate team, had graduated with a 3-plus scholastic average (4 was straight A) while working my way through college, and was appointed head of a children's home only two years after graduation, that I was newsworthy for Iowa Staters.

He received a curt reply from the director of alumni affairs that they only printed stories that reflected honor to Iowa State.

The Sentencing

I was president of the student body at Iowa State, the first man to win that election who was not a member of a fraternity. I was a lifelong member of the Religious Society of Friends but denied classification as a conscientious objector by the Burlington, Iowa, draft board. The Iowa Civil Liberties Union (ICLU) took on my defense. All of this generated newspaper publicity.

The judge who had my case in U.S. District Court in Des Moines had a set pattern of sentences. If the CO pleaded not guilty, he would be found guilty and sentenced to four years in prison and fined $500. If the CO pleaded guilty, he would just be sentenced to four years in prison. The ICLU had done all they could for me without success, so I pleaded guilty to save $500 I didn't have. My crime was failure to report for induction into the army.

After my sentencing, a federal marshal took me into an office in the building where a number of women were working, and there was a holding cell for prisoners waiting to be taken to the regular jail facilities.

There was one man already in the small cell, and he was obviously very angry, which gave me a bit of uneasiness as I was locked in with him. It turned out that the women workers had been laughing about my publicity doing me no good, as I still got a four-year sentence. The prisoner poured it out to me how crass it was for anyone to laugh about a man going to jail for four years. "Crass" is not the actual adjective he used for the women, the laughter, and the sentence. I received great comfort from the feelings of my newfound friend and felt reinforced to live with whatever was ahead.

Later in the day after being sentenced, my friend and I were taken to the Des Moines City bullpen, a large room meant to hold prisoners for a day or two before they were taken elsewhere. I was there for a week. The room was filled with steel double bunk beds. I forget exactly how many men were there; maybe 25. The sleeping area on the bunks was a crisscross of narrow steel straps with 3" gaps between the straps. The bunks had no mattresses, nor blankets, nor pillows. It was impossible to stretch out and try to sleep for an hour or two without getting up and walking around the room to ease aching muscles.

I became a short-term celebrity as my companion from the cell in the office told my story. My fellow inmates wanted to be helpful and, unlike officialdom and the laughing office women, were sympathetic about my wife and daughter. They asked around to see if anyone had served time in Sandstone, Minnesota, where I was headed, but nobody had, so they couldn't help my orientation there. Nobody had served a sentence as long as four years, so they couldn't help me understand how that would be either. They were stunned to learn that a man could be sent to prison for refusing to kill.

Jail Transitions

I was moved from the bullpen to a county jail where I stayed for three weeks or so. It was good to get to a place where there was a mattress and blankets on my bunk. I was being held until transportation was arranged to take me to Sandstone. The jail was crowded, the inmates friendly, and the stay uneventful.

I had no idea what to expect for the trip to Sandstone, a distance of about 250 miles. I was used to seeing men coming and going from jail in handcuffs. On the day of the trip, a U.S. marshal in civilian clothes came for me. He just asked me to go with him. We went to the office for him to check me out. We then went out to his car where he introduced me to his wife who was going along for the ride. At no time with them was I treated as other than a family friend, except that night.

I had told the marshal that I would appreciate mailing a letter to my wife if there was an opportunity. He stopped about a quarter of a block from a mailbox. I just sat there not knowing what to do. He told me to go ahead and mail my letter, which I did while they waited for me.

That night they planned to stay in a hotel in St. Paul, 80 miles south of Sandstone. When the time came to stop for the night, the marshal was very apologetic but said they'd have to leave me at the local jail for the night. The night was uneventful, and they took me the rest of the way in the morning.

Sandstone

The federal prisons have a grading system of institutions ranging from camps to maximum security. The "camps" are not like what Boy Scouts know. They have buildings, but not with walls surrounding them. They are relatively open. These are the "country clubs" we hear about. Sandstone, a Federal Correctional Institution (FCI), is the next notch up the line. It is walled, although a number of inmates work outside of the walls during the day. The primary physical difference between FCIs and other federal prisons is that most inmates are in dormitories rather than cells. To be lucky enough to have a private cell you must have a night assignment such as working in the hospital. Danbury, Connecticut, where East Coast Selective Service violators were usually sent, is a duplicate of Sandstone.

FCI inmates tend to be younger men, first offenders, or men who committed relatively passive crimes. There are a few older men ending long sentences whom the Bureau of Prisons is trying to prepare for reentry into the other world.

Selective Service was overloading the FCIs. There were three huge dormitories at Sandstone filled with Selective Service violators. The dorms were gymnasium-style and -size, with locked doors. At one side of the room was a long wall lined with double bunk beds just far enough apart to get around and pull out the drawer under your bunk where you kept your clothes, old letters, etc. I can't remember how many men were in a dorm, but I would guess more than 50.

One of the Selective Service dorms was filled with black Muslims, mostly from Chicago. They did not register for the draft, and most of them had refused to register for Social Security. Another dorm was filled with Jehovah's Witnesses. Most of them were not COs but had unsuccessfully claimed ministerial status for exemption from the draft. I was in the third dorm with COs and Selective Service violators of other types.

I give the Bureau of Prisons credit for having the good sense to segregate the Selective Service inmates into relatively congenial groups. The segregation did not carry over to the recreation area, dining room, or elsewhere. COs got along well with the non-Selective Service inmates. We played softball with them. Their team was called "The Thieves," ours "The Dodgers."

Parole I

Soon after I entered Sandstone, the Bureau of Prisons offered me a parole to Civilian Public Service, the CO program for which I had first applied but was denied the proper classification. I turned down the parole. I told the Bureau of Prisons that I had learned my mistake and would never again cooperate in any way with a military conscription system.

Psychologists

Among the staff members at Sandstone, the psychologists ranked at the bottom of the list for all inmates. Early in their stay each inmate had an interview with a psychologist. There were many stories among inmates about what they told the psychologist. None of us felt any need to be truthful in this interview, which had references to the personal sex life of the inmate. Even more than the COs, the "regular" inmates would regale each other with lurid sex experiences they had dreamed up for the psychologist.

The psychologists were the butt of many jokes. Arlo, my brother, was in and out of Sandstone before I got there. A number of inmates told me about a skit Arlo had been in. In the skit, Arlo visited a psychologist. Arlo had a serious tic and was continually opening and closing an eye as he screwed up his face. At the end of the skit, Arlo walked out OK, and the psychologist was sitting at his desk with a serious tic, continually opening and closing an eye as he screwed up his face.

The disrespect for the local psychologists was not totally unearned. Before going to Sandstone, I had been the superintendent of Quakerdale Farm, a home for dependent and neglected boys. This Quaker-run home had been in operation for decades, first in southeast Iowa as White's Institute and later in New Providence, Iowa, as Quakerdale Farm. When I answered the psychologist's question about my employment, I told him I had been the head of a boys' home. His immediate response was, "Boys! Only boys? Why boys?"

Mail

I was allowed a limited amount of correspondence with a very few family members only. I could write one or two letters a week, a single sheet (lined grade school paper provided) with writing permitted on both sides. I could receive a similar amount. Prison officers read all mail—outgoing and incoming.

Visits

We were allowed limited visits, but visits were emotional hazards. You sat in a room with other inmates and their visitors, supervised by a prison guard. You were allowed no physical contact, not even a welcoming or farewell kiss. Bickie made a few visits. We had a cousin living in the Twin Cities with whom she would stay. At my request, Susan never came along. I did not feel that I could take the emotional impact of such a visit from my little girl.

Work

All of the inmates had work assignments. Often the work was in teams that would be accompanied by a guard or two. There was no pay for work, unless you count room and board. Most of the work was productive for the institution. I was assigned to a garden crew, which brought in large quantities of vegetables. If we caught up on the garden work for a day or two we would be given some other manual labor job outside. I was pleased to have that assignment, both for the work and for getting outside of the walls for much of the day.

As the fall weather started to cool, I was eager to get an inside job. As I suspected, and found out later to be true, outside crews in the winter were often working in subzero weather. There were two men from Frank Lloyd Wright's group in my dorm. One of them worked at making drawings in the powerhouse. He told me the institution had lost its chemist, it seemed impossible to hire one, and they wondered if anyone in our dorm could do the job. The engineer in charge of the powerhouse had no chemical training. I got the job on the basis of starting my college work in chemical technology. It was actually a low-tech job doing routine things like testing boiler water, drinking water, and sewage processing plus writing a manual for the inmate who might get the job when I left and have even fewer qualifications than mine. I spent the rest of my time in Sandstone as the institution's chemist.

Doing Time

Doing time is the universal synonym for being in jail. It is an apt description of what happens. The worst thing about doing time is doing time. The prisoner has a single objective—move through time to release. Although a day may bring a good dinner, great news from home, or the defeat at chess of the man who usually defeats you, it's all irrelevant. The good thing is that another day has passed. As an inmate's release date nears, time becomes all the more overwhelming. Time begins to take on new ways of expression, such as yards of spaghetti to be eaten and the number of times to line up for count before you leave. If you are a prisoner, time is a totally different concept than it is on the other side of the wall. Time is the oppressor.

Tensions

There were many tensions in Sandstone, as should be expected, particularly between inmates and guards (usually called screws by the inmates). Tensions often broke through, as they did for me in the vignettes "Christmas" and "I'm Shot."

One day when I was working outside, a Jehovah's Witness on the crew was giving the guard a rough time. He and some others were aggressive and abrasive about their religion, trying to get converts or, as in this case, taunting people about the inadequacies of beliefs held by those who were not Jehovah's Witnesses. In this instance, the guard took the taunting quietly, without reproach when most guards would have pulled him off the crew and charged him with a disciplinary infraction to be settled by the institutional disciplinary board.

Each evening as we went back inside the walls we were searched for contraband. We would take our handkerchief out of its pocket, hold our hands up over our heads, and be "shook down," hands run over our pockets.

One time I had a green onion secluded in my handkerchief, taking it in for a friend who longed for a fresh green onion. I was, of course, in serious violation of the regulations. The guard who was searching me was the one given a hard time by the Jehovah's Witness. I thanked the guard for the patient and gentle way he handled him. The guard didn't say a word, dropped his hands, and I left hurriedly afraid he was about to burst out in tears. Kind words for guards from inmates were rare.

An Exception

Although World War II was a popular war with a cause that was widely considered just, unlike Vietnam, the churches, with varying degrees of enthusiasm, gave some support to their conscientious objectors. The Christian Science church was an exception. Their national headquarters issued a statement that there was nothing in Christian Science doctrine that would cause a man to become a conscientious objector. Yet, there was one Christian Science CO in Sandstone.

Christmas

There was a hallway across the end of our dormitory with heavy steel fencing setting the hall off from the dorm and the inmates. There was a space of perhaps six or eight inches at the bottom of the fence through which guards would pass out our mail. The only time we were allowed packages was for Christmas. Each inmate could receive one gift. The gift had to be solicited by the inmate and approved by the institution. When the gift arrived, it would be shoved under the fence by a guard's foot. I asked my family not to send me anything for Christmas, as I thought Christmas was badly polluted by Sandstone. There were also inmates, with whom I wished to identify, who had nobody to send them gifts.

Next door to home in Oskaloosa lived our neighbors, the Ruby family. They owned the United Delivery Company for which I worked on Saturdays and during Christmas vacation through high school and for a year after high school delivering groceries with a team of mules. The Rubys were not Quakers nor pacifists. They had three sons who went into the army. I had seen none of the Rubys for six years. Each Christmas they made very professional chocolates to share with their friends.

It was nearly Christmas, and my name was called as having received a gift. I thought it must be a mistake, but it was a box of chocolates from the Rubys. A box of homemade chocolates had made it past the restrictions of the Bureau of Prisons and my own personal restrictions for

Christmas. I wept.

I'm Shot

I learned some new vocabulary in Sandstone. Part of that was getting shot. To be shot had nothing to do with handguns or rifles but meant you'd been written up by a guard for an offense. That puts you before a disciplinary board for possible punishment.

I was working with a crew outdoors on some kind of digging job when the guard in charge came over to me and told me that I needed to work faster, because we were in front of the warden's office. I responded that maybe he felt he should work harder in front of the warden, but I would work the same way in front of the warden or back of the building. Bang!! I was shot for insubordination, or something like that.

I appeared before the disciplinary board, three guards as I recall, a couple of days later. There was no disagreement about what happened. This was a context within which the board didn't seem used to working. The guard who had accused me wasn't present.

There was a little discussion, and I was asked if I didn't realize they could take away some of my "good time," and I would have to stay longer, I replied that I knew that and when I did get out I would probably be back if the war was still going on. There was a void in the conversation. By refusing to be intimidated I seemed to have threatened their authority.

I presume there was some hesitancy about raising a public issue about how one worked in front of the warden's office. I was dismissed with a warning but no penalty.

Parole II

At the time, federal prisoners were eligible for parole after serving one-third of their sentence. A new plan made COs eligible for parole at any time to acceptable assignments with nonprofit institutions. The salary limit was board and room plus $15 per month. It was a Civilian Public Service kind of plan but totally devoid of any relationship to Selective Service.

Wistar Wood (unknown to me at the time), a Quaker, was superintendent of the Pennsylvania School for the Deaf in Philadelphia and desperate to find a boys' supervisor. He seemed to be well-connected politically and got permission to review some files of COs in prison who might be qualified for the job. He selected me. The Bureau of Prisons told him that I probably wouldn't take the job, as I had already turned down parole. Typical of the problems the Bureau had with COs, they couldn't see the difference between a parole to a Selective Service assignment and a parole to a regular job.

I was glad to take the job and left Sandstone after one year in prison. Bickie was a graduate of Iowa State with a degree in dietetics and was immediately employed by the school as the dietician, so everything worked out fine with my $15 per month salary. Susan, then two years old, went to a Catholic daycare center for children. When we left the school after a little more than a year, with the war over and my parole terminated, to return as superintendent of Quakerdale Farm, Susan was crossing herself before meals.

Lyle Tatum, a member of Haddonfeld (N.J.) Meeting, held a variety of posts with American Friends Service Committee between 1956 and 1983, including: executive secretary of the Middle Atlantic Region, 1956–60; International Affairs Representative in Southern Rhodesia (Zimbabwe), 1960–64; secretary for the Peace Education Division, 1972–75; AFSC special representative to the Constitutional Conference on Rhodesia in London, 1979; and executive secretary of the Dayton, Ohio, Regional Office, 1981–83.

Queries

How shall we define "war"? Is the loss of life that occurs because of the policies of our national government related to war? Is anyone's life of greater or lesser importance than another's is? Who is my neighbor?

As a member of a democratic republic, what is my responsibility concerning the policies of my national government?

Am I willing to spend time pursuing inquiry into understanding war and peace, or am I anxious for closure on the questions involved?

What kinds of commitment do I and do my meeting have to systemic change so people around the globe may enjoy their lives more equitably?

How do I resist reducing complex truths to easy slogans or catch phrases, thus avoiding learning about the issues involved in complex truths? How do I witness to that of God in each person in the face of torture?

When is my witness political and when is it religious? How do I define the differences? Of what importance are the differences to me and to my meeting?

What definition of pacifism have I developed for myself that I could articulate to a friend whose beliefs are not grounded in Christianity?

Do I speak of peace in a voice of love and with a sense of the sacrifice such a testimony may demand? Do I acknowledge the fears and courage of my countrymen and women who may disagree with me, yet never assume that they will necessarily disagree with me?

After Worship, Action

"We rest in God when we worship. We worship when we find our still center, the quiet we seek and which we can offer to others. There we find our capacity to act, in small and sometimes hidden ways or in public witness."

(*New York Yearly Meeting Worship and Action Update 8/18/04*)

There are two traps we can fall into. The first is silence. This was articulated clearly by the Catonsville Nine, as they came to be called, in a challenge they issued to churches and synagogues as they took action during the Vietnam War: "We confront the Catholic Church, other Christian bodies, and the synagogues of America with their silence and cowardice in the face of our country's crimes.

The other trap is taking on more than what is truly ours to do. Recognizing that becoming overly involved leads to greater agony rather than greater clarity, Red Cedar Friends headed its monthly action announcement sheet in 2003 with the following statement:

> Remember to stay close to the Light you are given. Don't get caught up expecting more of yourself. When you're being led to a concern, it will be something you can do—not a burden you think you "should be able to do." Your leading may take courage, but trust the "way will open" if it's right. That's one hallmark of being led . . . .

As you read the following articles, you may want to recall these admonitions—the first not to be silent or cowardly, the second not to take on the task that is not yours.

No one, young or old, should overlook Megan Oltman's article on "Peaceful Parenting." Almost all of us deal with children in some capacity—as parents, grandparents, aunts, uncles, or friendly presences. Children should be greeted just as any other family member or visitor, or as any other meeting attender or member. They should have their own name tags. Try to sit at eye level with a child and make conversation as you would with anyone.

Intergenerational "study" meetings or family worship times can be designed so everyone can participate. For instance, if everyone in an intergenerational group has an 11" x 17" piece of paper and some crayons, each can color a picture of a time or place he imagines he could feel God or the Spirit. Afterwards, make pairs of an older and younger person, or go around a small circle of mixed ages, and have each one tell about his or her picture. Listen to one another's stories.

"Learning Peace in Time of War: A Classroom Retrospective," by Judith Yarnall, is especially rich as a basis for intergenerational discussion. It speaks directly to our learning about and discussing peace and war in adult groups and in youth groups. It provides a rare opportunity for youth and adults to study an article together with equal interest. The issues in it are many, varied, and provocative.

Jeanne Lohmann's poem reminds us of stories we need to acknowledge and share with our youth in quiet moments. Lyle Tatum gave us the same reminder: "The new generations have a right to know more about their father/grandpa/uncle/friend who sometimes walked the road less traveled." So, he shared simple stories of his experience during World War II as a conscientious objector. There may be stories in your meeting like Lyle's, stories of "Jimmy's grandfather" or "Ann Marie's uncle." Today, too, there are stories of young men who are not registering. What do they experience at school or in trying to get a driver's license or in a conscientious objector workshop? And what of the young women?

Keith Helmuth's article on "Human Solidarity" takes us beyond what we have known of the Peace Testimony as he presents us with the problem of acting with a "commitment to the ethics of human solidarity." His last paragraph poses a major challenge to today's Friends. Michael True also encourages us to extend our thinking about peace. In "Peacemaking: Public and Private," he suggests that instead of the "peace" testimony we think of the "peacemaking" testimony.

Arden Buck's question, "What Do We Do Now?" and Chuck Hosking's challenge to us to contribute our dollars as well as our talents and time present us with the nuts and bolts of living out our faith. We "make peace" daily, but after worship and study, we may be able to do so in an ever more meaningful way, so that we feel like one of Mariellen Gilpin's winter onions:

Clean
New
Full of juice and flavor
Of life lived
Only the good part
Harvested.

Parents' Corner: Parenting within the Peace Testimony: Practical Tools for Creating a Peaceful Home

by Megan Oltman

"We utterly deny all outward wars and strife, and fightings with outward weapons, for any end, or under any pretense whatsoever; this is our testimony to the whole world."

—*Quaker declaration to Charles II of England, 1660*

While I utterly deny all outward wars and strife, the wars and strife within my own household are the ones that I must face on a daily basis. When my children begin pushing and kicking, when I feel stressed out and face their whining, or their refusal to do chores, the Peace Testimony seems unattainable.

Bringing peace into our homes is a challenge to most of us who have children. Despite our earnestly held beliefs and convictions and our moments of gathered peace, peacefulness itself can evaporate on the spot. And in the face of increasingly complex lives and too little time in which to live them, we may find ourselves dealing with our children in an angry fashion.

Parents in our meeting have often grappled with the difficulties of being Quaker parents in a world that does not support peace and reflection as a way of life. We must decide how to deal with war toys, with violent movies and television shows, with a consumer culture that pushes us all, adults and children alike, to want things and things and more things.

Most of the time we seem to muddle along without much guidance. But recently my husband, Dan, and I met Naomi Drew, author of *Peaceful Parents, Peaceful Kids* (Kensington Books, 2000). In one of those occasions of divinely inspired serendipity, I joined Naomi's writers' group, and my husband designed a website about her book and consulting work. Curious about what she had to offer, Dan and I read the book and found that Naomi's work is a perfect bridge between our beliefs as Friends and our needs as parents.

Naomi, who also wrote *The Peaceful Classroom in Action* and *Learning the Skills of Peacemaking*, has worked for about 20 years in peacemaking education. Initially interested in peacemaking as a teacher who wanted to resolve conflicts in the classroom, Naomi began with a notion of Gandhi's, that if we want to have real peace, we have to begin with the children. Her book is divided into 12 chapters, each containing one or more practical principles Naomi calls the "keys" to peaceful parenting.

As I delved into Naomi's book, I was affirmed and delighted. The keys are easy to remember and implement—and just reading the first chapter cut down arguing in my house by about half in a week's time!

The first chapter is called "Becoming a More Peaceful Parent: Getting Started." It contains the first key, "Peace begins with me," which is the foundation of the book. The key is solidly grounded in our spiritual practice as Friends. Exercises are to center down, use abdominal breathing, and envision a peaceful place where you can go when your stress level begins to rise.

A second exercise for the key "Peace begins with me" is to envision yourself 20 years from now, and then to write about what you want to be able to say about yourself as a parent, what you want your children to be able to say about you, about their childhood, and about themselves. Using this vision, look at the priorities in your life, Naomi suggests, and see if there is room to rearrange them to produce the outcome you want for yourself and your children in 20 years.

What a thought! My kids are 11 and 7, and they love each other deeply, but getting along involves compromises they often seem unwilling to make.

On a recent morning, for example, the kids' arguing was the first thing I heard after the alarm clock. I had slept badly, and not long enough, so my first thought was, "I can't handle this today." And it was true: I ended up yelling at both children, which only escalated the arguments.

But I had just finished the first chapter of Naomi's book the night before. So I took myself into the bathroom for a minute, and repeated the first key: "Peace begins with me." Then I stood barefoot in the bathroom doing abdominal breathing and envisioning my peaceful place—a corner of the front yard where I grew up, a corner of full green shrubs and a stone wall. A few minutes later, I was able to go back and deal calmly with the kids. And the minute I calmed down, they did, too.

Amazing.

Listening Is Powerful

As I worked my way through Naomi's book, chapter by chapter, I found other tips that worked just as effectively at helping me create the peaceful home we all needed.

I found, for example, that subtle things make a huge difference. Reflexive listening, contained in the 11th key, is both subtle and powerful. It showed me how often I try to fix my children's issues or conflicts, which, in effect, denied them the chance to be heard or the opportunity to learn how to resolve conflicts on their own. In reflexive listening, however, you listen and repeat back what you heard, without trying to fix, change, or argue with it. This, as I found, encourages the kids to express themselves more fully so that problems can be fully identified, solutions developed, and conflict avoided.

For instance, Dan and I were going out one Sunday night after Rachel had been out with her best friend all day. She came home and said, "You go out too much, you never spend any time with me!" and went up to her room crying. My usual reaction to this sort of statement would be to explain and defend myself. But whenever I try to address her upsets with my explanations, she doesn't want to talk to me.

Fearing she wouldn't talk to me, I nevertheless went up to her room. But this time I went with a commitment to listen rather than explain. She was crying; I said, "Do you want to tell me about it?"

She replied, "I'll never get as much time with you as I want," and I responded, "So you feel like you'll never get as much time with me as you want." I just reflected it back, without arguing or trying to fix it. Then my mature and independent daughter told me for the first time that she misses me during the day when she's at school.

I never even guessed. But I calmly reflected that back as well, and then I said, "This week I have to be out three nights, and I know you don't like it, but that's what the week looks like. So how can we plan it to be sure we have time together? And what are some things we can do together?"

Then the two of us put our heads together and mapped out the week. This was a breakthrough for us. We didn't argue, I went out without guilt, she let me go, and we had great times together.

As I reflect on Naomi's final key, "I remember daily that we have an impact on the world around us and I teach this to my children," I truly understand her vision: Peaceful families have peaceful relationships. We bring our relationships into small groups, larger groups, communities, and nations. And together with our children, we impact the world.

Megan Oltman, a freelance writer with two children, ages 11 and 17, is a member of Princeton (N.J.) Meeting.

Learning Peace in Time of War: A Classroom Retrospective

by Judith Yarnall

For four years I've been teaching a required interdisciplinary course on violence and nonviolence, called Peace and War, at Johnson State College in northern Vermont. The course, planned as an inquiry, invites students to take a long, dispassionate look at the human penchant for organized violence, to analyze its roots and explore alternatives. By now almost 800 students are its veterans. Most other U.S. colleges and universities that have courses or programs in Peace and Conflict Studies offer them as electives and thus reach only a self-selected clientele, but at JSC every upperclass student is part of the course's flock. In any given classroom, a student experienced in meditation practice may be sitting next to someone who's gone through Army basic training, who may be right behind someone who prefers not to let life be disturbed by the front page of any newspaper. How did this benign coercion come to exist at a small, public, nonsectarian institution? And what have been its results?

The answer to the first question is "opportunity seized." The Johnson faculty revised the school's General Education Plan in the 1990s to include a specification that each student take the same capstone "thematic interdisciplinary course," their hope being that this common intellectual experience would provoke a cross-campus, beyond-the-classroom dialogue. When the call went out for topic ideas, my suggestion of Violence and Nonviolence, influenced by my Quaker affiliation and my adolescence in the 1950s shadowed by nuclear weapons, was the only one to excite committed interest. Our design team of four History, Biology, Psychology, and Writing and Literature professors delighted in learning from each other during 1999 as we planned the general outline of a syllabus beginning with the shock of Hiroshima and ending with the Universal Declaration of Human Rights, with many historical forays along the way. (The syllabus is at <www.jsc.vsc.edu>.) Mindful of the rise in domestic and school violence, and of the fact that over three-quarters of the deaths in modern warfare are those of civilians, we were sure our topic was timely and right.

But we weren't prescient; none of us foresaw September 11, U.S. military involvement in Afghanistan and Iraq, or even the likelihood of teaching Peace and War when our country was practicing the latter. That circumstance has now confronted seven out of the course's ten full-time and adjunct professors. The heightened charge of classroom air in wartime can close down thought, as those of us teaching in fall 2001 felt happened once U.S. bombs began falling in Afghanistan, or it can be used to energize moral inquiry, as both we and our students experienced in spring 2003. The Iraq War, of course, did not catch us by surprise.

The course's results? By now there are thick files of student evalua-tions in the dean's office in which the word "irrelevant" never appears, although "frustrating" and "confusing" sometimes do—for the course is meant not to provide closure, but rather, tools for continuing the inquiry. A much-repeated remark—"I'm very glad I took this course, though I wouldn't have chosen it on my own"—expresses the prevailing willingness of most students to rise to the challenge of thinking about material they might prefer to avoid, reflecting on their own experience with violence, and talking with others who don't necessarily share their assumptions. Many have commented on wonderful guest speakers we've had: among them Hanne Liebmann, who was sheltered as a teenager during the Holocaust in Le Chambon-sur-Lignon, a sanctuary village in France described in one of our texts; John Balaban, a poet and conscien-tious objector who did alternative service in Vietnam during that war; Loung Ung, who was a child during the Khmer Rouge's massacres and now speaks passionately against landmines; Curtis Whiteway, a local Vermonter who at the age of 19 was among the first U.S. troops to enter Dachau. And other students over the years have said simply, "My eyes have been opened."

So have the eyes of Peace and War's teachers. Annegret Pollard, who hid from U.S. planes strafing her German town's streets on her way home from elementary school, now finds herself united with Curtis Whiteway in delivering a "war is hell, don't go there" message to her students. Though Victor Swenson brought a historian's perspective and a degree in International Relations from the School of Advanced International Studies (SAIS) to the course, his first semester of teaching was one of significant personal change. After dwelling intellectually with Mohandas Gandhi, Martin Luther King Jr., and the citizens of Le Chambon, and being moved by what they did, he came to see "energetic, purposeful, ingenious action based on refusal to do harm to another person as the fundamental obligation of all human beings."

For myself, though I had studied nonviolence and participated in such actions for years, the experience of teaching Peace and War during spring 2003 exposed limitations in my understanding. Our semester was bracketed by President George W. Bush's State of the Union address in January fervently justifying war with Iraq and his "tailhook" speech on the U.S.S. Abraham Lincoln claiming the war's triumphant conclusion in May. In the midst of such times, seeming to demand committed action, how does one clear and maintain a communal space for reflection?

No matter what my students and I were discussing—the warrior ideal in Homer's *Iliad*; the tradition of Holy War in the three major monotheistic religions; the disillusionment of Paul Baumer, Erich Maria Remarque's narrator in *All Quiet on the Western Front*, and his comrades in the trenches of World War I; or Gandhi's practice of Satyagraha—a consciousness of the impending, then actual, invasion of Iraq hung over our seminar table. It was a constant temptation to argue, to arrange ourselves into the Us/Them configuration we had become so adept at recognizing from our readings as "tribal thinking."

In this case, since the campus was mainly dovish, "Us" were those who regarded this war and a national security policy calling for preemptive strikes as appallingly bad ideas. I took part in the peace march in Washington on January 28; on February 15 about a third of my class of 18 went either to the massive rally in New York or to an antiwar gathering in front of Vermont's statehouse in Montpelier. We came back flushed with righteous energy. I began the semester badly torn between my role as an activist and my role as a teacher responsible to every member of this non-elective class.

It included Sarah, whose doubts about the rightness of this war were painfully outweighed by the presence of her boyfriend in Iraq. She had urged him to join the Marines two years before, when enlisting looked like his only road to a college education. And Justin, who was about to be commissioned as an Army lieutenant and trusted the government's case, though he regarded war as a last resort and wrote that he had a personal history of staring down bullies, not swinging at them. Several class members felt caught in a tug between conservative home or church milieus and the more questioning atmosphere on campus. Another, in a court diversion program because of a domestic violence offense, was already engaged in a personal version of the more historically based inquiry the class was undertaking. Only two or three like Jess, who had attended 1982 Nuclear Freeze rallies in her stroller, had grown up in peacenik families.

Immediately prior to our first vacation week in mid-February the class nearly exploded. I began the period with my usual exhortation to expand one's perspective by exploring non-U.S. news sources, then passed out a sampler of recent items from British websites—exposure of the plagiarized "dodgy dossier" on Iraqi weapons of mass destruction issued by Prime Minister Tony Blair's press secretary; news that the pope refused to declare the upcoming conflict a just war; mention that the U.S.A. Patriot Act II had already been drafted. "Maybe our President cares more for democracy in Iraq than in the U.S.," I speculated aloud.

In an atmosphere I had already politicized, we began discussing the essay "The Myth of Redemptive Violence" by Walter Wink. He analyzes a belief permeating U.S. popular culture: that "violence," as Dick Tracy puts it, "is golden when it is used to put evil down." The leap between gumshoe quip and the rhetoric of post-9/11 foreign policy swiftly got made. When Janet, whose feisty but searching voice had enlivened earlier classes, asked how, then, do we deal with tyrants (as a volunteer at a battered women's shelter she had extensive vicarious experience with them), a chorus drowned her out. At that moment I neglected to intervene effectively on her behalf. Our period over, the class broke into heated conversational groups and Janet left for the academic dean's office, intent on transferring to another section of Peace and War.

An alert administrative assistant there suggested she talk this over with me. How often does a student confront a professor, the one with power in the classroom, the one who hands out grades, about an unhappiness with that professor's performance? When Janet knocked on my office door, her bravery needed to be honored by serious listening. "You should have toned it down," she said and went on to make a broader point: that she felt she was being spoon-fed my point of view. Our conversation, grueling for both of us, ended with her deciding to remain in the section and my pledging to be more welcoming and protective of divergent student voices.

Twelve days later our class reconvened. By then, nearly 10,000,000 people worldwide had taken to the streets to protest war with Iraq, their voices heard by each other but seemingly not by policymakers. The last thing I wanted to do was replicate in the classroom the pain of not being heard. I began with an apology, acknowledging my conflict of roles and vowing to deal with it more professionally. First-hand reports on the New York rally followed, and then we were back to the syllabus.

Fortunately, it offered the protections of history. The lethal righteous-ness of Holy War in the Book of Joshua or in Pope Urban II's call for crusade struck students as more curious than controversial—these things happened centuries ago—but they appreciated the dark light it shed on the concept of jihad. (The lesser jihad, that is, of struggling against unbelievers—not the greater jihad of struggling with oneself, which was also practiced by Mohandas Gandhi and, indeed, by several people sitting around our table.)

Immediately before the U.S. attack began on March 19, the class was midway through a unit on World War I, focusing on the soldier's experience. What war, other than the Trojan War, has had such power-ful tellers, ones who sound the terrible, familiar chords of sorrow, love of comrades, lust for survival in a way that freshly pierces the reader? After Wilfred Owen's great poem "Dulce et Decorum Est" was read aloud—in which he counters "the old lie" that it is sweet and fitting to die for one's country with the image of a young man who has just inhaled mustard gas, whose blood comes "gargling from the froth-corrupted lungs"—none of us knew what to say. We believed then that Iraq had chemical weapons.

Once U.S. soldiers and Iraqis started to die, it seemed necessary to acknowledge that gravity with a depth of our own. At the beginning of our next class I suggested a modified form of Quaker meeting, where silence is the ground of speech and response is pure listening, not direct reply. Each person spoke in turn, Sarah out of raw pain and several others out of a confusion groping for shape:

"I want to support our troops, but how can I do that if I'm against the war?"

"There's so much information and hype, how can I tell what's true?"

"We're overwhelming our children."

"I'm scared of what happens in war."

"What's going to happen afterwards?"

Justin, who recorded these comments and gave everyone a copy on the last day of class, spoke eloquently about the preciousness of free speech and the United States' mission to share it.

Cliché or dog-eared truth, it hardly matters: attentive listening is a necessary step towards healing. We had already been leaving the Us/Them stuff behind, but after this day the class became a community, bringing a curiosity braided from many points of view to our remaining material, which at last centered on nonviolence. (Besides Mohandas Gandhi, it included the sanctuary village of Le Chambon, France, during World War II; Martin Luther King Jr. and the Civil Rights movement; the words of Jesus; and essays by Thich Nhat Hanh). When Jessica gave a presentation about a nonviolent protest she had taken part in, occupying a doomed Oregon redwood forest—and showed footage of police using pepper spray against the protestors—I was impressed by her self-discipline. She never let her passionate commitment block communication. "I felt a lot like Jess," Justin told me when I interviewed him after the course was over. "She was firm and whole-hearted. I always wanted to hear what she was going to say."

I also met later with both Janet and April, who shared the home-vs.-campus tug of opinion. Janet and I laughed about her yo-yo days at the beginning of the semester, when her vocal working-class parents complained on weekends, "You were never this liberal before." Now, she says she's more skeptical about all points of view and wants to get at facts. "It's upsetting that our country's credibility is shot." And she still wishes peace activists had more effective ideas about what to do with people who are committing evil acts. "Peace is a verb," she says, not some wispy kingdom.

April, slightly older than most other members of the class, and a Mormon with two young children, experienced the tug as "invigorating." For her, Peace and War was an invitation to build up a tolerance for complexity, to grapple with questions that have no easy answers but must, nevertheless, be asked. "Sometimes it seems hopeless, but I also believe people have goodness—I saw that in our class." "War is a crime against innocence," she added: words backed by troubling thought, for she could imagine her own children at Hiroshima or Nagasaki.

I thought not only of the civilians who are the majority of the dead in all modern wars, but of the lost generation of young men in *All Quiet on the Western Front*, of our U.S. youths picked off on the streets of Baghdad or Fallujah, of my students—unborn during the Vietnam War, kindergartners during the Iran-Contra years—who are inclined to trust and love their country.

The next time I teach this course, will I park my political views at the classroom door? Not a chance; they provide an animating passion. But I plan to hold myself to much stricter account about remembering a Gandhian caveat. Truth, he believed, is absolute. Though he had faith that it is approachable by determined seekers, he held that the only truth we human beings are privileged to know is relative. I thank my students for helping me to understand that purging righteousness from one's truth is part of nonviolence.

Judith Yarnall, a member of Middlebury (Vt.) Meeting, is currently attending Beacon Hill Meeting in Boston, Mass. She has recently retired from full-time teaching at Johnson State College in Vermont, but will continue teaching there part-time. She expects to be teaching American Literature in Ankara, Turkey, in spring 2005.

Testament: For One More War

In a despairing time, try to use necessary words.
Refuse the immense incomprehensible images
of terror, and while you can, answer the quiet
of your own heart that has somehow gone on
steadily beating through so many wars.

Be thankful that you do not know how to
speak the new physics, the new chemistry,
and cannot tell the absolute truth of agony,
the screams that may one day be ours. They could
multiply, if that's what it takes, until we hear
and repent, do justice, forgive each other.
Until we find the courage to change.

But because you have been given many years
and are a poet who remembers much,
much will be required: that you not forget
the dying soldier's hand reaching after
a butterfly in No Man's Land, that you say
although phosgene smells like pear trees in bloom,
it is deadly, and mustard gas burning lungs and eyes
        and skin
is nothing like the yellow flowers
that take your breath away in California fields.

Describe if you can, the up-ended skeletons of ships
you saw in 1948 in the harbor of Bremen. Tell about
clearing rubble with shovels and carts and wheelbarrows,
making a playground with students from many countries,
the flying brick that sent you to a hospital with no supplies.

Tell about your friend, a medic on his way to Vietnam,
how he sat at your kitchen table polishing his boots and
belt buckle, and when he left, left you the box
of brownies from his mother. Say when he was
wounded and came back, he did not talk.

You could mention Hiroshima, Babi Yar, cemeteries
in other countries, the DP barracks and orphanages
you visited, stories exchanged with enemies,
museums dedicated to history and atrocity.
You could open the floodgates.

And after telling, after trying to speak for the dead
and the walking wounded, the mourner's bench
with faces you know and voices you remember,
then, if you make poems, say nothing pretentious
or solemn. Be honest and angry. Be clear of lies.

But because you are alive and are for the moment
safe and able to speak, do what you can with letters
and messages, with marches and stories and prayers.
Take time to listen to the unknown bird
in the cedar you bow to each morning.
Attend to the sounds of water, the playful
voices of children, the questions in their eyes.

Remember to say that the scarlet poppies
nevertheless returned to the ravaged fields,
and sunlight and rain entered the broken houses.
Find words simple as air and hope, nourishing
as good bread, green coming slowly back after fire.

—Jeanne Lohmann

Jeanne Lohmann is a member of Olympia (Wash.) Meeting.

U.S. Exceptionalism vs. Human Solidarity

by Keith Helmuth

The attack of September 11, 2001, on the World Trade Center and
the Pentagon has generated a range of responses among Friends on the
Peace Testimony and on the commitment to nonviolence. Some Friends
have concluded that this situation goes beyond the relevance of the Peace
Testimony and have laid it to one side in order to support military action
against terrorism. We have been given nuanced interpretations of the
history of the Peace Testimony showing how the tradition, from the
beginning, has allowed for military action—a kind of Quaker just war
theory. Others, who have recoiled against war, have agonized over the
sense that some effective response must be made, but have been unable
to see how such a response can emerge from the Peace Testimony or any
kind of pacifist stance. Still others have argued persuasively that even in
this case there was plenty of scope for effective nonviolent response,
including the use of international law. A few Friends have suggested that,
at a minimum, we should recognize the role U.S. policy and its military

expression in the Middle East has had in setting up this conflict. According to this understanding, reducing the incentive for terrorism would include a fundamental change in U.S. policy—a change from military and economic domination to support for equity and justice in the region.

As I have listened to, read, and thought about these various responses, and considered them against the policies and actions of the Bush administration, another level of concern has emerged that goes beyond the Peace Testimony. The crisis for Quakers that arises from 9/11 and its aftermath is not just a matter of the relevance of the Peace Testimony or whether a commitment to nonviolent action can be sustained in the face of terrorism. Behind this crisis is another crisis, a crisis brought on by the way the current U.S. government is setting itself up openly to oppose and deny human solidarity.

Gregory Baum, Dominican priest and cultural historian, asks the question: "What is the primary spiritual discovery of the 20th century?" His answer is "human solidarity." I think it is fair to say the whole history of Quakerism has helped advance this spiritual discovery within Christendom. This new spiritual grounding, this advance in moral understanding—now framed by the ecological realities of the human/ Earth relationship—is a real cultural achievement. But it is an achievement that is now being challenged by "U.S. exceptionalism" and the will to domination that flows from this worldview. The overarching policies of the U.S. government are now being set in deliberate opposition to human solidarity.

The idea of U.S. exceptionalism that is guiding the Bush administration has been present in varying degrees within U.S. political culture and policy for a long time. The events of 9/11, however, became a new golden opportunity for U.S. exceptionalism and its "natural right" of domination to be brought into full force.

The policy framework now being put in place by the Bush administration is clearly based on this "natural right" of domination. In watching the progress of this policy formation, and in watching the behavior that flows from the policies, it is easy to see that a "master culture" syndrome is emerging. It is this master culture stance of the U.S. government that confronts Friends with a crisis that goes deeper than the Peace Testimony: It goes to the heart of the question of what it means to be in relationship to the social, economic, spiritual, moral, and ecological realities of the human world. It goes to the heart of human solidarity.

If we look at the behavior of the U.S. government and fully consider the range of economic interests reflected in its actions (and inactions), the following zones of policy come into view.

1. The institutionalization of war. The War on Terrorism has become an opportunity to make war an institution of U.S. life in the way education and healthcare are institutions. Those who profit from war will be assured of continued contracts and increasing business. The business of war as a regular and acceptable feature of U.S. life makes it possible for the policies of domination to be quickly implemented at any point in which U.S. interests are threatened. Opposition to U.S. military domination is now considered to be supporting terrorism.

2. Economic development as a triage process. Because the U.S. government and its associated interests have taken the view that there is no alternative to the political economy of the capital-driven market, a policy of writing off the impoverished, marginal, and excluded people of the world has become a clear and logical necessity. This is made evident by the use of the expression "nonviable economies." Regions that cannot participate in and contribute to the capital-driven market economy are not being assisted in becoming better subsistence economies. If they cannot get with the program of capital-driven economics they will be allowed to fail. The pitifully small aid programs of the G8 nations, even considering their recent face-saving pledges of increased assistance, is clear evidence of this triage policy.

3. Enclave strategy. The Bush administration has finally admitted that global warming is an environmental problem. But its response to this, and to other examples of ecological deterioration, is just to plunge ahead and tough it out from a position of strength. The administration seems to think that maximum use of fossil fuel and nuclear technology for as long as possible will put the U.S. economy in as strong a position as possible for coping with the disruptive events that are bound to occur. There seems to be little place for risk reduction or preventive action in the governing policy framework. This same attitude is clearly evident in the administration's response to the terrorist problem—reinforce the fortress, create defensive and offensive enclaves around the world. Equip them with the best technology. Plan for war in perpetuity. No sense of systemic problem solving. No sense of risk reduction. Add to this, the Bush administration's refusal of the Kyoto Protocol on global warming, its abrogation of the ABM treaty with Russia, and its opposition to the development of international legal institutions, and the rapidly expanding dimensions of the enclave strategy come into view.

4. Human health and development advantage. With the rise of biotechnology, wealthy U.S. residents, and their peers around the world, now have a dramatically increasing health and human development advantage over poor and low-income people. Not only will the rich continue to enjoy superior medical attention, but, with biotech enhancement, they will increasingly realize a human development advantage with regard to learning, skill development, intelligence, emotional balance, quality-controlled reproduction, physical strength, stamina and longevity. Since the technologies that make these kinds of enhancements possible have been developed within the political economy of the capital-driven market, their availability will naturally be restricted to those who can afford to pay for them. As the benefits of biotech enhancement continue, and the functional potential of affluent populations is pushed to extraordinary heights, the human world will become increasingly divided between a class of wealthy, objectively superior people, and a class of impoverished people who, by comparison, can only be regarded as deficient and defective. Already the language of "enhancement" has begun to describe those left behind as "naturals." The advance of market-driven biotechnology (once it is accepted as inevitable) leads directly to a further polarization of the superior rich and the deficient poor. The logic of eugenics, around which Germany's National Socialist government formed many of its policies, is implicit in this polarization. Biotechnology, along with its eugenic implications, fits perfectly within the program of U.S. exceptionalism. It is apparent that the current U.S. government is comfortable with this increasing polarization of rich and poor, and willing to accept the write-off implicit in this world picture.

The question must be asked, however; are Friends comfortable with U.S. government policies that advance the interests of the rich, deliberately write off the poor, and increasingly program a highly inequitable human world, both domestically and globally? How do Friends relate to a government and a political process that, as a matter of policy, are willing to write off "nonviable" economic situations and the people who inhabit them? How do Friends relate to a government and a political economy that range over the Earth seeking to command and sequester resources for the benefit and aggrandizement of those already among the favored rich, while large populations want for basic goods and whole regions remain impoverished?

The four zones of political, economic, and cultural life noted above all have a range of public policies that define and support them. These policies are rooted in the worldview of U.S. exceptionalism and expressed in the "natural right" of domination. Taken together, they describe a rejection of the moral evolution of Christian and other religious traditions. Taken together, they add up to a denial of human solidarity.

Is it not the case that a part of the agonizing conflict for Friends over 9/11 and its aftermath has been a sense of a wounded United States and a genuine feeling for its collective identity on the one hand, and, on the other, the realization that the collective identity of the United States is wrapped up in a doctrine of exceptionalism that rejects and denies human solidarity? This doctrine expresses itself in worldwide military and economic domination, itself a primary factor of the context in which terrorism has emerged.

I am reminded of the situation for people of faith in Germany just prior to the Second World War. Although the situation in the United States today is very different, the similarities are disturbing. Many good people had no idea that their elected government was about to plunge their homeland into Holocaust behavior and Europe into a catastrophic war. If we look now at the overarching policies of the U.S. government and the way they are shaping U.S. political culture and global behavior, we should ask: Where will these policies and these actions take the country and the world? In particular, what will happen if the U.S. uses "tactical" nuclear weapons in its War on Terrorism (a policy option now under serious consideration)? In 5, 10, or 20 years will a surviving remnant say, "Why didn't they see the trajectory? Why did they plunge headlong to such a disaster? Why didn't they take the 20th century's lesson of human solidarity to heart? Why didn't they make human solidarity and a reasonable equity the foundation of political, economic and intercultural life?"

Can Friends help intervene and preempt these haunting questions? Can we see what may be written if the trajectory of U.S. exceptionalism is played out? In the past it was possible to think that U.S. policy, although sometimes inept, was basically a positive force in world development. The evidence now unfolding makes it extremely difficult to maintain this view. A commitment to human solidarity is now increasingly at cross purposes with the mainline trajectory of U.S. government policy.

The challenge to Friends in the aftermath of 9/11 is not just about the efficacy of the Peace Testimony. It is about something even more central to the identity of Quakerism. It is about whether Friends still understand Quakerism to be rooted in a universal and transcendent experience of faith that makes human solidarity a first-order reality. It is about whether, under the imprint of the Divine, human solidarity is still the "unwobbling pivot" that centers and balances all our work for human betterment.

I think Friends in the U.S. are confronted with the uncomfortable choice of retaining support for the U.S. political economy or a full commitment to the ethics of human solidarity. Unfortunately, these two realities do not, at present, coincide. Although many good things still occur in the U.S., the trajectory of its public policies around economic behavior seems to diverge more and more from any sense of human solidarity. It seems likely that a full commitment to the ethics of human solidarity—a commitment to which Friends have traditionally aspired—will require the laying down of the last vestige of U.S. exceptionalism. This is not an anti-American thought. It is rather the hope that the U.S. might come to embody a different kind of political economy and culture, that it might become a focus of equity and justice, a beacon of human solidarity, and a citizen nation in the commonwealth of life.

Can Friends come to see what may be written if the present trajectory of U.S. exceptionalism is played out? Can Friends help build a movement that will create the future in a different way? Can Friends, as a people of faith, help keep human solidarity in central focus, and work unremittingly for public policies that advance equity, justice, cooperation, peace, and the integrity of Creation?

Keith Helmuth is a sojourning member of Central Philadelphia (Pa.) Meeting and a member of the coordinating group of Quaker EcoWitness.

What Do We Do Now?

by Arden Buck

It's a discouraging and ominous time. On November 5, 2002, frightened voters in the United States handed our administration unfettered power: to hasten environmental devastation, to increase the flow of wealth from the poor to the rich, to pack our courts with right-wing ideologues, to subject residents to invasive government scrutiny under the rubric of homeland security, and to embark on a global military rampage, starting with Iraq.

And what do we do now? How can we keep our spirits up and our hearts open in the midst of all this, and what can we do now to make this a better world?

It's tempting to become cynical and bitter, or to pull back and await the onslaught, as many German citizens did in the '30s. But—as writer and peace advocate Bruce Mulkey has pointed out—cynicism, denial, and hopelessness amount to victimhood. We can rarely control what life sends our way, but we can control how we respond to it. We can make ourselves miserable, helplessly wishing things were better, or we can do everything we can and feel the satisfaction of those efforts regardless of the outcome.

Many have offered lists of how one can respond. Here is my contribution, distilled from the thoughts of many others, past and present:

1. Allow yourself to grieve. Accept the pain, frustration, and anger you feel about what is happening. It is a necessary step for healing and moving on. But don't get stuck there.

2. Don't despair.

• Despair is a human notion—it doesn't exist elsewhere in nature, and it doesn't exist when one is immersed in the present moment. By simply doing one's work, one can move beyond despair, and also beyond fear.

• Taking a long-term view can be comforting: "This, too, will pass." The world, albeit somewhat changed, will go on.

• Corporate/military power is vulnerable because it's large, monolithic, and single-minded, and it relies on a few power-based tactics to maintain control. It is weakened by the light of truth; it is vulnerable to creative, adaptable strategies; and it presents a large, clear target.

• We are dealing with an outmoded mentality based on raw power, greed, and isolation—a dinosaur doomed to die. Our job is to do what we can to limit the damage caused by its death throes.

• Surprises are everywhere—change for the better may be just around the corner.

3. Be persistent. Even when the situation seems hopeless, effort often pays off in the end—sometimes when least expected, and sometimes in surprising ways. Patiently keep tapping away. Be willing to give it several years—plant seeds. Understand and use the concept developed by writer Malcolm Gladwell in *The Tipping Point*: major changes often develop as undercurrents with little visible indication, and our actions may seem to be futile. But if one keeps pushing, things can reach a critical point and abruptly shift in the desired direction, seemingly out of nowhere. Examples of tipping points: the fall of the Berlin Wall, and the transformation of Nelson Mandela from prisoner to president.

4. Help people become aware. This is especially crucial in the media-drugged U.S. I use the word "drugged" advisedly—our media make us into passive spectators, dull our critical thinking ability, implant ideas such as "violence is the best way" and "be afraid of everything," entertain us instead of informing us, and lead us to believe we're getting straight stories. It's more than simple information overload. Most people in this country, though well-intentioned (albeit sometimes immature and self-indulgent), have been herded into a fearful, self-protective state of mind by official pronouncements of various threats. Make holes in this worldview.

Share thoughtful articles and magazines. Look at the website <www.commondreams.org>. Write letters and op-ed pieces (when appropriate, mention your representatives by name). Attend vigils and demonstrations. Encourage people and groups to join a fact-finding delegation to a critical area to see for themselves and report back to their friends and groups to which they belong (check out Witness for Peace and Global Exchange). Find other ways to help people understand what's going on.

5. Build bridges. Reach out to those who think differently rather than just preaching to the choir. People already know something's wrong, but don't know exactly what. Those who believe differently can be softened by emphasizing common ground. Hear their concerns, find points of agreement, and then expose them to new thoughts.

Form coalitions with other groups, even those with whom we don't agree on other issues. We can make our connections with them more solid by showing up at their meetings, helping them hand out flyers, etc. Choose a specific issue that has a good chance of success, that many people care about (e.g., loss of privacy), that appeals to a variety of potential coalition partners, and where opposition is vulnerable.

6. **Continue working on your representatives.** Talk with them about the unanswered questions about this war and about other related issues.

7. **Work for campaign finance reform, and seek out worthy candidates to support.** Maine, Vermont, Arizona, and Massachusetts now provide public financing for candidates willing to follow stringent fundraising and spending guidelines. Bringing public financing to your own community and state is a project worth undertaking. We cannot allow our political representatives to continue to be bought and sold to the highest bidders. For more information, visit <www.publicampaign.org>.

8. **Look for and support good things.** There is plenty of bad news, but a lot of good things are also happening, although they don't often appear in the mainstream press—thoughtful, caring, and compassionate words and deeds by ordinary and not-so-ordinary people and local, national, and international groups.

9. **Add your weight to push for change.** Seek out and help support good ideas and programs that people can get excited about and involved in. Examples of successful actions can be found on <www.dbsst.org> (Database of Sucessful Strategies and Tactics).

10. **Cut off the fuel supply.** Giant corporations are fueled by money and profits. Withdraw your bit of energy from the bad ones. Whenever possible, buy from local vendors and from socially and environmentally responsible businesses. Avoid chains and megastores. Apply this approach in your banking and investing as well. A good resource is <www.coopamerica.org>.

By far the most important item is food. Avoid factory food and seek out food that is produced locally or by small producers, and/or that is free of chemicals, hormones, and genetic modification. You thereby help your community and the world, while enjoying healthier, better-tasting food.

Buy less. Live more simply and develop a lifestyle based on satisfactions other than having lots of stuff.

11. **Think outside the box.** Find creative new ways to deal with our situation, and help others implement their innovative concepts. Our

thinking needs to be dramatic—unexpected—outside the box. It can be a creative new tactic, an unexpected response, or an unexpectedly quick response.

Practice indirection. The war/greed machine is too powerful to confront head-on, but grassroots efforts can make the road so muddy that the machine bogs down. Perhaps we can find leverage points, vulnerable spots, or redirect its motion so it does less damage or self-destructs.

12. Multi-pronged actions can have a synergistic effect. For instance, a combination of demonstrations, op-eds/letters, and legal action all happening together may produce better results than the same actions done one at a time.

13. Use triage. Go for greatest possible effect. Spend time on people who might be energized or changed rather than on the already committed or those who are hopeless. Zero in on one specific issue or target rather than everywhere at once. Savor small successes—they all help, and they may lead to larger successes later on.

14. Don't demonize our adversaries. Consider opposing points of view. While we may be correct in what we affirm, there is usually a kernel of truth in our opponent's viewpoint. And we need to be especially mindful about what we deny, because this is often where our blind spots will be.

We are all in this together—there is no "enemy." We all want to be safe and loved. Any action that is fear-based—e.g. abusive language, intolerant behavior, or a violent act—is a cry for love and security, whether it's coming from George W. Bush or someone down the street.

15. Put joy into your work. Share your joy and allow it to warm others. Move from anger and despair to compassion and love. This is not to deny the legitimacy of outrage at injustice; but it is more effective to work from compassion than angrily to fight against evil. The Dalai Lama said, "A positive future can never emerge from anger and despair."

16. Broaden the circle of caring. Most of us care deeply about our small circle of friends, family, etc. We usually also care about our neighborhood or community. Some care deeply about the well-being of their country. However, our circle of compassion must expand beyond the familiar to include human and nonhuman, living and nonliving—to match our expanded influence in the world. Find ways to encourage concern about the life of a little girl in Baghdad or a coral reef in the South Pacific as well as about one's own loved ones.

17. Be kind to people everywhere, the good and the not-so-good. The world needs role models for kindness as never before. Nurture others, and surround yourself with those who nurture you and who understand and respect your hopes and dreams.

Be especially kind to yourself. Keep yourself grounded and burnout-free by giving yourself down-time: meditation, a quiet walk, exercise, music, time with a friend, creative time, etc. Self-renewal is an essential part of your work.

18. Detach yourself from the results of your efforts. Make the commitment, do the work, follow through as needed, and then let go. Let the universe make of it what it will. Do it for the doing, not for the outcome. Do it simply because it's the right thing to do, and because it's good for your soul. This is a lighter, freer, and more effective way.

As an added bonus, your good work may in fact produce unexpectedly good results, it may inspire others, and it almost certainly will expand your own capabilities and wisdom.

19. Enjoy life. An ancient parable tells of a Buddhist monk who is chased by tigers to the edge of a cliff. As they close in, he spots a small bush growing at the very edge, grabs it, and jumps over. As he hangs there, the tigers paw the ground above but can't reach him. Looking down, he sees more tigers below. Then he notices a mouse gnawing on the slender root that holds the bush. As the bush slowly gives way, the monk spots a berry on it. With a delighted smile, he picks the berry with his free hand and eats it slowly, enjoying every morsel. In reality, we are all caught between tigers above and tigers below, but like that monk, we can and should live fully and with delight in this moment, in spite of it all.

Discover your unique gifts—what you can do most effectively—and share them where they're most needed. You have much to offer—your time, energy, money, talents, possessions to share, etc.

As Will Keepin, co-founder of the Satyana Institute, tells us, we can serve as hospice workers to a dying culture, and also as midwives to an emerging culture. These two tasks call for us to maintain an open heart, offering our light and joy, and being present for grief and pain. When we root our actions in both intelligence and compassion, we reach a balance of head and heart that combines the finest of human qualities.

Our task is not easy—but we must do it anyway. We do make a difference—individually and collectively. Every positive thought and action changes the world we live in, and therefore changes the fabric of our own existence for the better.

As Margaret Mead said, "Never doubt that a small group of thoughtful, committed citizens can change the world. Indeed, it's the only thing that ever has."

Israeli activist Uri Avnery observed, "It always starts with a small group of committed people. They raise their feeble voice. The media ignore them, the politicians laugh at them, the respectable parties distance themselves. But slowly, with persistence, they start to have an impact. This finally compels the leaders of the mainstream organizations to respond, and the message spreads."

A cloud of mosquitoes can send a rhinoceros running.

Arden Buck is a member of Boulder (Colo.) Meeting. An earlier version of this article appeared at <commondreams.org>.

Forum: Investing in People: Using Weapons of Mass Construction to Avert the Next War

Need I even ask? Are there any Friends who are not outraged over our government's behavior since the tragic 9/11 attacks? On the assumption that outrage makes very few of us happy, let me suggest an avenue along which to channel our energies.

The President has decided to lash out against terrorism by investing our tax dollars in weapons of mass destruction in pursuit of peace through strength. We all know this doesn't work: like the Hydra of Greek mythology, when you bomb hate, it just multiplies. So citizens of the U.S. empire and its allies will surely be targets of future terrorist actions, and the challenge arises of how best to counter these threats.

What if Friends chose to fight back against terrorism with weapons of mass construction in pursuit of peace through global sharing? Would it succeed? The world's lowest-income people rarely become terrorists. They don't have the time; survival dominates their lives. But terrorists are parasites on society, producing nothing and consuming vast resources—sort of like the Pentagon. Terrorists rely on the world's teeming masses for both moral and material support. As long as the U.S. goal is global economic domination (bolstered by shock and awe when necessary), terrorists can indict our evil empire and rally much of the world to support their holy war. Only by putting the lie to their accusations can we hope to undercut the terrorists' support base. Happy, well-fed people don't hate with as much intensity.

Global sharing is no substitute for public protest, of course. We must continue to oppose the institutions of global dominance, be they economic (WTO, IMF, World Bank), military (Pentagon and its arm-twisted "willing" allies), or cultural (Hollywood and its perverted yet seductive values). But we all yearn for balance in our lives, especially when so many of our efforts are directed toward opposing government policy. We need something we can affirm.

In October 2001, the President suggested that people could be helpful by consuming—anything. Instead of spending mindlessly, perhaps Friends could agree to invest mindfully in global projects that benefit those of lowest status in the belief that we are all better off when we are all better off. After all, we're all consumers, and no one is (yet) pointing a gun at our heads, telling us what to buy. Everyone from Bush to Bangladesh wants "peace" and "security," so these words lack meaning unless qualified (e.g., peace through strength vs. peace through global sharing). Why not reject the myth of "fortress America" security through military might as well as the myth of economic security by gambling in the stock market and instead invest in people—the world's lowest-income people—in a common-good approach toward global societal security?

Fortunately we have the avenue to do so. I know of no group that better embodies the brand of peace and security we seek than our own Right Sharing of World Resources (RSWR). On a project budget of just $2 per U.S. Friend, RSWR consistently invests in innovative, environmentally sound efforts to partner with those of lowest income and status to enhance the global common good. Could we set a modest goal of $5 per U.S. Friend for the RSWR coffers? Is this too much to ask? Averting Washington's next war will require a redirection of financial resources away from taxes for weapons toward an investment in global equity. Let's test to see what love can do. RSWR can be reached at 232 College Ave., Richmond, IN 47374. Please contact RSWR and see how much your soul can be uplifted by partnering with them to work toward a better world.

—*Chuck Hosking*, Albuquerque, N.Mex.

Reflection: Peacemaking: Public and Private

by Michael True

In addressing this topic, I turn to the theme of a workshop/retreat with Bennington (Vt.) Meeting in August 2002, as a way of asking Friends for help in understanding and clarifying the relationship between personal transformation and social change.

As Quakers our basic testimony, it seems to me, is not "peace," but "peacemaking." Although the differences in the two words may appear unimportant, for our language and present needs, they are fundamental. Why? Because the English word "peace" no longer conveys the essential weight and power once associated with that word.

Figuratively speaking, "peace" died on the Western Front in 1916, in what Ernest Hemingway called "that senseless slaughter." The implications of that tragedy were first recognized by Wilfred Owen, who died in battle there two years later, after writing several extraordinary lyrics, including "Dulce et Decorum Est" and "Futility." Almost a century later, his poems are still essential to our understanding of the horror and waste of modern warfare.

A few years later, T. S. Eliot, in *The Waste Land* (1922), used a Sanskrit word *shantih* rather than the English word "peace" to name the concept that surpasses all understanding. It was a fundamental insight into the corruption of the word, a casualty of war, and thus of our loss, linguistically speaking. Perhaps coincidentally, the year that T. S. Eliot published his epic poem was the same year that the word "nonviolence" entered our language.

This discussion may sound rather abstract, given the plight of the United States involved in war once again. But I think that it is an issue that must be dealt with by anyone trying to offer alternative ways of being in the world in a violent century. The language we speak, the words that we use, have consequences and implications beyond the mere naming of things.

"Peacemaking" is both clarifying and exact, whereas "peace" is ambiguous. The latter word implies that peace is something that just happens, usually between wars, not something that must be created or it will not exist. Kenneth Boulding, among others, tried to address this matter by talking about "negative" and "positive" peace, in a way that was helpful. But for the common reader—the ordinary person, including me—this alternative doesn't fully meet a fundamental need to name our proper work.

Toward this goal, the writings of Adam Curle, British Quaker and peace researcher, provide some guidance, in a series of publications that deserve to be much better known in the United States than they are at present. I have in mind his pamphlet *Peacemaking: Public and Private* (1986) and a more recent book, *Another Way: Positive Response to Contemporary Violence* (1995). In the former, Adam Curle says, for example, that "Public peacemaking is what we do; private peacemaking is what we are, the two being interpenetrating." Drawing upon his long experience mediating violent and intractable conflicts in West Africa, Sri Lanka, and the former Yugoslavia, he concluded in the latter work, "It is an absurd illusion to consider that we can work for peace, which means to be actively involved with people who are behaving in an unpeaceful way, if we are inwardly in turmoil and ill-at-ease; or to help people change their lives for the better if our own experience is disordered and impoverished."

Although one may demur at the sweeping nature of Adam Curle's conclusion, it is a useful reference point, particularly when set beside his resonant definition of peacemaking as "the science of perceiving that things which appear to be apart are one, and the art of restoring love to a relationship from which it has been driven by fear and hatred."

An important implication of this line of reasoning, for me, is its stress on the intimate relationship between peacemaking and nonviolence and between personal transformation and social change. It suggests what nonviolent theorists from 19th century pacifist Adin Ballou to Mohandas Gandhi and Martin Luther King Jr. have implied about personal behavior and community building. The poet Muriel Rukeyser says, similarly, in "It is There":

Meditation, yes, but . . .
Generations holding to resistance, and within this resistance,
Fluid change that can respond, that can show the children
A long future of finding, of responsibility.

It is a truism in peace studies that strategies for resolving and transforming conflict within ourselves and our families are surprisingly similar to strategies at the international level. Both involve silence, listening, and being attentive to language and context, especially in distinguishing the conflicts from the persons involved. The goal is to restore equilibrium and harmony—to heal ourselves and the wider community, while recognizing the interdependence of the so-called spiritual and secular realms: to make peace, to act, to clear a space where peace might happen.

Michael True, a member of Worcester (Mass.) Pleasant Street Meeting, is the author of An Energy Field More Intense Than War: The Nonviolent Tradition in American Literature *(Syracuse University Press, 1995), and writes for* Peacework.

Winter Onions

Bright spring day
Seated by the garden
Cleaning winter onions
First thing to grow.
Planted in fall
In rich loam
Green shoots in February
Tall spears in April.
I dug the onions
Shoved the spading fork deep
Half-lifted, half-pulled
Roots clinging to the soil
Now, knife in hand,
I clean each one,
A quick slice taking off the roots
Then peeling the tough skin
Layer upon layer
Til bulb and long neck
Shine white.
Last I lop off the leaves
So a green whorl tops each.

Anger
Buried in heart-loam
In the winter of my life
Uprooted now
Feeder roots cut away
Tough parts peeled away
Layer upon layer
Til only the memory
Without the hurt
Clean
New
Full of juice and flavor
Of life lived
Only the good part
Harvested.

—Mariellen O. Gilpin

Mariellen O. Gilpin is a member of Urbana-Champaign (Ill.) Meeting.

Forum: The Right Security Comes From God

I have been a member of Friends meetings for almost four years. I recently became a clerk for the Eastern New York Correctional Facility's Friends Meeting.

Recently, a friend brought me the November issue of FRIENDS JOURNAL. As soon as I saw it, I became selfish. I quickly put it into my prison net bag and then, when we finished our worship, I returned to my housing unit and immediately started to read it. I had a stack of *New York Times* and Chinese newspapers that I needed to get caught up on, but I pushed them all to the side to read the JOURNAL first.

I started by reading the way Friends responded to the tragedy of September 11th in "Finding Our Way." I felt so touched by Carol Holmes from 15th Street (N.Y.) Meeting. Before my incarceration, I used to live on East 60th Street, and I used to like to walk around too. Sometimes, I said to people, "How's it going with you?" Normally, I got strange looks. I think people thought I was crazy.

People sympathized with people in the U.S. on September 11th. But now there is a feeling that the U.S. is making the same mistake and killing innocent people. Can't we all get along? I agree with David Hartsough, from San Francisco, Calif. He believes that the only way we can build real security for the U.S. is for our country to become a real friend to all of the world's people. Instead of spending hundreds of billions of dollars for weapons of destruction, the U.S. should allocate hundreds of billions for feeding the hungry, housing the homeless, healing the sick, and helping heal the wounds of war and hatred around the world. This would do more to win friends and real security than Star Wars and all the other weapons in the world combined.

The most important thing is respect and understanding each other. Also, the right security comes from God. God is Love, so there cannot be hatred. In the Kingdom of God, there are no terrorists; everyone is a child of God. I see myself as God's child.

—*Chun H. Lam,* Napanoch, N.Y.

Forum: The Flag Belongs to All of Us

Thank you for your thoughtful and inspiring December issue on the aftermath of September 11th. (I could say the same of every issue!) Our community of faith is more needed than ever.

I wish to respond to Eleanor Dart's letter in the Forum of that issue. She says, "Flying the flag today would mean I support war." No!! It does not mean that! It will only do so if those of us who support other approaches to terrorism allow the war supporters to take it over. The flag belongs to all in the U.S.

I am a Quaker, opposed to violence, but I wear a flag pin to show that I too am a loyal American who loves her country and supports our precious freedom of opinions, thoughts, beliefs, and who is free to disagree with her government.

Friends, don't let our flag be turned into a jingoistic symbol! Fly it to signify our solidarity with all who grieve and suffer and who work for the restoration of peace and justice for all.

—*Carolyn W. Mallison,* Newfield, N.Y.

Forum: Peace Testimony Isn't Logical

The Peace Testimony isn't arrived at through careful logic. It stems from the realization that we are living in the Kingdom now. Knowing that this is the Kingdom changes our viewpoint, and with this new paradigm comes an awareness of the connections that exist in all of creation. We are not separate beings, but all part of a whole that has existed forever and will continue to exist forever.

I enjoy Scott Simon's commentary and reporting on world events, and value his vast experience in observing violent conflicts. I will continue to rely on the still small voice, rather than logic, when it comes to killing.

—*Nils Pearson,* Ogema, Wis.

Forum: Opt-out from Military Recruitment

Friends and their communities should be aware of the provisions of the Federal No Child Left Behind Act, which requires school districts, or private schools getting certain Federal funds, to give to military recruiters the names, addresses, and telelphone numbers of high school students. There is an exemption for private schools with verifiable religious objection to service in the armed forces. There is also a provision that students or their parents may opt out, requesting in writing withholding of the student's name and information.

Once a young person's name is given, parents have lost the right to deny recruiter contact with their child. So parents and children need to consider exercising their opt-out rights promptly.

The law requires that the educational authorities inform parents of the right to request withholding of the student's name. But school districts may handle this obligation in a variety of ways. Friends have the opportunity to encourage making it convenient for rights to be understood and exercised. Our Peace and Social Concerns Committee has contacted our local newspaper and school administration.

More information is available from the Center on Conscience and War at <www.nisbco.org> (e-mail: <nisbco@nisbco.org>). The address is 1830 Connecticut Ave., NW, Washington, DC 20009; phone (202) 483-2220.

—*Clarkson Palmer,* Swarthmore, Pa.

Forum: Let's Support the UN

We would like to follow up on J. William Frost's article on "AFSC and the Terrorist War" (*FJ* Jan. 2002) with thoughts for further Quaker tactics.

In our understanding of the history of Quaker response to war, we should not forget our work at the United Nations and its precursor, the League of Nations. The UN was born as a response to World War II. Quakers have had a continual presence there for the nearly 50 years of its existence and, through its Geneva Office, since 1922 in relation to the League of Nations.

The Quaker United Nations Office has worked steadily on issues of concern to Friends: world peace, development, and elimination of nuclear and conventional arms, the environment, racism, and the prevention of deadly conflict. Over the years we have become respected for our impartial, quiet diplomacy. Quaker House, which is just a few blocks from the United Nations, is used as a safe, comfortable place to bring people from the United Nations community together for off-the-record meetings on sensitive issues.

We must continue to support and strengthen these activities as we try to raise awareness of the need for a global response to terrorism. The UN is fragile from lack of support and in danger of domination by a U.S. determined to use it to its own ends. Yet it is still the only world body we have. We as Friends can play an important role in raising awareness of the need for more creative and enlightened global foreign policy in this country. The recognition of the importance of the UN, its agencies, and its legal institutions is essential if we are to really minimize the threat of terrorism and achieve a more peaceful and just world.

—*Scilla Wahrhaftig,* Quaker United Nations Office,
New York, N.Y.

Forum: We Need International Policing, Not War

My response to Scott Simon (*FJ* May 2003) is to propose that the world must not accept the violence of wars, but seek only nonviolent solutions. How can the world form an international body that would exercise police functioning among nations that would stop evildoers? Must we continue to have military forces to "take out" evil and then bring the evildoers to justice? Scott Simon seems to dismiss the development of an international system of justice and policing as ineffective.

Many of us would prefer such an international system, just as we accept police and the limitation of police power in our society. Why do we as a nation approve sending a military force with its terrorizing firepower and the subsequent acceptance of "collateral damage"? It has been a dangerous habit of U.S. society (and many others) to rush into short-term solutions. We lack the patience, the planning, and the persistence to develop long-range planning for cooperation for the future good. We know that a civilized society will not—does not—permit its police to use helicopter gunships using rockets against civilian cars and to enter neighborhoods with tanks to crush and enter civilian homes. How should, or can, we allow other nation-states to exercise such violence? I'm sure that many remember the outrage after Philadelphia police used a helicopter to drop a bomb on the MOVE house a decade ago.

I will continue to support actions that encourage local, national, and international groups to formulate a consensus that will make possible such nonviolent solutions to conflict. There will be many different views as to the format of the solution, such as the International Court of Justice and the International Criminal Court. Our country needs to accept their jurisdiction. There is work to be done, politically and diplomatically, before the world can have justice and be able to have nonviolent solutions. Sometimes we have very wide differences among Friends about how we put our principles into action, but I know we have the patience and persistence to find our way as we respect the Truth and mind the Spirit.

I feel that I am to witness to groups as I am able, to bring about a community of persons to change things for the better. This Friend finds himself among Friends unwilling to compromise the principle of non-violence or to allow military force to replace police action. We would limit the violence of police power with judicial and civilian control.

—*Charles Peterson*, Newtown, Pa.

Forum: Let's Take Effective Steps to Avoid Further War

Congress may be considering expansion of U.S. military aggression to Iraq and Somalia. I think of the scars our men and women in uniform suffered from Gulf War syndrome and during the failed Somali occupation of 1992–4; I hope that we don't have to send them back there.

Of course the U.S. government must work seriously to reduce weapons of mass destruction and the training of terrorists worldwide. Yet terrorism is committed by individuals, not by entire nations. Supporting the Rome Statute for an International Criminal Court, so that such individuals could be indicted and fairly tried, would be cheaper and less bloody than war.

Iraqi civilians have already suffered a decade of bombing, and harsh economic sanctions have led to the deaths of hundreds of thousands of Iraqi children. Somalia has had no functioning government since 1991. U.S.-led war in those areas would likely increase humanitarian suffering and decrease international stability. It would increase animosity between U.S. citizens and Muslim peoples worldwide.

We in the U.S. must answer hatred with proactive solutions. Implementing Article VI of the 1968 Nuclear Non-Proliferation Treaty, which calls for a "treaty on general and complete disarmament under strict and effective international control," should be one of our top priorities. The U.S. military should also de-alert our Trident nuclear submarines, which only threaten our neighbors and promote international insecurity. Legislation that provides enforcement for the 1972 convention to ban biological weapons is an important next step.

Senator Feinstein's "Security and Fair Enforcement in Arms Trafficking Act of 2001" (S 1555), and the "Landmine Elimination and Victim Assistance Act of 2001" (S 497, HR 498) are vital steps toward increasing international stability. When considering the Foreign Operations Appropriations Bill for FY02, we must reduce U.S. military assistance in Colombia and the Andean region, which numerous human-rights organizations have linked to the arming of terrorist right-wing paramilitaries there. Finally, HR 1594, the Foreign Military Training Responsibility Act, is a necessary tool providing Congressional oversight to ensure that U.S. military trainees worldwide do not spawn terrorist networks like bin Laden's al-Qaida.

These are simple, effective steps that the U.S. can take right here at home to reduce the world's supply of weapons of mass destruction, to stop the arming and training of terrorists, and to promote respect worldwide for international law. Shouldn't we consider these steps before involving ourselves in another bloody and costly war?

—*Susanna Thomas,* Warren, N.J.

Forum: Long-range Partnerships?

The article by Arden Buck, "What Do We Do Now?" (*FJ* April 2003) offers some much-needed encouragement. My fear has been that once the present crisis has subsided, we will turn our attention to other important matters, and put the question of peace aside until the next conflict develops. Two ideas are especially welcome: building bridges (coalitions), and thinking outside the box.

Does anyone know of any Quaker group, committee, or organization that is exploring ways to build coalitions that will work towards preventing future wars? Experience teaches us that once the dogs of war are baying, it's too late to prevent war, and many thousands may die before the war machine can be made to grind to a halt. If we are serious about actually ending war, we have to 1) join with others, and 2) find new paths.

There are organizations working internationally to build democracies, and some working on techniques of international crisis intervention. Still others are trying to keep our own democracy from failing. The present peace coalitions (American Friends Service Committee and Friends Committee on National Legislation with MoveOn and True Majority, for example) show that we can work effectively with organizations that may not have exactly the same overall philosophy, but share the same immediate goal. Can we also build long-range partnerships to protect the future?

—*Martha Maas,* Columbus, Ohio

Queries

In what ways has my understanding of the Peace Testimony deepened throughout my lifetime? Since the year 2001?

How do I define pacifism? Where do I stand in relation to my definition?

How do I relate my definition of pacifism and my stand on issues surrounding it, such as:

- Registering for the selective service?
- Supporting individuals who refuse to register?
- Paying taxes for war?
- Supporting individuals who refuse to pay taxes for war?
- Participating in political life and issues?
- Supporting others who participate in political action?
- Confronting bullies?
- Dealing with perpetrators of violent crimes?
- Respecting the rule of law within nations, among nations, or between individuals of differing nations?

What does my faith tell me about my relationship to other people, their welfare, and their religious and cultural beliefs?
In what ways do I and my meeting "work . . . for public policies that advance equity, justice, cooperation, peace, and the integrity of Creation"?

Do I think before I speak? For example, have I thought carefully about what seeing the U.S. (or any other) flag means and doesn't mean to me? Do I know or care about "flag etiquette" as our elders learned it? What of flag etiquette is important or not important today? Many school children are asked to salute the flag every day at school. Has the meeting listened to the children's questions?

Is my meeting aware of the policy concerning military recruiting in the local schools? Have we listened to our pre-teens and teens tell about what they hear and what they see concerning the military at school, on the streets, on the television, in their play time? Have we developed a voice that speaks to these issues?

When I read or hear a list of suggestions for action, am I able to discern which one(s) are for me to act on and which ones for others?

In what ways is my voice heard? In what ways is the voice of my meeting heard?

Afterword

> . . . But peace, like a poem,
> is not there ahead of itself,
> can't be imagined before it is made,
> can't be known except
> in the words of its making,
> grammar of justice,
> syntax of mutual aid.
>   A feeling towards it,
> dimly sensing a rhythm, is all we have
> until we begin to utter its metaphors,
> learning them as we speak. . . .
>
> *—Denise Levertov*

Making peace and making poetry are similar in that they require of us the most ethical, precise, and respectful use of language. Each grows from and expresses truthfulness. We negotiate peace by finding the form of words by which we can bind ourselves to pledges we can keep. Peace grows as we find the right words for the right deeds and put them together in the right order. "A line of peace might appear," Denise Levertov says, "if we restructured the sentence our lives are making. . . . Grammar of justice, syntax of mutual aid." Peace comes about through treaties and promises made and kept. To make peace we must make a self that is trustworthy, a self that persists in trusting.

Confucius taught that our great ethical work is to call things by their right names; to recognize and use the most accurate and truthful words for our actions, for our social inventions, and for the institutions we have created to serve us. Every generation has its particular struggle to reclaim and rehabilitate its most precious words from the cynical, the power brokers, and the oppressors and their tame rhetoricians. Every generation has to find ways to live by the great words, the great promise-words, with courage and integrity. Truth is a complexity, but our work is to seek the truth sincerely; to listen to even the most painful truth-claims and weigh them against our own convictions; to demand of ourselves sincerity and accuracy in what we say; to learn to speak the truth in love; and to speak it to each other, to the world, and in our own hearts. —*Paul Lacey*

> . . . A cadence of peace might balance its weight
> on that different fulcrum; peace, a presence,
> an energy field more intense than war,
> might pulse then,
> stanza by stanza into the world,
> each act of living
> one of its words, each word
> a vibration of light—facets
> of the forming crystal.
>
> —*Denise Levertov*

Paul Lacey, member of Clear Creek Meeting in Richmond, Ind., is emeritus professor of English at Earlham College and clerk of the national board of directors of American Friends Service Committee. He is also the literary executor for Denise Levertov and edited her Select Poems. *The two excerpts presented here are from the poem* "Making Peace."

About the Editor:

Sharon Hoover, professor emeritus of English at Alfred University, Alfred, New York, has had a long career in many facets of education—publishing, teaching, and administrating. She has also been active in the Western American Literature Association and in Willa Cather Studies.

She is a longtime member of Alfred (N.Y.) Monthly Meeting, Farmington-Scipio (N.Y.) Regional Meeting, and New York Yearly Meeting. For Sharon, that has meant participating in First-day school to clerking yearly meeting committees to serving as a trustee of Friends World College. She has also been blessed in sojourning for several months in meetings in Santa Barbara, California; Missoula, Montana; Lincoln, Nebraska; and Ft. Lauderdale, Florida; and studying in writing workshops at Earlham College, Pendle Hill, and Powell House.

After September 11, 2001, Sharon volunteered with American Friends Service Committee in New York City, where she helped cook for the police all night near the towers, explored the web for informative sites about peace, and stuffed envelopes. She stands in the Alfred, N.Y., village weekly peace vigil, writes letters to the local newspapers, and talks to audiences interested in peace issues. Currently Sharon lives in the country with her husband, Dean; a daughter; three grandchildren; and five dogs. She is working on a web-based bibliography of Willa Cather's reading, and she meets with a small "faithfulness" group that worships together for three hours about monthly.